Weidenfeld (Publishers) Ltd., London, for excerpts from Rudolf Hoess' *Commandant of Auschwitz*.

Doubleday, New York, for excerpts from Joseph Goebbels' *The Goebbels Diaries,* translated by Louis P. Lochner, copyright 1948 by Fireside Press, Inc. Reprinted by permission of Doubleday and Company.

Atheneum Publishers, Inc., New York, for the U.S., for excerpts from Kitty Hart and John Burke's *Return To Auschwitz*. For Canada and the British Commonwealth, by Sidgwick and Jackson, London.

Belmont Books, New York, 1962, for excerpts from Willi Frischauer's *Himmler*. (copyright holder Odhams Press Ltd., London).

Mr. G. Hausner, for excerpts from his *Justice in Jerusalem*, Schocken Books, New York, 1968.

Editions Calmann-Levy, Paris, and Simon and Schuster, New York, for excerpts from J.F. Steiner's *Treblinka*, published in 1967 by Weidenfeld and Nicolson, London.

Mr. Aleck Goldberg, Executive Director of the South African Jewish Board of Deputies, on behalf of the late Arthur Suzman, Q.C., for passages of his and Denis Diamond's *Six Million Did Die*, Johannesburg, 1978.

Other published sources from which quotations have been taken:

Odd Nansen, *From Day to Day,* first published in 1949 by G.P. Putnam's Sons, New York.

Fania Fenelon, *The Musicians of Auschwitz*, Michael Joseph, London, 1977; originally published in French as *Sursis pour l'Orchestre*, by Opera Mundi, Paris, 1976.

William L. Hull, *The Rise and Fall of Israel*, copyright 1954 by Zondervan Publishing House, Grand Rapids, Michigan.

Smolen Kazimierz, Chief Editor, *KL Auschwitz Seen by the SS;* translated from the German by Constantine Fitzgibbon and Krystyna Michalik, copyright 1972 and 1978, Panstwowe Muzeum, W. Oswiecim.

——, *Auschwitz Museum Guide-Book, 1940-1945,* 4th edition: Auschwitz, 1972.

Gawalewicz Adolf, informative brochure inserted in *Adam Bujak's Photo-Album* of Auschwitz-Birkenau, Wydawnictwo Sport and Turyskyka, Warsaw, n.d.

Deportation railway lines to Auschwitz, in use March 1942 to November 1944.

NEW
STAR
BOOKS

Vancouver
Canada

First printing November 1986
1 2 3 4 5 90 89 88 87 86

Canadian Cataloguing in Publication Data
Francq, H. G., 1904-
Hitler's Holocaust, a fact of history

Bibliography: p.
ISBN 0-919573-58-4 (bound).—ISBN 0-919573-59-2 (pbk.)

1. Holocaust, Jewish (1939-1945). 2. Antisemitism -
Canada. I. Title.
D810.J4F6 1986 940.53'15'03924 C86-091532-8

The publisher wishes to thank the staff of *Canadian Jewish Outlook*
for their generous help in the production of this book.

Production co-ordinated by Catherine Ludgate

This book is published with assistance
from the Canada Council and
the Department of Communications.

Printed and bound in Canada
by Gagne Printers, Louiseville, Quebec

New Star Books Ltd.
2504 York Avenue
Vancouver, B.C.
Canada   V6K 1E3

Grateful acknowledgement is made for permission to quote from the following,
granted by:

Doubleday and Company, for excerpts from John Toland's *Adolf Hitler*.
Macmillan, London, for an excerpt from Ann and John Tusa's *The Nuremberg
Trial*.
Grafton Books, London, for excerpts from Olga Lengyel's *Five Chimneys*.
Ballantine Books, New York, for excerpts from Miklos Nyiszli's *Auschwitz*.

Contents

DEDICATION

When Hitler came to power in 1933 and brought the
brutal Gestapo onto the scene, the German Jews were
mocked, insulted, hooted and harassed. They were
chased through the streets, evicted from their shops;
their businesses, bank accounts and valuables were
confiscated. Thus robbed of their property, they were
pushed to the depths of humiliation and despair. Those
who were magistrates, civil servants, school teachers,
doctors in hospitals and professors in universities were
stripped of their positions and authority. Jewish
families were torn apart as parents were arrested and
separated from their children.

From 1939 onwards, with rifle butts at their backs
they were driven in "herds" or hauled in trucks to
ghettos which eventually were shelled and put to the
torch. Those who tried to escape through the roofs, the
windows, the cellars, the sewers, were shot at like birds;
the others were burned alive, perished asphyxiated in
the smoke, jumped to their deaths from buildings or
were crushed in the rubble. Such was the fate, in part, of
the Jews locked in the Warsaw ghetto.

All the while, mass collections of people of all ages,
the rich and the poor, were organized across Europe.
From Germany and the occupied countries, hundreds of
thousands were packed in cattle cars and transported to
the hell of concentration camps. Before they arrived
many died of asphyxiation or starvation. Tormented by

*the guards who awaited them, the survivors were then
made to suffer unimaginable abuses and indignities, and
in their flesh the worst and most varied cruelties.
Obeying the orders of the Fuhrer, a screeching and
howling maniac, SS "doctors" submitted the emaciated
inmates to sterilization and to heinous so-called medical
experiments, all part of the plan of the Master Race to
exterminate those whom they deemed inferior to
themselves.*

*The stronger men and women in the camps were
commonly used in the vicinity as slave-workers but
eventually, like the sick, the weak and the old, while
they stood or knelt in a trench that they had been forced
by the whips of their torturers to dig for themselves,
they too were shot in the back of the neck or mowed
down by the salvos of the SS squads in attendance.
Sprayed with petrol, their bloody cadavers were then
incinerated and the excavated earth was pushed back by
bulldozers into the anonymous mass grave.*

*Countless multitudes were starved to death in the
camps, walking about like skeletons until they fell and
breathed their last. Others were hanged, drowned or
poisoned; they were attacked by dogs trained for the
purpose, and at times electrocuted when they were
pushed or stumbled or threw themselves onto the high-
tension wire fences. In Himmler's death factories,
millions were gassed and their corpses reduced to*

cinders in twenty minutes in the ovens of crematoria working round the clock. Infants were strangled at birth and their bodies thrown into the inferno. Nor were other children spared.

Before such horrific massacres were being carried out during the years 1942 to 1945, the Jews still at large in the General Government were hunted down like animals and machine-gunned by special units, the Einsatzgruppen, operating in 1941 in the wake of the Wehrmacht advance through Soviet territory. Others, caught up with as they fled, and those assembled in villages or in town squares, were brutally made to climb into enclosed vans where they stood, like so many herrings in a barrel, until they were gassed with the exhaust fumes of the moving vehicles.

Such is the infamous and terrifying story of the Jewish people's genocide by the shameless, barbaric Nazis, blindly devoted to the beloved leader of their Master Race.

> So that younger generations may know and never forget the martyrdom those innocent victims endured, this book has been written. It is dedicated to the imperishable memory of the millions who succumbed in Hitler's Holocaust.

Acknowledgements

Special thanks are here extended to Mrs. Alice Brancewicz and other members of the Brandon University Library staff in charge of the Interlibrary Loan Service for having provided a number of source books in the course of my research.

Thanks are also extended to Mrs. Marilyn Wilson for the careful attention she has given to the typing of my original manuscript as it was submitted to New Star Books.

Also to those persons whose spontaneous help and encouragement have been greatly appreciated:

Ms. Ora Acalay, Head Librarian, Yad Vashem (The Holocaust Martyrs' and Heroes' Remembrance Authority), Har Hazikaron, Jerusalem

Mr. Jan Brancewicz of Brandon, Manitoba

Mrs. Olga Lengyel, former inmate at Auschwitz, author of *Five Chimneys*

Mr. Kazimierz Smolen, Director of Panstwowe Muzeum, Oswiecim-Brzezinka, Poland

Special thanks are due to Dr. Werner Entz, professor emeritus, Brandon University, for his assistance in the preparation of the glossary.

Last but not least I am particularly indebted to Dr. Mary (Hrenchuk) Pankiw for her friendly helpfulness in reading and correcting the original manuscript of the present book, before it was typed and sent to the publisher.

Publisher's Note

Hitler's Holocaust is the product of Professor H.G. Francq's research conducted to answer neo-Nazi Ernst Zundel's claims that the Holocaust of World War II never happened.

Professor Francq's compelling project, based on indisputable evidence, has another goal as well, an educational one. It is intended to prevent postwar generations of Canadians from falling prey to the deceptive, anti-Semitic propaganda spread by Ernst Zundel and other pro-Nazis. The author writes mainly for those younger readers, many of whom are unapprised of the reality of the original Nazi Master Race ideology, and more specifically of the SS implementation of a long-planned and deliberate genocide of the Jewish people.

In order to present a clear account of the events of 1933-1945, Professor Francq quotes directly from the testimonies of the Holocaust survivors and the works of contemporary investigators and historians. In addition to making use of secondary sources provided by scholars and other writers, he uncovers German archival material and the exact statements, speeches, diaries, directives, orders and, later, admissions of those Nazi and SS executives and executioners who blindly and joyfully obeyed the Fuhrer and were involved in the extermination of millions of innocent victims.

The facts speak for themselves and their impact is

unmistakable. The record of Nazi atrocities cannot help but arouse emotions of anger, disgust and outrage in anyone exposed to it. In the text that follows, the reader will recognize that the author shares these sentiments deeply, though they are necessarily tempered in the interest of conveying a mass of historical facts in an economical way.

Subsequent to his selection from the enormous amount of evidence available (which Ernst Zundel has ignored or denied), Professor Francq also reports on the trial of Adolf Eichmann in Jerusalem and on those of other infamous Nazi criminals who appeared before the International Military Tribunal in Nuremberg or before other courts— American, British, German or Polish.

Finally, the author has supplied detailed notes and appendices which will aid students of all ages in pursuing their inquiries into additional facets of the Nazi Holocaust.

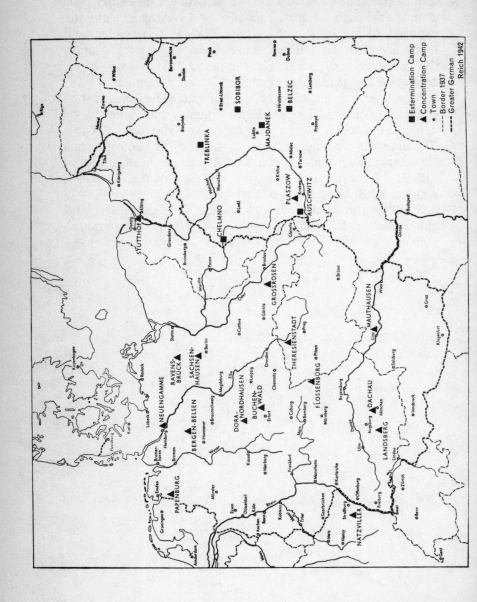

Extermination Camp
Concentration Camp
Town
Border 1937
Greater German
Reich 1942

FOREWORD

Under the cloak of freedom of thought and expression, civil and human rights, Ernst Zundel* published a booklet in the early seventies entitled *Did Six Million Really Die?* The author of this infamous little publication, a Richard Harwood, declared that his purpose was to present "irrefutable evidence that the allegation that 6 million Jews died during the Second World War, as a direct result of official German policy of extermination, is utterly unfounded."

Harwood's chapter headings, crafted in the best tradition of yellow journalism, include the following:

> Legal principles ignored—Confession under torture
> Jews called emigration "extermination"
> Twisted words and groundless assumptions
> Fantastic exaggerations—Absence of evidence
> Treblinka fabrication—Best seller a hoax (Anne Frank's Diary)
> Fake photographs—The imposture of gas chambers
> Six million falsehood rejected—No evidence of genocide
> Imaginary slaughter—Enormous fraud

Any aware and critical-minded individual realizes at once

---

*A German landed immigrant residing in Toronto.

17

what tune Harwood has chosen to play (and Zundel to echo). He claims peremptorily that the Holocaust never existed; it was merely Israel's postwar propaganda aimed at pocketing "compensation for six million dead, each one representing an indemnity of 5,000 marks."

Also basing his argument on French Professor Paul Rassinier's work, *Le Drame des Juifs europeens*, Harwood repeats to the reader that Dr. Kubovy, Director of the World Centre of Contemporary Jewish Documentation at Tel-Aviv, "recognised that not a single order for extermination exists from Hitler, Himmler, Heydrich or Goring."

This surprising discovery Harwood has characterized as *"the truth at last."* Nothing but the truth, of course, in the minds of the author and his admiring neo-Nazi publisher, Ernst Zundel, since "the preeminent value of [Rassinier's opus] lies firstly in the fact that [this inspired man] actually experienced life in the German concentration camps, and also that, as a Socialist intellectual and anti-Nazi, nobody could be less inclined to defend Hitler or the National Socialism. Yet, for *the sake of justice and historical truth*, Rassinier spent the remainder of his postwar years until his death in 1966 pursuing research which utterly refuted the *Myth* [!] of the Six million and the *legend* [!] of Nazi diabolism" (emphasis added).

Diabolism indeed! But rid of any straight-jacket, Harwood has gone on undaunted. With one stroke of his pen, he does away with all Holocaust survivors by proclaiming, for instance, that Olga Lengyel's *Five Chimneys* is "absurd" and that Dr. Miklos Nyiszli is "apparently a mythical and invented person." Harwood also names Philip Friedman as one of those "ad nauseam" spinners of false tales, and feels that *This is Auschwitz: The Story of a Murder Camp*, Friedman's vivid and dramatic narrative of what he endured and what he saw in the infamous extermination camp, should be dismissed as a fraud and thrown into the flames.

On the opposite side of the diptych, however, Harwood

proudly presents an "eye-witness account of Auschwitz" by one Thies Christopherson whose testimony, according to Harwood, is "certainly one of the most important documents for a re-appraisal of Auschwitz." Sure enough! "I have never observed the slightest evidence of mass gassings," the man has ventured to say, and of course, "the odour of burning flesh...is a downright falsehood."* This is curious logic inasmuch as this "witness" had not seen the crematorium when he left the camp in December 1944. So saying, Christopherson contradicts himself by having written just a few pages earlier in his book, that "200,000 people lived there and in every city with 200,000 inhabitants there would be a crematorium."**

Finally, of what value could Christopherson's testimony be, when Harwood himself reports that his key-witness "was sent to the Bunawerk plant laboratories at Auschwitz to research into the production of synthetic rubber"? The Bunawerk was some five kilometres away from the extermination camp,*** where Christopherson would not have been in the first place.

On the other hand, as *Kommandant* Hoss† testified in Nuremberg, Dr. Duerrfeld, who was the temporary director of the Farben Buna plant, did visit the camp as did managers of other Farben factories in the vicinity of Auschwitz. Duerrfeld, the witness said, "knew about the

*This is just *one* testimony—and a pack of lies at that. What about the tens of thousands of survivors and even SS guards who have testified or confessed to the contrary?
**There were four crematoria in the Birkenau camp and one, the smallest of all, was in the mother-camp (Auschwitz). There had never been any existing crematorium in the *town*, whose population in 1939 was some 12,000 people, not 200,000.
***Actually at Monowice.
†Many German words, including proper names, can take a number of different written forms in English. For example, "Hoess" can be rendered "Höss" or, informally, "Hoss," which is the style adopted in this book. The same applies to "Goering," "Göring" and, as used here, "Goring." Similarly, the renditions of "Mueller" are "Müller" and "Muller," the latter adopted here.

gassing of people and worried as to how he could explain these *dreadful things* to his colleagues and subordinates." As he had already testified, Hoss was referring to "the foul and nauseating stench from the continuous burning of bodies which permeated the entire area and all the people living in the neighbourhood knew [except Christopherson evidently] that exterminations were going on in Auschwitz."

Another fraudulent invention of Harwood's—he who likes to point to the "frauds" of Holocaust victims and their defenders—is his story of the Warsaw tragedy. Referring to Himmler's order in the summer of 1942 to resettle all Polish Jews in detention (labour) camps, "over three quarters of the Warsaw ghetto inhabitants were *peacefully evacuated* and transported, supervised by the Jewish police themselves," and "after six months of *peaceful evacuation*, when only about 60,000 Jews remained in the *residential* ghetto, the Germans met with an armed rebellion" (emphasis added). At this juncture, the reader is told that after SS General Stroop had taken action with armoured cars and torched the ghetto, "a total of 56,065 inhabitants were captured and peacefully resettled in the area of the Government-General."

Harwood's peaceful evacuation and resettlement is laughable, for 56,065 Jews had not been resettled anywhere; they had "peacefully" been burned to death or shot in the ghetto. Do Harwood and "civil rights" activist Ernst Zundel assume their readers are idiots?

In a similar vein, Harwood regards "the so-called Hoss memoirs" as another hoax, and calls those papers of the former Commandant of Auschwitz "a forgery produced under Communist auspices." Hoss, so Harwood's version goes, was "ordered to write the story of his life, [and] was subjected to torture and brainwashing techniques by the Communists...." Hoss' deposition in Nuremberg was "a catalogue of wild exaggerations" as the witness "is supposed to have 'confessed' to a total of 3 million people exterminated at Auschwitz."

This is how Harwood handles Auschwitz statistical data:

"The exterminations...are alleged to have occurred between March 1942 and October 1944; the figure of half of six million, therefore, would mean the extermination and disposal of about 94,000 people per month for thirty-two months.* This kind of thing is so ludicrous that it scarcely needs refuting."**

And Harwood persists in his demonic juggling act, distorting and opposing several authors' figures and reports, except Professor Rassinier's in which Harwood has shown blind confidence:

> Since the war, Rassinier has...toured Europe in search of somebody who was an actual eye-witness of gas chamber extermination in German concentration camps during World War Two, but he has never found even one such person.... Not one of the authors of the many books charging that the Germans had exterminated millions of Jews had even seen a gas chamber built for such purposes, much less one in operation, nor could any of these authors produce a living authentic witness who had done so.

In this paragraph, Harwood is caught at his own tricks, hoping the reader will forget that no one, of course, ever came out of a gas chamber alive.*** Such was the fate, for instance, of the inmates who served as members of the *Sonderkommando* in charge of the gassing and cremation operations in Auschwitz and who, after a short time on the

*Compare with Kraus and Kulka's table of figures, page 124, *The Death Factory*.
**More ludicrous still is Harwood's last claim, *in fine* of his work, namely, that "the majority of the 3 million Jews who experienced the Nazi occupation of Europe are in fact very much alive...a resounding confirmation of the fact that Jewish casualties during the Second World War can only be estimated at a figure in thousands."
***And anyone who would have been nosing around a gas chamber would certainly have been shoved into it or shot, and turned out in corpse form.

job, were themselves put to death by the relieving squad, so that not one single man of the former group would ever speak up to tell the truth to the world—and Professor Rassinier.

Harwood has also made a great affair of faked atrocity photographs, one of which is reproduced on page 26 of the booklet released by the enthusiastic Zundel. That photo-montage, if it is one, represents a group of standing skeletal figures taken from one photograph and, so Harwood claims, subsequently grafted onto another photo showing "a heap of corpses super-imposed in front" of the background group.

Harwood is not quite as convincing as he may have hoped to be since the miserable condition of the living skeletons was proof enough that those creatures, victims of SS treatment, would soon end up as the corpses lying in front of them. There was no need of a photomontage! Harwood's implication is that the hundreds of thousands or the million other photographs released in postwar years by the media, or otherwise published worldwide, were *all* faked atrocity documents. Many of the lies of neo-Nazis do not seem even remotely intended to be convincing. For whatever twisted psychic reasons, they appear moreso to have the objective of keeping old wounds open and adding whatever grains of salt they can.

Finally, Harwood insists that "documentary evidence" is in fact an "absence of evidence." Contemporary witnesses such as Kurt Gerstein, Felix Kersten, Himmler's masseur, SS General Erich von dem Bach-Zelewski, SS Captain Dieter Wisliceny, Eichmann's assistant, SS General Otto Ohlendorf, the commander of the *Einsatzgruppe* D in Ukraine, and, in a second group, writers like Gerald Reitlinger, Leon Poliakov, Manvell and Frankl, and Willi Frischauer, have done nothing but exaggerate or lie. You understand, readers, only Harwood's truth, as he has made it up, is genuine and commendable!

The items I have selected from Harwood's material are just the tip of the iceberg. A fuller portrait of the man must

include dishonesty and abuse as a researcher, his contrived
interpolations, his distortion of facts, events and testimonies, his use of excerpts out of context, his snarl of
half-truths, false truths and plain lies, his systematic
repudiation of survivors' and historians' reports and
testimonies, and his vicious claims that some war criminals
and witnesses were tortured to fit the indictment and verdict
of the judges.

Let us turn to the Nuremberg Trials and Harwood's claim
that the mountain of evidence they produced was a fraud. I
have studied some twenty works dealing with the Nuremberg Trial, including Colonel C. Burton Andrus' two
books, *The Infamous of Nuremberg* and *I Was the
Nuremberg Jailer*. Nowhere in the entire material have I
found a single reference to extracted statements or
confessions under torture or duress applied to any witness
or defendant.*

*There is an excellent picture of the defendants in the dock at Nuremberg
in Bradley Smith's *Reaching Judgment at Nuremberg,* New York, 1977.
The accused do not seem very happy but they bear no stigma of violent
interrogation.

There was, however, a complaint of Hoss' at the time of his arrest on
March 11, 1946. He claimed in his autobiography that at his first interrogation, evidence was obtained from him through beating. He said he
did not know what he had signed, although it was found that his eight-
page admission hardly differed from what he said or wrote later in
Nuremberg or in Cracow.

Nevertheless, he said that "alcohol and the whip were too much for
me." Then he received "further rough treatment at the hands of the
English public prosecutor, a major," when he was taken to Minden-on-
the-Weser for further questioning. Three weeks later he was "taken by
lorry to Nuremberg....My imprisonment by the International Military
Tribunal was a rest-cure compared to what I had been through before."

On July 30, when he was taken to Cracow, he was treated "quite well"
but after a week "the attitude of the prison-officials changed completely
and overnight....I gathered that they wanted to finish me off." Hoss'
complaint concerned the little food he received and also "the mental
torture inflicted by the...devils was too much for me." Fortunately,
things turned out for the best when the prosecutor's office intervened.
Until then, "they had nearly got me at the end of my tether [but] I must
admit that I never expected such decent and considerate treatment as I

Before the defendants were imprisoned in Nuremberg at the time of their trials they had been assembled at Mondorf-les-Bains in Luxemburg in the Grand Hotel which, for the occasion, was called Ashcan. Their jailer there, the same Colonel Andrus, took all possible measures of protection, even against lynching. The only inconvenience the defendants experienced while in Ashcan was to be denied any communication with the outside world. They were not permitted to receive letters, parcels or newspapers or to listen to the radio. As an exception, they were permitted to watch films that the Allies had shot of Nazi concentration camps. The viewers, with the exception perhaps of the sadist Streicher, did not much like the sight of those abattoirs.

Otherwise, Goring, whose health was improving, and his companions, who were getting fatter all the time, had no complaints to file. The Soviets, who were dispensing treatment to prisoners in their Lubianka prison in Russia, had personal ideas as to what a prisoner's diet should be. They also felt the insolence of those war criminals unbearable.

During the Nuremberg hearings themselves, great care was taken to ensure the full rights of the accused to a fair trial. At no time did they complain of having been mentally or physically maltreated, nor was a formal protest of any kind from their counsels ever received by the Tribunal.

I would not have wasted my time collecting specimens of Harwood's prose except to make use of them as a warning to the reader. In the pages to come, I will recount and analyse the documentary evidence gathered after the war from survivors and other witnesses of SS crimes and

---

received in Polish custody, once the public prosecutor had intervened.''

So much for the treatment Hoss complained about after the one he had inflicted on the Auschwitz inmates during several years. The fact remains that the story he wrote in Cracow, as he waited to be tried in Warsaw, was a spontaneous, detailed and voluntary account of his life and his commandantship in Auschwitz.

atrocities, by investigators, members of the armed forces and rescue teams, psychologists, journalists, historians, politicians, prosecutors and magistrates. In other circumstances, the documentation would stand as indisputable truth and the Holocaust as historical fact utterly unnecessary of substantiation. But Harwood and his neo-Nazis are a fact of life and there is a controversy over the indisputable.

However, my contribution to the controversy is a modest one considering the more thorough and comprehensive examination of Harwood's arguments, his deceptive system of misinforming his audiences, and his techniques of misrepresentation, which were exposed in 1978 by Suzman and Diamond in their book, justly entitled *Six Million Did Die*, from which I shall now refer to two examples as a final illustration of Harwood's viciousness.

The first concerns *The Diary of Anne Frank*, which Harwood claims is another hoax, based on a New York Supreme Court case that took place seven years after the book's initial publication in 1952. During that period of time, Otto Frank, the girl's father, had made a fortune from its sale, but then, in 1959, he had to face a court action initiated by Meyer Levin, a Jewish novelist, who claimed "he had written the dialogue of the diary and was demanding payment for his work." According to the Swedish journal *Fria Ord*, which had made those revelations, Meyer Levin had been "awarded $50,000 to be paid him by the father of Anne Frank as an honorarium for Levin's work on the *Anne Frank Diary*," and the defendant, Anne's father, had promised to pay because "he had used the dialogue of Author Levin just as it was and implanted it in the diary as being his daughter's intellectual work."

Suzman and Diamond unravelled Harwood's twisted account: Otto Frank, in his affadavit, had testified "to the authenticity of the Diary and the circumstances in which it came into his possession." In fact, Samuel G. Fredman, the American lawyer who took the plaintiff's case before the court, "made it quite clear that the authenticity of the Diary was never at issue in the case which was solely concerned with an alleged breach of copyright of a *stage and screen script based on the Diary*" (emphasis added).

As Suzman and Diamond stressed, Harwood's spurious attack was "yet another example of [the man's] unscrupulousness."

The second specimen of Harwood's infamous techniques, which Suzman and Diamond have also elaborated upon, is incorporated in the former author's chapter on "a factual appraisal of the Red Cross." Most of the report of the International Committee of the Red Cross, on which Harwood has concentrated, dealt with what the committee witnessed during their visit to a number of concentration camps, after which investigation, relief supplies were shipped to those camps for the benefit of the internees; "until the last months of 1945, letters of thanks for which [food relief program] came pouring in from Jewish internees."

But the "three-volume Report" of the committee also mentioned "that the delegates of the International Red Cross," according to Harwood, "found no evidence whatever, at the camps in Axis-occupied Europe, of a deliberate policy to exterminate the Jews. In all its 1600 pages, the Report does not even mention such a thing as a gas chamber. It admits that Jews, like many other wartime nationalities, suffered rigours and privations but its complete silence on the subject of planned extermination is ample refutation of the six million legend. Like the Vatican representatives, with whom they worked, the Red Cross found itself unable to indulge in the irresponsible charges of genocide which had become the order of the day.... Incidentally, it is frequently claimed that mass executions were carried out in gas chambers cunningly disguised as shower facilities. Again the Report makes nonsense of this allegation. 'Not only the washing places, but the installation for baths, showers and laundry were inspected by the delegates. They had often to take action to have fixtures

made less primitive, and to get them repaired or enlarged.'
(Report Vol. III, p. 594.)''

Suzman and Diamond again expose Harwood's misrepresentation. Regarding this last claim, they point out
that Harwood had ''deliberately sought to create the
impression that the camps referred to in the above passage
of the Report were German Concentration Camps. A
reference to vol. I, p. 594 (incorrectly cited by Harwood as
vol. III) reveals that the camps referred to. . . far from being
German concentration camps, were in fact Allied camps for
civilian internees in *Egypt*!''

Further findings of Suzman and Diamond are elaborated
in their work. One of Harwood's usual tricks is exemplified
in the case of the Red Cross Report where he deliberately
suppressed passages from which Suzman and Diamond
have quoted (from vol. I, pp. 641, 642, 645, 647 and 653;
from vol. III, pp. 513 and 514). These examples, to which
many others could be added, lend an idea of Harwood's
''scholarship,'' his distortions and misrepresentations, and,
in Suzman and Diamond's words, indicate the length to
which ''he has gone to further his pro-Nazi propaganda.''

In volume I, page 641 of the Report, for instance, it is
stated that ''under National Socialism, the Jews had
become in truth outcasts, condemned by rigid racial
legislation to suffer tyranny, persecution and *systematic
extermination*. No kind of protection shielded them;. . . they
formed a separate category without the benefit of any
Convention. . . . They were penned into concentration
camps and in ghettos, recruited for forced labour, subjected
to grave brutalities, and sent to *death camps*. . . .''

Throughout his work, Harwood has one recurrent and
obsessing thought: that the six million Jews who were said
to have died as a result of the official policy of
extermination implemented by the Nazi apparatus during
World War II was a fraudulent invention of postwar
propaganda. The author, ostensibly a writer and specialist
in political and diplomatical aspects of World War II,
claimed to be ''with the University of London.'' Upon

investigation, it was discovered that such a person had never been a student, a graduate or a teacher at that university or in any of its constituted colleges. Harwood, in a word, is a phoney; his real name is Richard Verrall. Further, no other publication bearing his alias has ever been found.

Nevertheless, his single pamphlet amply reveals the dishonest techniques he has at his command.* A few have been itemized by Suzman and Diamond: "Outrageous lies; misquotation and quotation out of context; false attribution; falsification of statistics; deliberate suppression of adverse passages in the very writings upon which he relies. The techniques vary, but all have the same end in view—the perversion of the truth."

In one instance, Harwood thought it clever to claim that the Jerusalem Court, at Eichmann's trial, had carefully avoided mentioning the figure of six million as being the total number of Jews who had been exterminated by the Nazis. Yet again, Harwood was caught lying since Gideon Hausner, the prosecutor, had indeed mentioned the figure in *the very first sentence* of his opening remarks.

More malicious still was Harwood's claim that the Holocaust was basically a story designed to extract financial reparations from the West German Government—"a fraud," he said, "which defies description in any language."

Suzman and Diamond have shown in their work the enormity of his falsehood.** The truth is that German reparations were first envisaged and offered by Chancellor Adenauer on September 27, 1951, at a session of the *Bundstag* and, as the authors recalled, "a sharp conflict of opinion subsequently arose within world Jewry as to the moral propriety of accepting restitution from Germany."

*It has been shredded by critics: "A mishmash of doctored statistics, fantasy and outright lies." (John Toland) "A tendentious publication which avoids material evidence and presents half-truths and distortions for the sole purpose of serving anti-Semitic propaganda." (H. Trevor-Roper, Regius professor of Modern History at Oxford)
**See details in Suzman and Diamond, pp. 51-55.

Eventually, after a three-day debate in January 1952, the Israeli Parliament passed, by a small majority, a resolution to enter into direct negotiation with the Federal German Government on an issue which the latter, and not the former, had raised. An agreement was ultimately signed in Luxemburg between the two governments on September 19, 1952, whereby the funds would be allocated to aid and rehabilitate Nazi victims and rebuild Jewish communities: cultural, educational and other institutions devastated by the Nazis. There was no compensation offered or claimed in respect of the dead.

Therefore, Harwood's "allegation that the number of Jewish dead as a result of Nazi persecution has been deliberately exaggerated to inflate the restitution claims is not only false," wrote Suzman and Diamond, "but an insult to the living and to the memory of the dead."

In a one-page preface to Harwood's 50,000 word booklet, Ernst Zundel, addressing "all Canadian lawyers and media representatives," calls their attention to the "Hate Law" Section of the Canadian Criminal Code, and stamps it "not so much an instrument against hate as an instrument against truth."

As self-appointed "writer, artist, publisher and Civil Rights activist," Zundel offers a booklet free of charge as "a public service," intended, "whether the reader agrees or disagrees," to help Zundel's company—Samisdat Publishers Ltd.—to defend "freedom of enquiry and freedom of access to information by striking the terrible sword of censorship from the hands of those who would slay truth in pursuit of their dubious aims."

This appeal ends, of course, with a solicitation for a "contribution to the Samisdat Legal Defense Fund," the money to be used in Zundel's defence against the criminal charge of "promoting hatred against an identifiable group," expected to be laid against the company. Such

contributions, it was said, would help Zundel foot the
"attorneys' fees and the reimbursement of witnesses who
must be flown in from Australia, Israel, Europe, and from
both American continents." If provided, this financial
assistance would make 1984 "a much better year for your
children and grandchildren—a year of freedom of thought,
a beautiful reality!"

So far, however, Zundel, who is no Canadian but speaks
like one,* has cautiously kept a mantle of secrecy over the
subject of his announced booklet. When the reader
discovers what Harwood's topic really is, he will perhaps
wonder why pro-Nazi literature is precisely what Zundel has
chosen to use to prove his point, if not to cover up his dear
friends' crimes against humanity.

And again, Zundel's two-page vindication of the Nazis,
appended to the 30-page diatribe of Richard Harwood,
reminds the reader that the brochure now in focus was also
sent to all members of federal and provincial Parliaments,
and all *Attorneys-General* in Canada.** In other words,
Zundel has deliberately sought trouble by challenging the
protectors of the law to let him, "in the interest of Freedom
of Speech and Human Rights," vindicate the Nazis of their
crimes. This ambition certainly calls for protest, and here it
is. Canadians are not prepared to consider it acceptable that
human rights be invoked in their country by a German
citizen and neo-Nazi whose plan is to bludgeon Canadians
with the blunt axe of Nazi propaganda.

But the bellicose Zundel boasts that "since that time"
(1968), he has "devoted increasing research, study and
effort into illuminating the events of German and world
history, particularly in the 1933-1945 period, with a view

*"*Our* laws . . . *we* Canadians . . . *We* have grown older as a country." He
writes about "*our* passage of the Hate Law," and worries that a country
"that so distrusts the majority . . . becomes a police state in the worst
tradition of police states."
**Also to 8,000 Canadians in all walks of life, and all clergymen. Why
clergymen?

toward defending Germans and German-Canadians against
the hateful lies surrounding the alleged gassing of six
million Jews by the Nazi government of Germany.''

So, here we are at last! That's what was bothering
Zundel—not the alleged denial of freedom of speech in
Canada, but the world's awareness of the gassing of six
million Jews by the Nazi government during the Second
World War. Yet Zundel continues, ''Zionists and their
sympathizers. . . are using words like 'hate' and 'racism' to
conceal their very attempt to suppress the truth.''

Zundel does not of course admit that suppression of the
truth is precisely his own aim—in defence of his Nazi lambs.
And, carried away by his own obsession, he concludes that
the ''Hate Law'' ''is being invoked to prevent the exposure
of the biggest money-raising racket of all time, namely the
Holocaust Lie.''

And having thus spoken, he asks his readers once again to
send donations to his Samisdat Legal Defense Fund.

Here ends Ernst Zundel's case and Richard Harwood's
distorted version of the facts.

What follows is the result of my research.

H.F.

INTRODUCTION

On Thursday, February 28, 1985, after a trial which lasted two months, the Toronto District Court, presided over by Judge Hugh Locke, convicted Ernst Zundel, 46, a landed immigrant of German origin residing in Canada since September 2, 1958, on a charge of having wilfully published a pamphlet denying the mass slaughter of the Jews by the Nazis during World War II. Zundel had also dismissed accounts of this Holocaust as a hoax and a Zionist conspiracy intended to claim financial reparations from Germany.[1]

The reader is already aware that Zundel's published material belongs in fact to Richard Verrall, alias Harwood, author of the infamous brochure *Did Six Million Really Die?* Having discovered that it reflected his own concoctions very precisely, Zundel took as his own Harwood's ideas, theories, deceptive techniques, misrepresentations and aims, and stood up, de facto, as co-author of Harwood's poisonous writings.

This is the aspect of the case which has allowed Zundel's supporters to protest, when he was brought to trial, that he had been deprived of his freedom of speech. However, since Zundel, professing the same views as his pony-writer, had distributed the brochure without at any time having been prevented by anyone in Canada from lying and misrepresenting the historical facts, as was his wont, the claims of his friends do not stand to reason. Besides, any landed immigrant or citizen in this country has always been left entirely free to make a fool of himself and to show his audiences his ignorance or bad faith on any subject matter. At bottom, genuine freedom of expression in Zundel's case was never a point in doubt. On the night the verdict of the jury was rendered, CBC entitled their program on *The Journal* as History on Trial and, indeed, what really was at issue with respect to the unforgettable and tragic genocide, was the *Historical Truth*, which the culprit in furthering his malicious purpose had pretended to ignore.[2]

At the beginning of the war in 1939, when the Jews had already been persecuted by Hitler for several years, Zundel was still in his mother's womb, and an uneducated child of five when the war ended. What did he personally know of the horrific sufferings the Jews had been put through?

Zundel emigrated to Canada in 1958, at the age of 19. Since then he has produced and distributed thousands of anti-Semitic publications, and came to be regarded by the Canadian Jewish Congress as the world's largest exporter of such hate material to West Germany. In Canada, he had, by the same token, revealed himself as a neo-Nazi, working to vindicate the father of the Master Race, Adolf Hitler, a man he had never known, but whom he loved dearly and whose "genius" he admired.[3]

Finally, in 1981, Zundel, as has been seen, released Harwood's infamous pamphlet. One may wonder with reason how the man has dared pretend that the master minds of the "final solution"—Himmler, Heydrich, Eichmann and their henchmen—never existed, never ordered any execution. How can he, in good faith, brush aside the enormous amount of evidence: the thirty million pages of documents filed at Yad Vashem in Jerusalem, the world's foremost research institute devoted to the study of the Holocaust?; the speeches of the SS planners, the lies and threats screamed at enthusiastic audiences by the Fuhrer himself, years before and during the war?; the thousands upon thousands of photographs which were taken at the end of the hostilities in the Kazets, of the gas chambers, the ovens, the ditches and the corpses piled mountain high or lying on top of one another in trenches 50 to 100 yards long, or on concrete floors, pending cremation? These photographs, shot by the military, by reporters and other civilians and by members of the many commissions of investigation established by the Allies, all are conclusive documents which have been reproduced in perhaps a million newspapers, magazines and books, and which are still available in archives, libraries and war museums all over the world.

How can Zundel, this helmeted author,[4] ignore Eichmann's confession to SS Colonel Dr. Wilhelm Hottl, who swore in an affidavit in Nuremberg that Eichmann had admitted that four million Jews had been liquidated in concentration camps and two million more by the *Einsatzgruppen* sweeps? Indeed, Eichmann had added, Himmler was convinced that the six million total figure was too low.

In 1961, at Eichmann's trial, Hottl did not appear but his deposition at home to an examining magistrate was used in Jerusalem. The witness recalled that in August 1944, in Budapest, Eichmann had come to see him and had already admitted what the slaughter of Jews had amounted to. The ''forwarding agent of death'' had then said that he had no hope to be considered other than a most wanted war criminal when collapse came.[5]

Six months later, in February 1945, Eichmann, the angel of death, in a better mood had boasted in Berlin to Dieter Wisliceny: ''I will leap into my grave laughing because the feeling that I have five million human beings on my conscience is for me a source of extraordinary satisfaction.''

But all of this, Zundel feels, is rubbish; Hottl and Wisliceny are liars, traitors to the cause of the Nazis, and Eichmann beyond reproach!

Of course, it continues to boggle the mind how Zundel dare discard the testimonies recorded in Nuremberg of confessed Nazis and of some of their victims who survived the SS atrocities and killings; the interrogations and

depositions of German officers and civilian officials; the
thousands of affidavits signed by the guilty; the 485 tons of
captured German archival documents;[6] the 42-volume
record of the trial of the major war criminals; the report of
SS Major General Stroop boasting how proud he was for
having eliminated 56,000 Jews who remained in the Warsaw
ghetto in the spring of 1943, plus an additional unknown
number who, having been incinerated, could not be
counted; the diaries of Hans Frank, the Governor of the
General Government in Poland, overflowing with details of
his crimes; the tragic accounts of the liquidation of Jews by
the SS units of the *Einsatzgruppen*; the narratives of Dr.
Miklos Nyiszli, of Olga Lengyel, Kitty Hart, Fania Fenelon
and many others who lived long months in the inferno of
Auschwitz or in other concentration camps; the confessions, during his trial in Warsaw in January 1947, of
Rudolf Hoss, and his candid as well as revolting memoirs,
Commandant of Auschwitz, published in 1959; the stories
of some of the ghettos in Poland, Czechoslovakia and
Hungary, and hundreds of research works by historians; the
history of the hecatomb of Jews and other victims of the
bloodthirsty Nazi beast; a record from which Reverend
William L. Hull has given the following short example:

"After six years of Hitler's regime during which the
German Jewish population decreased from 540,000 to
240,000, the estimated Jewish population of Europe in 1939
was 9,739,200. By 1947 this figure was reduced to
3,920,100. Six million dead; six million who suffered the
torrent of hell and died. The Jewish population of Poland
alone decreased from 3,250,000 to 105,000!"[7]

In court, Zundel needed a lawyer who shared his ideas.
He found such a man in the person of Douglas Christie—a
man on record as having said that he doubted the existence
of the Holocaust. Going beyond the usual demeanor of a
defending attorney, it must have appeared to Judge Hugh
Locke, the jurors and the public that Christie, in effect,

chose to put himself also on trial, demonstrating during the hearings and his summation how wholeheartedly he espoused and applauded his client's theory.

Thirty-nine year old Mr. Christie was born when the military and the civilian commissions of investigation, having just visited Hitler's and Himmler's concentration camps in 1945, wrote their conclusions after having realized what the "final solution" had been in the minds and plans of its Nazi initiators, and even more what it had meant to millions of Jews and non-Jews whom the assassins had starved, tortured, gassed and burned, shot, hanged, poisoned, and even butchered and mutilated by doctors for the sake of the Reich's pseudo-science applied to the improvement of the Master Race.

It is a pity that Mr. Christie himself did not have the opportunity to witness the appalling spectacle in 1945 of the last and still alive skin-and-bone, staring-eyed prisoners who were fortunate enough not to have suffered the fate of those other men, women and children of all ages who had been, not long before, their companions in misery, and who had ended their calvary in death-pits and in gas chambers. It may be assumed that Mr. Christie would then have understood what today he denies ever existed, and would not have undertaken Zundel's defence.

This did not come to pass, and being a strong believer in the sacrosanct freedom of speech (though a never-heard-of privilege in Nazi country), the lawyer had the gall to call witnesses of the prosecution liars. Then, looking down his nose at them, he treated them as if they were idiots because they had *seen* crematoria chimneys spitting smoke and flames, and they had *smelled* burning flesh and scorched hair, though it was claimed by his client that there had never been any oven or gas chamber in Auschwitz, in Treblinka, in Majdanek, or anywhere else in Hitler's Third Reich Paradise. In Zundel's own secluded den, in his "bunker," he had on a table a miniature replica of the main buildings in Auschwitz. The model was shown on television without, however, any evidence of smoke clouding out of the chimneys. This is what must have irremediably convinced Zundel and his attorney that no corpse was ever burned in the Auschwitz ovens.

It is ironic that a lawyer insulting witnesses enjoys his freedom of speech while denying it to former victims of the Nazi fury. And, effectively, since *all* survivors from Himmler's KZs had lived the same hell and have harboured the same tragic memories as the victims who testified in Toronto, *ipso facto* they are *all* liars and idiots. Tens of thousands, actually three hundred thousand of them! They had not seen anything, they had not smelled anything, nor suffered any cruelties of the SS under the whips, bludgeons and guns of those sadists: such is Christie's contention as it is Zundel's.

One witness on the stand, however, had the wherewithal not to let himself be intimidated by Christie's aggressive examination and cross-examination strategy. Christie's target was Professor Rudolf Vrba, from the University of British Columbia, who replied, as the lawyer fired questions at him, that he had seen 1,766,000 people walk to their death in a space with no way out. Smoke was all that resulted from the SS routine treatment. And when Professor Vrba, too, was called a liar, he coolly asked the agitated interrogator: "Would you perhaps suggest that they are still there?" Of course, they are still there, Professor, silvery ashes, bones and even the blood of millions of them!

"In the courtyard of Hut No. 11," wrote Adolf Gawalewicz, "some 20,000 prisoners were shot against what was known as the Black Wall...Sand removed in April, 1944, from under [it] was soaked to a depth of two meters in the blood of victims."[8]

Yet, the unanswered question did not stop the unbridled defence lawyer, prejudiced in favour of the *Totenkopfs* of yesteryear, from accusing another leading authority, Raul Hilberg, author of one of the most thorough accounts of the Holocaust. Mr. Christie suggested that the University of Vermont professor had relied on "madness and liars to create a selective account of history" after a research study which the professor had carried on for 37 years.[9]

Thus, the impudent Mr. Christie, in one sweeping gesture, showed in what contempt he held the mass of cross-referenced evidence of American, British, French, Polish, Hungarian and Russian sources. It is no wonder Mr. Christie could do that! He had his own witnesses who showed how devoted they were to racial thinking and history falsification. Fancy! One of those trustworthy witnesses—a faithful partisan of racial hatred—even claimed he had seen "secret areas" in Auschwitz where the skeletal inmates danced, bathed in a pool and had fun. Fun!

In *The Musicians of Auschwitz*, French author Fania Fenelon, who was a member of an inmate orchestra established by the Nazis, gives dramatic testimony of what exactly their performances were. There were concerts at night for the SS who, poor men, needed this kind of relaxation after their hard work. "It was these sessions," wrote the author, "that earned the orchestra its reprieve." Otherwise, the main purpose was to play an *Arbeitsmarsch* for the group of prisoners leaving for work in the morning, and in the evening upon their return to the camp.

An outdoor platform had been built at the intersection of camps A and B, and there the musicians assembled and played for the wretched creatures who were required to give their step a military gait. The orchestra also played in the block of the insane, and in the hospital huts for the sick. "After our departure," the author said, "a hundred or two hundred of these women would go to the crematorium."

In the summer of 1944, "the camp entirely emptied of its occupants who were confined to their blocks"; the group had once to play for the "arch-enemy," the "king-sized assassin," the "savage defender of the superiority of the German race," Heinrich Himmler in person. "Under the sun," Fania Fenelon recounted, "on the platform, beneath watchtowers, amid barbed wire in front of these men in uniform, it seemed to me incredible, ridiculous, grotesque ...*He* looked bored."

On another occasion, "the black triangles"[10] were giving a party, and they wanted music. "We would be paid in sauerkraut...Music to dance to and to eat to!"

This event is perhaps what Christie's trustworthy witness referred to. "Most of the women," wrote Fenelon, "were German prostitutes—Aryan naturally—of all kinds: young, old, toothless, fat, thin, redheads with green eyes, blue-eyed blondes, black-eyed brunettes, something for every one." The ones who impersonated the males wore silk pyjamas.

"At the first bars, some 'gentlemen' decided to invite the 'ladies' to a waltz, and in a few minutes the buffet was deserted and the whole block, old and young, was dancing ...Between dances they drank. There was no shortage of alcohol."

After a three-hour performance, the evening had turned into an orgy. "...If the SS had burst in during the revelry, the punishment would have been devastating."

There was no pool to bathe in, and while the party was in turmoil, it happened that it was on the same night of the black triangles' party that the SS herded the Gypsies to the gas chambers.[11]

The text, which follows, is not intended to convince Zundel or his lawyer of what life and death in the biggest concentration and extermination camp had been because one just can't convince people whose minds are not open, who operate in bad faith and are motivated by racial hatred.

During my research I have simply selected significant material for the sensitive and objective readers of *Did Six Million Really Die?*, and more particularly, for those uninformed readers of post-war generations. It is the result of a compilation of works which cover the real historical events, and the political and social philosophy imposed upon the German people by Hitler and the Nazi hierarchy.

Apologies are, however, extended for the many episodes which could not be treated in this concise history of the

Holocaust and, on the other hand, for the unavoidable repetitions which occur when different authors are quoted or referred to. Many of the repetitions, however, were made wilfully, both for emphasis and to show how evidence from diverse sources reinforces each other.

A short bibliography concludes this research work. It lists a number of selected sources which, for the sake of historical truth, must be considered indispensable reading for those who have reached the age of reason. If Ernst Zundel knows how to read, he could start with those marked with an asterisk.[12]

Chapter I
PRELUDE TO GENOCIDE

Hitler had not waited until the year 1939 to express his views in regard to the *Judenrein*[1] (Jewish Purge). As early as September 1919, immediately after the Treaty of Versailles was signed (June 28), Hitler, still a mere soldier, was assigned as lecturer in a Munich regiment. As he himself was to say, he had just been offered the opportunity of speaking to large audiences. He was about to deliver speeches in which the Versailles disgrace, the Jewish-Marxist world plot, and his hatred of the Jewry were his favourite topics. In September he was accepted as a member of the German Workers' Party—the *Deutsche Arbeiterpartei*—the embryo of National Socialism. He was still far from power at the time but he had a "big mouth," as Anton Drexler, founder of the DAP had remarked, and Hitler was soon expounding his ideas with the forceful and loud ebullience which was to make his reputation in the years to come. In his mind, as in his words, the Jews, who worshipped money, were sucking the masses dry. One had to consider them as members of a foreign inferior race and, therefore, an anti-Semitic program should be set up to deprive the guilty of privileges they did not deserve. Here was a solution to the Jewish question which must irrevocably lead to the *Entfernung* of the despised race—in a nutshell, its very liquidation.

One year later, on August 13, in Munich, at a mass meeting which took place at the Hofbrauhaus, Hitler spoke

41

for two hours explaining why his party was against the "despicable, immoral and parasitic" Jewry, and he promised the people that the party would free them from that plague. "He called for an all-out struggle to the death. . . a battle against the entire Jewish race." Again he insisted on the complete, thorough solution, the one which meant the removal of those suckers "from the midst of our people."[2]

In June 1922, a pistol shot sounded the beginning of a campaign of extermination of the Jews; the German Foreign Minister, Walther Rathenau, a Jew, had just been gunned down. The Nazis took his death as good riddance, since they accused him of plotting the Jewish domination of the world. The shooting occurred on the same day Hitler was imprisoned in Stadelheim for having incited a riot. Five or six weeks later, scarcely out of jail, he thundered again in front of an audience against the Jews, calling them robbers, destroyers and exploiters. There was nothing new in this outburst but his virulence seemed boundless when that same year, as he talked to Josef Hell, an acquaintance, he said, almost shouting, that if he were ever in power "the destruction of the Jews will be my first and most important job." He would have as many gallows erected in the streets of Munich as the traffic would allow. The Jews would be hanged and stay hanging until they stank "as long as hygienically possible." When they'd be untied, "then the next group will follow and that will continue until the last Jew in Munich is exterminated. Exactly the same procedure will be followed in other cities until Germany is cleansed of the last Jew!"[3] One day this apocalypse would almost come true.

As is well known, Hitler had to fight ten more years to obtain power. In 1930, his party finally won a majority at the September election; the Nazis received 6,371,000 votes which, on October 13, gave them 107 seats in the Reichstag—"so many men with faces of criminals and degenerates. What a degradation to sit in the same place with such a gang."[4]

On July 31, 1932, the elections for the Reichstag returned more than double the number of votes Hitler's party had received two years earlier. The Democrats and Communists together received half a million votes fewer than the National Socialists.

Having finally obtained the seat of Chancellor, Hitler emerged as the master of Germany with—as he would soon show—absolute dictatorial power, and when, at Hindenburg's death, in 1934, a law was passed uniting the office of Chancellor and President, Hitler carried the double title of Reich Chancellor and Fuhrer. He boasted that in some five hundred years he would be looked at with respect as "the man who once and for all exterminated the Jewish pest from the world."

At that time, old Hindenburg protested Hitler's purge but to no avail. Hitler answered the venerable marshal that the Jews were swarming in 80 per cent of the major posts in high institutions, as civil servants, doctors, professors and lawyers. He wanted to cleanse the house in view of future political developments. The Jews were nothing but pernicious enemies not only of the State but also of the Church. They had to be ousted by all possible means. Suddenly "all Jews holding public positions were dismissed, including those in the judiciary, educational and administrative posts. About 11 per cent of the German doctors were Jews, among whom were some of the leading specialists in the world." They had to go, as well as over 16 per cent of the lawyers. "Soon, signs in large letters appeared in the streets of Berlin exhorting people to 'shun Jewish doctors and lawyers.'" They simply quit, and so did many Jews whose trades were boycotted. "In less than six months after Hitler's coming to power there was a decrease in the Jewish population of 11.5 per cent in large towns and 17.1 per cent in small towns. Some districts, where anti-Semitism was especially vile, showed reductions up to 45 per cent."[5] Even five Nobel prize winners were dismissed from office.[6] Albert Einstein, for one, was branded a dangerous man when a bread-knife was discovered in the course of a search of his house; henceforth, the persecutors considered "the weapon" a valid excuse to seize Einstein's bank accounts. The professor was also hooted by Nazi hooligan students as he lectured at the university in Berlin. Hitler came to sneer at Einstein's achievements as the "Jewish physics."

As Hitler was determined to eliminate all of the 540,000 Jews who breathed in the German Fatherland, the boycott of Jewish stores and offices was started on April 1, 1933. The *Judenrein* after Hitler's rise to power merely intensified and increased hatred and anti-Semitism, not only in Germany but also in Austria.

"We [the Nazi executives] ask you, German men and women, to fall in with this boycott. Do not buy in Jewish shops and department stores. Do not go to Jewish lawyers! Avoid Jewish physicians! Show the Jews that they cannot drag Germany's honour into the mire without being punished for it! Whoever does not comply with this demand proves himself thereby on the side of Germany's enemies."[7]

There was nothing new in the nature of the persecution, as one earlier report, from 1925, shows: "Jewish women have been forbidden entry to dairies and to bakeries and grocers' shops. Milk cannot be got even for tiny children. Some shops used to supply their Jewish customers secretly, taking orders on the telephone. But when this was discovered, as for example, in Elbing, the second largest city in East Prussia, the local papers published the names of the shopkeepers concerned. Since then the Jews in Elbing have not been able to buy food. Today there are at least fifty cities and towns, among them Magdebourg (300,000 inhabitants), Schwerin, Marienwerder, Dessau and Fursten-walde (near Berlin) where milk is not supplied to Jewish children."[8]

School children, of course, were not spared the effects of Hitler's hatred. Indeed, they were to be taught what social purity meant. "The teaching of racial principles," heralded Bernhard Rust, Hitler's Minister of Culture, "is to begin with the six year old children in their first term, in accordance with Hitler's pronouncement that no German boy or girl is to leave school without a knowledge of the necessity of racial purity.''[9]

On February 27-28, 1933, Goring put the torch to the Reichstag, watched it burn to its foundations and then blamed the Communists for the disaster. It was a political triumph, and the ''culprits'' were arrested forthwith. Then, on October 14, just five months after his ''Peace Speech'' in May, Hitler announced that Germany was withdrawing from the League of Nations, and fixed the date of the national plebiscite on the issue for the following month, November 12. On that day, 95.1 per cent of the votes supported Hitler's foreign policy; in the Reichstag, 92.2 per cent went to his party—the only one, it is true, on the ticket.

This plebiscite simply confirmed Hitler's totalitarianism, that is, fascism, which the people welcomed ''unconditionally and joyfully.''

Hitler had not even waited for the results of ''his'' elections before shutting down Social Democratic and Marxist newspapers and publishing houses. With the establishment of the Reich Press Chamber, freedom of the press and ''that of literature, radio, theatre, music, films and fine arts'' were eliminated.[10]

Scores of concentration camps were already functioning —beating, torturing and inflicting humiliating tasks on enemies of the new regime and, in particular, on the interned Jews.[11] Meanwhile, outside the camps, acts of violence and atrocities were carried on against the Jews by the Nazis, who took little notice of the reaction of the press in democratic countries. Two years later, on September 15, 1935, the Reichstag passed the Nuremberg decrees whereby the German Jews were deprived of and denied citizenship; after the persecutions they had suffered in the past, they were now made legally an outcast race. Some Germans, friendly to the Jews, defied the authorities, although it could hardly help the persecuted who were now compelled to wear the yellow badge, were forbidden to buy in German food stores, and were deprived of employment.

There was a timid initiative of the League of Nations[12] in an endeavour to handle the problem of Jewish refugees who were leaving Germany in increasing numbers, but Hitler, who thought only of exterminating the hated race, was opposed to any plan of other countries to offer asylum to Jewish refugees. A number of rich Jews, however, escaped to the Holy Land, having purchased, at any price available, pre-dated British passports and visas until the British decided in 1936 to stop the migration. This measure, however, prompted the Zionists to organize an underground route through which young German and Polish Jews were smuggled away, crossing Hungary and Rumania by rail and ending in Turkey whence they sailed to Palestine.

Nevertheless, Hitler had not changed his mind. In April 1937, Hitler addressed an audience of the district leaders in Vogelsand, and left no doubt as to what he intended for the Jewry. "I am not going to challenge my opponent immediately to a fight," he said to his open-mouthed audience. "I don't say 'Fight' just for the pleasure of fighting. Instead, I say: 'I will destroy you.' And now cleverness helps me to maneuver you into such a corner that not a blow will be struck until you get a thrust into your heart! That is it!"[13]

Indeed, in 1938, with the destruction of synagogues in Dortmund, Munich and Nuremberg, the Nazi racists were let loose. "The entire Kurfurstendamm was plastered with scrawls and cartoons. 'Jew' was smeared all over the doors, windows and walls in waterproof colours. It grew worse as we came to the part of town where poor little Jewish retail shops were to be found. The SA had created havoc. Everywhere were revolting and bloodthirsty pictures of Jews, beheaded, hanged, tortured and maimed, accompanied by obscene inscriptions. Windows were smashed, and loot from the miserable little shops were strewn on the pavement and floating in the gutter."[14]

About two months after the Evian Conference (July 1938), as if to challenge or to provoke the nations who had turned down the project of Jewish emigration, Goring announced a forthcoming plan to confiscate all Jewish property, estimated at two billion dollars. As a parallel measure, a special department would see to it that all Jewish businesses were liquidated.

In point of fact, the confiscation of Jewish property and the expulsion of Jews from the economy had already begun. Mass arrests, which began in June, were followed in October by mass expulsions of the *Ostjuden* (a minority among German Jews in Eastern Europe).

Another measure that the Nazi authorities undertook was their first "legal" deportation on the 29th of that same month. The Polish Government had just passed a law under which Jewish nationals living in Germany would lose their nationality, as of October 30. Army General SS Reinhardt Heydrich, chief of the Security Police of the Gestapo, therefore, did not hesitate; he had those Polish Jews rounded up and brought to the frontier. Thence, the SS men cracked their whips on the backs of the crowd as they escorted them. Anyone who lingered was whipped; blood was spilt on the road. Finally, after the Polish sentries had started shooting, they stopped and lifted the frontier roadblock.[15]

This episode was revealed at Eichmann's trial in Jerusalem, in 1961, by Zindel Shmuel Grynszpan, whose son had killed a member of the German embassy in Paris, in 1938. Indeed, on November 7, Herschel, whose parents had recently been deported to Poland, shot the German attache, Ernst vom Rath, who, in fact, was felled by bullets which had been intended for the ambassador himself.[16]

This daring coup called for a harsh punishment in Germany where, after 40,000 Jews had been arrested, some killed and wounded, the Jewish community was fined four billion marks. In addition, millions worth of property was destroyed, and in cases covered by insurance, where damaged property remained, this insurance was confiscated; the Jewish owners were left to repair the damages at their own expense.

On November 9-10, 1938, *Kristallnacht*, countryside pogroms broke out simultaneously across Germany, notably in the districts of Kurhessen and Magdeburg-Anhalt. All day and night, synagogues and Jewish stores were razed to the ground. "Beginning systematically in the early hours in almost every town and city in the country, the wrecking, looting and burning continued all day.[17] Nearly 200 synagogues were burned, a further 76 were totally demolished, eleven community centres and cemetery chapels pulled down, several thousand Jewish places of business destroyed, as well as 29 large stores. Thirty-six Jews were killed and 36 seriously injured. The police stood by and watched.[18] It was the shattered plate-glass, as it littered the streets of towns and cities, which gave the pogrom its name. It was later estimated by Lucy S. Dawidowicz that the quantity of plate-glass thus destroyed equalled the annual production of the plate-glass Belgian industry from which it originated.

At 1:20 a.m. on November 10, Heydrich had, as a precautionary measure, already sent a teletype to the State and Security Police apparatus regarding the "expected demonstrations against Jews." It ordered that businesses and private apartments of Jews could be destroyed though not looted, and that "not too old, healthy men" should be arrested and confined as fast as possible in "appropriate concentration camps"[19] (U.S. Prosecution Exhibit 240 at the Nuremberg Trial).

In Vienna, only one synagogue remained. Arrested were 5,000 Jews, among whom were those queuing at the British Consulate in the hope of securing a visa.

Months after *Kristallnacht*, suicides accounted for more than half the Jewish burials. All Jewish institutions were burned down or banned by order of the Gestapo. The Jewish media was suppressed. Finally, *Reichsvertretung der Jungen in Deutschland* (Federal Representation of the Jews in Germany), whose creation dated back to 1933, was transformed into the *Reichsvereinigung* (Federal Union of the Jews in Germany), whose tasks—emigration, welfare and education—were dictated by the Gestapo. In actuality, it foreshadowed the Holocaust in preparing for the final liquidation of German Jewry.[20]

Himmler, when told that Goebbels had ordered a pogrom, felt that it was not the right time, when the foreign political situation was at stake, to initiate such a violent action. Accordingly, he told his men to discourage excessive looting. It was an odd about face, since only a few hours earlier he had again attacked Jews in an impassioned secret speech to his SS generals. The Jews were simply to be wiped out from the Reich with all expedient ruthlessness. Germany had to win its battle against the Jewry for fear of being starved and butchered.

On November 12, Goring ended a four-hour meeting of the Council of Ministers by saying that if the Reich were ever in conflict with foreign powers, "it goes without saying that we in Germany should first come to a showdown with the Jews." But the Fuhrer, pressed by those nations which protested the inhumanity of the repression, had suggested deporting the hated Jews to Madagascar.[21] He had explained it to Goring three days before. "He [the Fuhrer]," concluded the marshal, "wants to say to the other countries: 'Why are you always talking about the Jews? Take them!'"[22]

It was precisely how Heydrich felt. He complained that only 19,000 Jews had been driven out of the country, compared with 50,000 who left Austria during the same period. Goring then came up with "a legal formula to make the Jews pay a collective fine of, say, a billion marks in expiation for their base criminal act!"

Meanwhile in Vienna, as Jewish doctors, lawyers and officials were being rounded up, Eichmann (according to Moritz Fleischmann, a witness who testified in 1961 in Jerusalem) arrived and spoke to a crowd which had been herded into a school. He was full of wrath. He said that the Jews were not disappearing from Vienna quickly enough and that he would know now what to do and what measures to take.[23]

The problem, at the time, was that the Western World did not want within its territory any more Jews than it already had. Hitler, whose hatred had not abated and whose policy had not wavered for years, could therefore declare that the vermin must be destroyed. "The Jews," he was saying on January 21, 1939, to the Czech Foreign Minister "are our sworn enemies and at the end of this year there will not be left a Jew in Germany."[24]

On the 24th, Goring nominated Heydrich to be head of the Central Office for Jewish Emigration for the whole Reich. As a direct consequence, Jewish leaders from Berlin were ordered by the Gestapo to visit the *Zentralstelle* in preparation for the installation of the system in Germany. Assailed by Eichmann, they were aghast. "I had to be everywhere and to deal with everything," the man recalled. "Heydrich said I was acting like a small prime minister. Anyway I could fix a special rate of exchange for a person, which even the Reichsbank could not do.... My subordinates treated me with such respect that the Jews thought I was really a kind of king."

In clear terms, if a Jew wanted to be admitted into a foreign country, he had to pay in German money on the basis of an exorbitant rate of exchange fixed by Eichmann, the future angel of death. Thus Germany, while getting rid of the vermin, was doing good business. Eichmann was intoxicated by the success he had already reaped in Vienna. He thought he had then found the answer to the Jewish problem. "So he coined the phrase that was to become the code name for an unspeakable crime [later to come]," writes Hausner, "a cover for the systematic murder of six million human beings. He called it the '*Final Solution*.' All his files bore this designation."

"I suggested these words," he told Sassen[25] when he was in Argentina. "At that time I meant the elimination of the Jews, their marching out of the German nation. Later... these harmless words were used as a camouflage for the killing."[26]

At about the same time, a circular originating from the

Reich Foreign Ministry was mailed to German embassies and consulates abroad to inform them there would be an international solution to the Jewish problem in the near future. It was dictated by the realization of the danger which the Jews represented for the racial preservation of all countries. Thus, the original 600,000 Jews of Germany, constituting less than 1 per cent of the country's population, were deemed a national danger, and this became the cornerstone of the Nazi propaganda.[27]

On January 30, 1939, Hitler shouted in the Reichstag: "I will once more be a prophet. If the international Jewish financiers in and outside Europe should succeed in plunging the nations once more in a world war, then the result will not be the Bolshevization of the earth, and thus the victory of Jewry, but the annihilation of the Jewish race in Europe!"[28]

This threat was just six weeks before Hitler's invasion of Czechoslovakia and eight months before *he* himself—and not the Jews or other countries—started World War II.

Chapter II
THE IMPLEMENTATION

In the case of the Jews, the defendants proved their own best prosecutors. No other section of the indictment was so clearly, comprehensively, and consistently proven by the Nazis' own words and their own orders, and I propose to let the documents speak for themselves.
—Victor H. Bernstein, *Final Judgement*, 1947

At the end of 1934, Adolf Eichmann had been hired as an expert on Zionism by SS-*Untersturmfuhrer* Leopold von Mildenstein, who was in charge of Jewish affairs in the Sicherheitsdienst (SD) Main Office in Munich.

Once in this *engrenage*, Eichmann soon realized that all matters relating to Jewish emigration should be centralized in one agency. By 1937 he had conceived the idea of forced emigration—a policy of expulsion which expressed the German people's wrath and hatred against the Jews. Heydrich agreed wholeheartedly. On paper, therefore, "everything relating to the Jewish question, it seemed, had been disposed of, except the Jews themselves." It is true, they had already suffered during recent violent demonstrations across Germany. Then, on January 24, 1939, Goring gave Heydrich the power to take all necessary measures for a stepped-up forced emigration of the German Jews, along the lines that Eichmann had already pioneered in Vienna after the Anschluss.

As a follow-up to the events of *Kristallnacht*, SS terror struck harder and more incessantly, and the flow of Jews into concentration camps increased to unprecedented figures.[1]

Eichmann, however, then came up with the idea of substituting emigration—a euphemism for expulsion and robbery—for terror. But once the war started, evacuation became another euphemism for forced deportation to death factories.

It was from his Central Emigration Office, with SS Major General (*Gruppenfuhrer*) Heinrich Muller, Chief of the Gestapo, acting as director, that Eichmann, entrusted with the actual day-to-day work, organized, scheduled and directed the deportation of European Jews to the camps.[2]

The process of destruction was applied in stages. The wearing of the yellow Star of David had been a preparatory measure. Then:

1. The local concentration of European Jews in ghettos.

2. Later, after the attack against the Soviet Union, the murder of individual Jews in ex-Soviet zones by the *Einsatzgruppen*.

3. The launching of the "final solution," which entailed the round-up of all accessible European Jews for deportation to designated areas.

4. Finally, the creation of death camps for the systematic massacre of all Jews.

The reader shall soon see how the program developed.

On the eve of the war, Heydrich's directives were formulated at a conference which Eichmann attended. A copy of the official minutes shows that Eichmann was the initiator of the ghettoization, a crucial instrument in the Nazi elimination of Jewry. It also proved to be a decisive step in the annihilation process.[3]

On the morrow, September 3, 1939, Hitler's panzers were rolling into Poland where they wreaked havoc. On the 7th, the Polish air force had been annihilated and the nation's

35-division army paralyzed. The Blitzkrieg ended. At this point, Hitler was preparing to transform Poland "into a massive killing ground." He lost no time assembling the German Jews "in specific Polish cities having good rail connections. Object: 'Final Solution', which will take some time as Heydrich explained to SS commanders on September 21. He was talking of the extermination of the Jews, already an open secret among high-ranking party officials."[4] In a directive to the *Einsatzgruppen* chiefs, however, referring to "the conference held in Berlin today" [September 21], Heydrich insisted that the planned joint measures [the killing of Jews in the occupied zone] were to be kept *strictly secret*. (U.S. Prosecution Exhibit Document 3363 PS at the Nuremberg Trial.)

Eichmann set to work without delay. The first deportees, coming from Morawska Ostrawa, Czechoslovakia, arrived in Poland at the Nisko Station. Eichmann was waiting for those Jews and he told them that the Fuhrer had promised a new homeland to them. But there were no apartments or houses. "If you will build them," he said, seething irony, "you will have a roof over head. There is no water. The wells are infected with cholera, typhoid, dysentery. If you will drill and find water, you will have it. Once you cross the river you will never come back." Such was the promised land.

From then on, during the hard winter of 1939-1940, other Jews were also transported in locked wagons to regions of the General Government, an appellation which designated the Polish territory left after Hitler's recent annexation to the Reich of the four western provinces of Poland (October 8). It was headed by Hans Frank, an able and energetic lawyer, one of the Nazi intellectuals, the legal adviser of the party and now—appointed by Hitler on October 12, 1939—he was in office as governor of the General Government.

Frank was told, though still in vague terms, that by February 1940, about a million Jews would be packed into the area between the San and the Vistula.[5] He lost no time in getting organized and two weeks after he had taken office, he issued a decree making forced labour compulsory for all Jews aged fourteen to 60. This measure was followed about a month later, on November 23, by an ordinance prescribing that all Jews over the age of ten wear ten-centimetre white bands with the Star of David on their right sleeve, and on both the inner and outer linings of their clothes.

On January 30, 1940, Heydrich called a meeting of all concerned with the planned migration, notably Eichmann and Frank's deputy. He promised to co-ordinate the evacuation of the General Government. The projected figures for the immediate future were 190,000 Jews, Poles and Gypsies. Heydrich rejected all suggestions "to put a break on what they called mass movements."

There was plenty of work for Eichmann, and by the middle of February, the Jews of Stettin and Schneidemuehl were rounded up and deported. Brought to the vicinity of Lublin, they were ordered to march some twenty to 30 kilometres in the snow at 22 below zero Celsius. The march lasted over fourteen hours; 72 people were left on the road to freeze to death. The survivors had to go on suffering the worst trial of their lives. This was one case of deportation among others which were in progress, and in the annexed zones, the German press was triumphantly announcing that one town after another had become *juderein*—clear of Jews.[6]

Immediate ghettoization was then carried out according to plans. Various ruses were adapted to local conditions to coerce the Jews into the designated ghettos—invariably the slum areas of the towns. It became a common sight to see women dragged off by their hair or a group of SS men driving at gunpoint a band of beaten Jews, weary to death. In actual fact, this was the meaning of enforced ghettoization.

One of the biggest concentration camps was set up in Lodz. In May 1940, the ghetto was fenced round and cut off from the outside world. More than 200,000 Jews were herded in; during the four years of the ghetto's existence, 120,000 died of hunger. Eichmann, ever zealous, undertook to push into Litzmannstadt another 20,000 Jews and 5,000 Gypsies. At the same time, the largest ghetto in Europe was being readied. When it was completed, Warsaw held half a million prisoners in it. As usual the round-up there had been carried out to the accompaniment of extortion and robbery.

At the Wewelsburg Conference of early 1941, Himmler addressed his senior officers and told them, under the seal of secrecy, that the Fuhrer had decided to strike a mortal blow at Russian Communism and to smash the Soviet Union. "War against Russia will start this summer," Himmler told his SS staff. "The purpose of the Russian campaign is to reduce the Slav population by thirty million. . . ." Clearly the Jews would be wiped out as they already had been in Poland and other countries overrun by the Nazis.

Despite Hitler's military operations, and his attack on the Soviet Union on June 22, 1941, the Jewish question was still constantly on his mind. At the beginning of July of that year, he said to Walther Hewel, Ribbentrop's liaison at the Chancellery: "I discovered the Jew as a bacillus and the ferment of all social decomposition. . .and one thing I have proven is that a state [Germany] can live without Jews; that economy, art, culture, etc., can exist even better without Jews, which is the worst blow I could give the Jews."[7]

Reinhard Heydrich could not agree more with his chief, Himmler, and his Fuhrer, since he felt that the mere deportation of Jews was an inadequate solution. He had complained about this project as definitely insufficient in his estimation, and on July 31, 1941, he received a signed order from Goring, Supreme Chief of War Economy, who acted only on Hitler's instructions, to the effect that he, Heydrich, was now charged with the job of making "all material, economical and financial preparations regarding organizations and financial matters to bring about a complete solution of the Jewish question in the German sphere of influence in Europe.'' Goring ended his letter by requesting Heydrich to submit, as soon as possible, ''an overall plan for the implementation of the desired final solution of the Jewish question.''

Obviously, Goring's order which ''supplemented the task assigned to you on January 24, 1939'' was the extermination pure and simple of European Jewry. As Hitler's troops swept through the borders of the Soviet Union, Heydrich ordered four SS *Einsatzgruppen*, each of battalion strength, to prevent and oppose any resistance of civilians in the military zone.[8] In particular, Bolshevik leaders at all levels were to be arrested and executed; the same fate applied to Jews and Gypsies, '''Asiatic inferiors' and 'useless eaters' such as the deranged and incurably sick.''[9]

Heydrich also met with Eichmann and informed him that Himmler had already given instructions to Odilo Globocnik, SS and police chief in Lublin,[10], and that he, Heydrich, believed the man was using the Russian antitank ditches to get rid of the Jews. Eichmann was asked to go and see. He must have discovered that, indeed, that method of killing had started in the wake of the advancing *Wehrmacht*. Three quarters of a million Russian Jews were thus to be liquidated. It proved to be an effective dragnet, whose catch would be added to the German and Polish Jews and those farther east who would fall into the hands of the SS. However, the killings in Globocnik's Lublin territory were also performed with exhaust gas from the diesel motor of a submarine, and eventually in mobile gas vans first employed in Chelmno. It appears that SS *Untersturmfuhrer* Rudolf Becker had suggested using these mobile gas vans,[11] which could be driven to a spot at some ten to fifteen kilometres from the main road, during which ride the gas fumes were directed inside the vans. On arrival, the victims were already dead and all that remained was to bury them. However, the method did not always work as expected and SS Major General Otto Ohlendorf, Chief of *Einsatzgruppe*

D, preferred a more military form of execution—a bullet in the back of the neck—not to spare the victims the strain and stress of their journey to death but rather to protect the SS executioners from the unpleasant task of unloading corpses and cleaning the vans which the doomed had dirtied.[12] Gas chambers would later be the answer to the problem.

The ironic side to this situation was that the Jews who were killed—either by shooting or by gas poisoning—were taken by surprise. They knew nothing of Hitler's program of extermination and found no account of anti-Semitic atrocities in the Russian press. In fact, those Jews initially welcomed the Germans as their liberators. Toland describes the process:

> The extermination proceeded with cool calculation. It was a tidy, businesslike operation; and the reports were couched in the arid language of bureaucracy as if the executioners were dealing with cabbage, not human beings.... [Some officers] took their task with excess enthusiasm and sadistically beat the prisoners in violation of Himmler's orders to exterminate as humanly as possible.... [Himmler] himself was a witness to the demoralizing effect of daily murder [on a number of killers]. That summer 1941, on a visit at Minsk to Artur Nebe's Einsatzgruppe B, he asked the commander to shoot a hundred prisoners so he could observe the actual liquidation.... The squad fired but Himmler, who had come to see, stared into the ground. He shuffled nervously.

He saw that two women still writhed in the heap and, feeling uneasy, he shouted to the men to get on with the job, to shoot quickly. SS General von Bach-Zelewski, police commander for Central Russia, was on the site beside Himmler and remarked that the firing squad was deeply shaken. They were "finished for the rest of their lives," said the general. "What kind of followers are we creating by these things? Either neurotics or brutes!"

Himmler impulsively ordered every one to gather around so he could make a speech. Theirs was a disgusting task, he said.... Their conscience, however, should be in no way affected because they were soldiers who had to carry out every order without question. He alone, before God and the Fuhrer, bore the terrible responsibility for what had to be done. Surely they had noticed that this bloody work was as odious to him and moved him to the depths of his soul. But he, too, was obeying the highest law by doing his duty.[13]

A few weeks later, in consideration of the Fuhrer's recent instructions, Himmler wondered what would be the best method of mass extermination. The SS chief physician whom he consulted stated clinically: gas chambers would be most appropriate.

At this stage, after a rather brief "experiment" of wholesale killing of the Jews behind the Russian front, there was no immediate retaliation from the free world. It was felt, therefore, that it was quite safe to proceed with the *Endgueltige Loesung*, also referred to as Aktion 14 F 13. This was the "final solution." The phrase was in fact *copyrighted* by Eichmann, as he boasted to Sassen. The solution was, of course, a euphemism for mass slaughter. It involved the concentration of victims in immense abattoirs and the administrative arrangements for getting them there. In other words, mass deportation to death factories.

Hitler had already ordered the killing of all Jews in the Reich and the pillage of their property.[14] Goring issued his directive to Heydrich.[15] Heydrich would only have to pass this order to Eichmann, his competent department chief, and the actual dirty work would be done. Virtually automatically, the whole machinery of the Gestapo was switched into action. The "final solution" now meant physical extermination. What property the Jews left behind would be looted.[16]

Gas poisoning, which Eichmann had seen used in the Lublin area, was still not the ideal means to achieve fast results. Rudolf Hoss,[17] who as early as May 4, 1940, had been assigned as *kommandant* to the future camp of Auschwitz, was asked what he thought of the carbon monoxide method of poisoning. He thought it would necessitate too many buildings in Auschwitz, the camp which had been earmarked for such an operation. Gassing? Yes, but which gas to be used and how to administer it was still uncertain. Soon, however, Hoss was called to Berlin in June 1941 to receive secret instructions for the planned extermination. Hoss had not to judge but only to obey. He knew beforehand and had heard Himmler reminding him that the Jews were the eternal enemies of the German people. Therefore, Himmler said, spelling it out, "they must be exterminated. Henceforth all Jews we can lay our hands on must be annihilated with no exception during this war. If we are unable today to destroy the biological bases of the Jewry, it will be the Jews who will later destroy the German people."

However, the Fuhrer had recommended that Himmler and Heydrich should proceed with the killings "as humanly as possible." The Jews already knew how *human* those killings were!

Thus, the gas chambers were seen as the answer to the Fuhrer's "wish," and Himmler had only to order these chambers built without delay. According to Dr. Rudolf Kastner's deposition in Nuremberg (U.S. Prosecution Exhibit 242), Kaltenbrunner commissioned SS *Standartenfuhrer* Blobel, in the fall of 1941, to work out the plan of the gas chamber system. But the initiative was Eichmann's. Hitler approved of the plan, and the responsibility for its execution fell back onto Eichmann, Himmler and Kaltenbrunner. Kastner also referred to Eichmann's meeting the following spring when Eichmann addressed the officers of the Jewish Affairs Office of the Gestapo and informed them that "the government had decided on the complete annihilation of the European Jews, which would be carried out silently in the gas chambers."

Meanwhile, the future victims, already arrested, were

deported in box cars to ghettos until the death factories in Auschwitz, Birkenau, Majdanek and elsewhere were ready to operate.

And Heydrich had time to set up his bureaucracy in view of the forthcoming liquidation. On December 10, 1941, he ordered a number of his SS subordinates and even State secretaries to a conference to communicate his final instructions. The meeting, however, had to be postponed, and Hans Frank, who headed the General Government of occupied Poland, was so impatient that he sent his deputy, Josef Buhler, to Heydrich to ask for details of the scheme.

Then, on December 16, Frank opened his own conference in Cracow and dealt with the migration of the Jews which was about to begin. He reminded his audience that the Jews had to be finished off one way or the other; there should be no feelings of sympathy for them. "We must annihilate the Jews," he declared, "where we find them and whenever it is possible in order to maintain the structure of the Reich as a whole.... The Jews represent for us extraordinarily malignant gluttons. We have now approximately 2.5 million of them in the General Government, perhaps 3.5 with the Jewish mixtures and everything that goes with it. We cannot shoot or poison those 3.5 million Jews; but we shall, nevertheless, be able to take steps which, one way or the other, will lead to annihilation, and this is in connection with the gigantic measures to be determined in discussions from the Reich."[18]

Heydrich's postponed meeting then took place in the Wannsee suburb of Berlin on January 20, 1942. Heydrich told his fifteen listeners that he had been vested with the responsibility for settling the so-called "final solution" of the Jewish problem, "regardless of geographical boundaries." Emigration of Jews, he explained, was no longer contemplated; instead, deportation would be carried on to the East. Heydrich then produced a chart showing which Jewish populations in Europe and in Soviet Russia would be evacuated and what would be their fate. He mentioned that the Jews were, in total, some eleven million, 8.5 million of

whom were in the occupied Russian zone. His figures were
not quite accurate. Actually the Jewish population across
his map was over fourteen million, and by Heydrich's
stroke of a pen, these people were now earmarked for
deportation and eventual murder in a SS death factory.
Population estimates and their locations:

5   million—USSR
3   million—Ukraine
2.3   million—General Goverment (occupied Poland)
1.2   million—Eastern Territories, White Russia
       and the Bialystok District
0.9   million—France
0.7   million—Hungary
0.35 million—Rumania

The remaining Jews were in other countries in Europe. As
for Estonia, it was acknowledged free of Jews because four
months earlier, when the country fell under German rule,
they had all been murdered.

The Nazis and in particular Heydrich were so confident
that to the above figures they added the 330,000 British
Jews, as well as Jews who lived in neutral countries: 18,000
in Switzerland, 6,000 in Spain, and some 4,000 in Ireland.
Portugal, Sweden and Turkey were also mentioned.
Heydrich had been speaking from Eichmann's draft[19] and
he reminded his audience of Eichmann's appointment as
plenipotentiary for the "final solution" in Europe.

To deal with such a mass of people scattered over Europe
and east of the Polish border, the plan was to put them to
work. While labour gangs would be formed of healthy men,
only as long as they survived the rigours of hard labour, it
did not mean that they would ever be released. At this
point, Heydrich implied that if they were set free, they
could form a new germ cell from which the Jewish race
would rise again.

The forthcoming system of deportation was clear
enough. Several listeners protested that such evacuations

could create serious problems in the Scandinavian countries, for instance. Other topics, such as mixed marriages and their offspring, were discussed but no one raised any question as to the killing of the Jews. In fact, it seems that all present acclaimed the idea of physical annihilation and concurred with Heydrich's plan. Dr. Josef Buhler, head of Frank's government, even asked to be the first in line to finally solve the problem of the Jews in his zone, "as we have already begun it." The Jews created a potential danger of epidemics in the area and they should be removed, he said. Most of his 2.5 million Jews were not fit for work anyway; extermination was the sole logical solution.[20]

It emerged later that Eichmann, according to his own testimony, had cheerfully talked things over with Heydrich and Gestapo Chief Muller, and said he felt free of all guilt. Like Hoss, he did not regard himself as judge of the matter. He would simply be like his superiors, obeying Hitler's orders in virtue of the laws of the land.[21]

Three days later, on January 23, 1942, it was Hitler's turn to speak out. With Himmler facing him, he repeated that the Jew must clear out of Europe. It was his favorite tune all over again. The Jew prevented everything, and the Fuhrer felt he was being "extraordinarily humane." Therefore, "I restrict myself to telling them [the Jews] that they must go away. If they break their pipes on the journey, and whether or not they went along I can't do anything about it. But if they refuse to go voluntarily I see no other solution but extermination." What Hitler did not say is that he would see to it that the Jews did "break their pipes on the journey," and whether or not they tried to oblige their persecutors, they would be exterminated.

On the 27th, he barked again that the Jews must disappear from all Europe, and a few days later at the *Sportpalast* on the Ninth Anniversary of National Socialism he, once more, spelled out that the Jews were their old enemies. The war (which he'd started) could only be ended by wiping out Germany or by the disappearance of Jewry from Europe. "For the first time," he shouted at his listeners, "it will not be the others who will bleed to death." It will be "an eye for an eye, a tooth for a tooth." "The more the struggle spreads," he predicted again, "the more anti-Semitism will also—the world Jewry may rely on this." Then as a promise of Holocaust: "It will find nourishment in every prison camp. . . and the hour will come when the worst enemy in the world will have finished his part for at least a thousand years to come."

On September 30, 1942, at the *Sportpalast* rally for Winter Relief in Berlin, at a time when Stalingrad was in doubt, "for the third time that year,"[22] Hitler [would reiterate] his prediction that if the Jews instigated an international war to exterminate the Aryan peoples it would not be the Aryan race that would be annihilated but the Jewry itself."

These were, of course, quite clear words "to those privy to the secret of the Final Solution. Each mention was a public acknowledgement of his program of extermination; each gave reassurance and authority to the elite charged with the task of mass murder.

"To those engaged in designing gas chambers," Toland concluded, "to those constructing the killing centres in Poland, and particularly to those who were being prepared to administer the mechanics of the final solution, his statement was a clarion call for genocide."[23]

Indeed, "in the meantime, preparations for the Final Solution were maturing, and Heydrich's *Einsatzgruppen* had begun another deadly sweep. While this second roundup of Jews, Commissars and partisans was carried out in a co-ordinated manner in the military areas, progress in civilian territories proceeded smoothly."[24]

It was now Eichmann's job to co-ordinate, concentrate and expedite the complex administration of the programs of deportation to the camouflaged abattoirs, with other camps remaining partially labour camps. Through occupied Europe and the satellite states, the process would be: confiscation, leaving the Jew isolated, humiliated and stripped of his possessions, and then taken on his last journey. There were practical difficulties from the outset, but those problems and those left undecided at Wannsee were taken up in two subsequent conferences chaired by Eichmann: on March 6 and October 27, 1942, when the adoption of administrative practices regarding forced sterilization and the dissolution of mixed marriages was discussed.

The operation continued and, as usual, robbery accompanied murder. It was a hand-in-hand process. The organized seizure of Jewish private and communal property was, in itself, an enormous organizational feat. Eichmann also had to plan and carry out the transport of the doomed. It would be a gigantic effort and Jews, after having been marked, screened, torn away from homes, detained and convoyed, still had to be loaded onto trucks.

In Germany, it went off with clockwork accuracy with the help of the Gestapo offices. The Jews learned that there was no way to escape deportation other than by suicide.[25]

The final roundup in Berlin took place in February 1943, when about 8,000 Jews were suddenly arrested either at home or at work, and concentrated in several places, pending their last journey. A similar fate befell all other communities in Germany, Austria and the Protectorate, and the looting went on, with Eichmann giving special care to objects of art possessed by some of those arrested.

In the spring of 1942, six slaughter camps—of which Treblinka, Sobibor, Belzec and Lublin were in Frank's General Government where the victims were gassed with engine-exhaust fumes—had already started operations.

In Belzec, the camp where Christian Wirth was the *kommandant*,[26] Himmler's orders were carried out with typical SS cruelty, as Kurt Gerstein witnessed. On August 18 and 19, 1942, Gerstein, head of the Technical Disinfection Service of the *Waffen* SS, had toured the four camps in the General Government where the action had speeded up on Hitler's and Himmler's command. Wirth told him there were not ten people alive who had seen or would see as much as he, Gerstein.

When a train of 6,000 Jews arrived, 1,450 were already dead. The survivors were then driven out of the box cars with whips, and ordered to remove money, jewels, spectacles, clothing and even artificial limbs. Females, old and young, had their hair cut. The entire stark-naked group were then marched to the gas chambers, where they were told they would be disinfected. All they had to do was to breathe in; the procedure would prevent them from catching infectious diseases. "But the odor from the death chambers," Toland remarked, "was telltale and those at the head of the column had to be shoved by those behind."

Wirth used his whip on the shoulders of the laggards and protesters, and the march went on. "By now," Toland continued, "the chambers were jammed with humanity. But the driver of the diesel truck, whose exhaust gases would exterminate the Jews, could not start his engine." When, finally, it did start after almost three hours, Gerstein waited some time and then peered through a window into one of the chambers.

> Most of the occupants were already dead. At the end of thirty-two minutes they were all lifeless.... The horror continued as one group of workers began tearing open the mouths of the dead with iron hooks, while others searched anuses and genital organs for jewelry. Pointing to a large can filled with teeth, Wirth said: "Just look at the amount of gold there is! And we have collected as much only yesterday and the day before. You can't imagine what we find every day—dollars, diamonds, gold! You'll see!"
>
> Gerstein forced himself to watch the final process. The bodies were flung into trenches, each some hundred yards long, conveniently located near the gas chambers. He was told that the bodies would swell from gas after a few days, raising the mound as much as six to ten feet. Once the swelling subsided the bodies

would be piled on railway ties covered with diesel oil and burned to cinders.

The following day the Gerstein party was driven to Treblinka near Warsaw where they saw almost identical installations but on a larger scale: eight gas chambers and veritable mountains of clothing and underwear, 115 to 130 feet high.[27]

Apart from the four camps in operation in Frank's General Government, the two other death factories were in German-incorporated territories in Chelmno and Auschwitz.

On March 27, 1943, a train of French Jews was already en route to Auschwitz. But finding the pace too slow in rounding up the Jews in France, Eichmann ruled that 100,000 of them should be moved. To this end, in May, he sent *Haupturmfuhrer* Brunner to Paris with orders to speed up this mass deportation. In fact, Eichmann himself installed his right-hand man in Paris and supervised Brunner's ruthless action. A specific timetable of deportations was laid down. Its effect, however, was disappointing, leading to the arrest during the month of July of "only" 13,000 people,* including 4,000 children.[28] This did not satisfy Eichmann, who returned on two occasions to France** to see how Brunner was doing.

By the end of the year, however, Brunner had the transit camp of Drancy firmly under his control; the departure of freight trains filled with condemned Jews, arrested and marked for annihilation in the SS death factories, was sped up. Thus, Eichmann got what he wanted: the 100,000 he had demanded from France, to which figure was added

*Since it had been rumoured that Jews were taking shelter in Nice, Eichmann travelled south to check on this possibility.
**At that time, as Bormann's decree of July 1 "deprived the Jews of all recourse to ordinary tribunals and placed them under the exclusive jurisdiction of the Gestapo," Eichmann's power over the Jews had become absolute. (Delarue)

25,000 Belgian Jews and 12,000 from Holland. Almost all of them were to perish in the camps.

Deportations of Slovakians had also started in March, and by June, about 52,000 people had been transferred through local transit camps in the Lublin area and forwarded to Auschwitz. The number increased to a total of 71,000 deportees by the last days of March 1945.

Rumania, like the others, suffered the same sweep. When the Russians knocked the Rumanians out of the war, there remained only 400,000 Jews, about half the country's original Jewish population.[29]

A case apart is Hungary, where the action against the Jews took place when the Germans were in full retreat from the East. At first, 50,000 Jews were put to work in labour camps. Half of them died there, but that was the extent of the Hungarian authorities' initial co-operation. Then, in March 1944, as the military situation was deteriorating, Himmler wanted things speeded up. So he ordered Eichmann "to comb the country from East to West; send all Jews to Auschwitz as quickly as possible. Begin with the Eastern provinces, which the Russians are approaching. See to it that nothing like the Warsaw ghetto revolt is repeated in any way." (Hausner)

Obediently, Eichmann arrived in Budapest on March 19 with SS *Standartenfuhrer* Dr. Edmund Veesenmayer, who had just been appointed Plenipotentiary of the Reich in Budapest in charge of forming the new government.

In a meeting with the Jewish Council, Eichmann said to the silent audience, "I have ordered ghettoization in all the boundary regions of Hungary. This affects 300,000 Jews. I won't leave 300,000 enemies loose so near the border.... Jews will have to remain in the ghettos and live there."

Upon this, Eichmann started on an extensive tour to visit the larger ghettos. Confronted with the dreadful conditions that prevailed, he was satisfied, and proceeded to Auschwitz to find out whether the camp was really in a position to "absorb" the number of Jews about to arrive. Actually, he is said to have accompanied the first transport of Hungarian deportees in person—although not in a cattle car.

Though some events from 1940 to the spring of 1942 have already been reviewed, the episodes which marked the beginning of the Auschwitz concentration and extermination camp in the spring of 1940, and its organization and expansion during the following four years should now be exposed.

The choice of Oswiecim, a town of 12,000 near Cracow, for a new concentration camp must be credited to SS *Oberfuhrer* Richard Glucks, the new concentration camp general inspector, who informed Himmler of his discovery on February 21, 1940, describing the place as an ideal one for a quarantine camp. Jan Sehn, however, has stated in his work that the Auschwitz camp was created upon the initiative of SS *Gruppenfuhrer* Erich von dem Bach-Zelewski, Commander-in-Chief of SS and the Wroclaw police. In fact, the Gestapo inspector, SS *Oberfuhrer* Arpad Wigand, who was Bach-Zelewski's subordinate, was the one who drew the attention of his chief to Auschwitz as early as the end of 1939 after the invasion of Poland.

Be that as it may, Himmler agreed to the choice and work was begun on the site in the middle of June 1940. During the spring of that year, SS personnel included Josef Kramer, the future beast of Belsen, and Rudolf Franz Hoss, who was appointed by Glucks on May 5 as *kommandant* of the future Auschwitz camp, arrived on the spot to develop plans for the project and to proceed with the building of a number of top priority plants.[30]

Hoss must have been the right man in the right place. Himmler had read his *curriculum vitae* which disclosed that Hoss had spent several years in prison after having been convicted of murder. Eventually, he was assigned to the post of jailer, probably as an SS promotion.[31] Now Hoss was to superintend the construction of the Auschwitz complex. The site consisted of a swampy plain holding up a handful of dilapidated shacks crawling with vermin. They were the vestiges of Polish military barracks and stables which were later used by the Polish Tobacco Administration.

To start cleaning up and rebuilding, Hoss needed thousands of slave convicts, whom he found in the Sachsenhausen camp (where he had been assigned on August 1, 1938); it housed prisoners of common law, most of them Germans. In fact, the idea was to use these convicts later as officers for the expected "herd" of Jews. Before this could happen, however, Hoss and his assistant, Palitzsch, applied the usual violent methods on the men to speed up construction of the camp.

Hoss had been warned that he would have to manage with whatever material he found on the spot. In Poland, however, the barbed wire necessary for fences was nowhere available. All he could do, to compensate for the lack of steel, was to dismantle what remained of the Polish fortifications in the countryside, and find what he could in former military depots. Meanwhile, the construction was taking a turn for the better; the population around the camp was dislodged—a state secret—and a second zone evacuated to incorporate some arable land into the complex.

Himmler appreciated Hoss' enormous job, and toward the end of November 1940, he called his Auschwitz *kommandant* to Berlin. It was then, said Hoss, that "I made my first verbal report to Himmler in the presence of *Sturmbannfuhrer* Vogel from the Economic Administration Head Office" (SS *Wirtschafts- und Verwaltungshauptamt* —WVHA). Himmler explained that Auschwitz was to become *the* agricultural research station for the eastern territories. Was this plan to screen the real purpose of Auschwitz? Himmler's intentions were soon made clear when the *Reichsfuhrer* arrived in Auschwitz on March 1, 1941. He told the *kommandant* that to ensure Reich security, the camp with its capacity to handle 10,000 evacuees was no longer sufficient. Himmler's plan now was to create two satellite zones for a total capacity of 30,000 inmates, including the original camp. But, of course, these inmates were temporary.

One of the new extensions would be Auschwitz II at Birkenau near a small forest of birch trees. The second site, a few miles away, would be near Monowice and would become Auschwitz III. There already existed, though not completed, the I.G. Farben plant for the production of Buna synthetic rubber and coal oil. What actually was needed in Auschwitz III was labour: more convicts were to be brought there.

As Himmler stood with his entire entourage—Glucks and Hans Frank among them—on the bridge above the railway tracks, he envisioned a new extermination camp established in the area below him.

Hoss strongly protested against a development which did not take such realities into consideration as the lack of water and drainage problems, but Himmler "snubbed him abruptly." The expansion of the camp to hold 30,000 prisoners was said to be only the working out of a "peacetime establishment," but the truth is that the construction which the *Reichsfuhrer* was ordering, in effect, was to create a "POW camp for 100,000 prisoners." I.G. Farbenindustries was to get 10,000 of them assigned to the construction work. Important branches of the armaments industry were to be transferred into the same region and, finally, space would be reserved for the agricultural research station and farms. Himmler would not hear of any drawbacks, technical difficulties or other grievances. The work had to be done and quickly. Questions were dismissed when Himmler stood up, brought down his fist on the table and demanded the immediate execution of his orders. Then, without further explanation, the *Reichsfuhrer* adjourned. All that counted was the aggrandizement of the camp. Turning to Hoss, the SS Chief said, "It is up to you to manage somehow."

In June that same year, Himmler once more called Hoss to his Berlin office, where they met in private. He told him that the Fuhrer had given the order to settle the Jewish question once and for all. The SS was to carry out the order. So far, the "final solution" had amounted to the forced emigration of the Jews, but now it would be no less than their annihilation. The SS *Reichsfuhrer* said that he had earmarked Auschwitz (Birkenau) as the site for those great actions because "the place destined to such operations can be easily isolated and camouflaged in that region. . . . It will be your task. It's a hard and painful job that you'll have to attend to; you'll have to involve your whole person and disregard any difficulty.[32] Details will be given you by the *Sturmbannfuhrer* Eichmann[33] of the RSHA [the *Reichssicherheitspolizeihauptamt*],[34] who will soon join you."

Hoss was to keep silent and was forbidden to discuss the matter even with *Gruppenfuhrer* Richard Glucks, his immediate superior and inspector of concentration camps. "This is a secret Reich matter," Himmler insisted. "You must not mention it to anyone; you would endanger your life. Henceforth the final solution of the Jewish problem will be the physical extermination of those people. There already exists centres of extermination in the east zone, but they are not equipped to undertake to the end the great operations which have been planned."

Hoss had just been made to understand that Auschwitz, in fact, had been earmarked to become "the largest human slaughter house that history had ever known."

Upon leaving, Hoss was asked to send Himmler the plans of the proposed installations following his conversation with Eichmann. The *kommandant* returned to Auschwitz to undertake at once the installations needed for the implementation of the program.

As Hitler was to say, there was a time when the German Jews mocked his predictions but they would soon stop laughing. On March 20, 1942, Hitler told Goebbels that Europe must be cleansed of all Jews, if necessary by the most brutal methods—it was no longer "as humanly as possible." In his diaries, Goebbels commented further on the 27th:

Beginning with Lublin, the Jews in the General Government are now being evacuated eastward. The procedure is a pretty barbaric one and not to be described here more definitely. *Not much will remain of the Jews.* On the whole, it can be said that about 60 per cent of them all have to be liquidated whereas only about 40 per cent can be used for forced labour.... A judgement is being visited upon the Jews that, while barbaric, [this solution] is fully deserved by them.... One must not be sentimental in these matters. If we did not fight the Jews, they would destroy us. It's a life-and-death struggle between the Aryan race and the Jewish bacillus. No other government and no other regime would have the strength for such a global solution of this question. Here, too, the Fuhrer is *the undismayed champion of a radical solution* necessitated by conditions and therefore inexorable[35] (emphasis added).

Months before Goebbels had entered these declarations in his diary, Eichmann had joined Hoss in Auschwitz not long after Himmler had told the *kommandant* his plans. Apparently, it was Eichmann's first visit but he lost no time initiating Hoss to the plans which he had drawn for the operation—"actions" as they were called—in the European countries. Hoss was later to recall in his memoirs that the SS *Obersturmbannfuhrer* always showed enthusiasm at the prospect of destroying every single Jew he could lay his hands on. It was a veritable obsession. The actions he was preparing were to start in High-Silesia and neighbouring regions of the Polish General Government. Simultaneously, German and Czech Jews were to be involved. Those of France, Belgium and Holland would follow. Eichmann now briefed the *kommandant* as to the number of convoys he should expect. As for the method of extermination, it would be asphyxiation by lethal fumes. It would be simply impossible, remarked Eichmann, to liquidate the herd with mass shooting. With women and children in the crowd, that

method would be too painful...for the SS executioners.
Therefore gas was ideal. At this point, Eichmann expounded
on what the *Einsatzgruppen* had already accomplished in
Russia, and he cited the example of Minsk.

When a train of the deported arrived, the inmates
climbed down and then got aboard trucks which travelled a
few miles to a meadow where there were a number of
waiting vans. In fact, these were well-camouflaged trucks,
on the side of which windows with drapes and shutters were
painted and each was fitted with a chimney. The crowd was
then ordered to climb in. When the vans were full, the steel
doors were noisily closed and locked. All that had to be
done then was start the motors whose exhaust fumes exited
inside the van through a pipe. Yet Eichmann did not think
the method was suitable for the mass liquidation
contemplated in Auschwitz. In the Reich, carbon dioxide
had been blown through bathroom shower heads for the
extermination of lunatics, but that system was not ideal
either. Eichmann just had to think of something else. But,
in Appendix I of his autobiography, Hoss wrote:

> We agreed that the farm located at the N.W. corner of
> the future Sector III at Birkenau was particularly
> appropriate for those operations. The premises, not far
> from the tracks, were isolated and protected by bushes
> and hedges. The bodies would be disposed of in long
> and deep trenches which would be dug in adjacent
> clearings. At the time, we did not yet envisage incinera-
> tion. According to our calculations, it was possible to
> kill about 800 persons simultaneously with the appro-
> priate gas.

After Eichmann left, Hoss sent Himmler a special report
with a detailed plan of the chosen site and an exact
description of the projected installation. But it was not until
November 1941, that the *kommandant* was again called to
Berlin. It was Eichmann who now chaired the meeting. All
the executives charged with the Jewish liquidation were

present, and one after the other they reported on the operations for gathering and transferring the Jews that they were responsible for in the occupied territories. Many difficulties had been encountered. One of the main problems was that the railroad gave priority to the army. This remark did not deter Eichmann, who reminded his listeners that the *Reichsfuhrer* had recommended they disregard all problems; the action simply had to be speeded up.

Hoss, in turn, announced that the work in Auschwitz progressed rapidly, and he asked if there was a date fixed to launch the program of annihilation. But there was no date because the ideal gas had not yet been discovered. When Hoss returned to Auschwitz, he acknowledged that his deputy, the *Standartenfuhrer* Karl Fritzsch,* had, on his own initiative, used gas to kill Russian prisoners, political commissars and Communist party members who had been arriving in Auschwitz in small groups. At first, they had been shot in the quarry or in the yard of Block II. Then Fritzsch had the idea of trying a gas, Zyklon B, which the Testa Company from Hamburg (TEsch and STAbenow) supplied to the *Wehrmacht* as disinfectant and insecticide to combat parasites and epidemics. A number of containers of Zyklon—simply a preparation of hydrogen cyanide, a lethal poison—were stocked in the Auschwitz administration building, and one day Fritzsch decided to test its efficiency on Russians. The result of this limited experiment impressed

---

*Because of the size of Auschwitz, there was, from the start, a first and a second prison commander under Hoss. Karl Fritzsch and Hans Aumeier, second in line, thus entered the scene. Fritzsch, in charge of Auschwitz I, the mother-camp, had words of welcome to newcomers. His words went into the record and have been quoted partly or totally by most historians of the Holocaust. "This is not a sanatorium you have come to," he spelled out to the doomed deportees, "but a concentration camp from which the only exit is through the chimney. If anyone does not like it, he can go right away and throw himself against the high-tension wires. If there are any Jews in this convoy, they are not entitled to live more than two weeks; priests are given one more month of life and the remainder will get three months."

Hoss. The product was a cheap, ordinary one. It needed no complex installation. The procedure was simple, silent and fast-acting. Zyklon B was in purple granulated form. Once in contact with air, it was promptly transformed into an asphyxiating, poisonous gas. Obviously, this was the stuff and the method which, at long last, could put the "final solution" into operation.

When Eichmann returned to Auschwitz, Hoss informed him of the good news. "We made the decision to use it [Zyklon B] for future mass extermination."[36]

The mother camp had already opened its gates on June 14, 1940, when the first prisoners arrived. They were Poles, political prisoners, and numbered 728.[37] They were given no illusions regarding their fate as they were driven toward Block 26, in front of which they had to undress; they had their heads shorn and were herded into the bath-house. "Regaled with beating and abuse, they were showered with boiling hot or ice cold water and... regardless of the season were driven naked into the yard."[38] They were given tattered, dirty prison clothes, and a camp number was tattooed on the left forearm. Later, they were marched to "quarantine" for six to eight weeks.[39] There they were drilled and incessantly beaten, since the idea was to terrorize them and "to break down [their] mental and physical resistance."

The camp was thus in operation, but it was not yet large enough nor ready for mass extermination. Still it handled what it could. When a cargo of deportees from Czechoslovakia (Brno) were joined in the month of August by others from Yugoslavia, as well as by Soviet prisoners of war, they were exterminated by injections of oxygenated water, benzine and evipan when found to be ill or unfit for work. From then until the end, in addition to Poles, who formed the largest single group of prisoners, there were Hungarian, Czech and Slovak, German, Greek and Dutch Jews. They were herded in crowds of 700 to 800 into every barrack of the camp. In periods of heavy influx, all that was left for newcomers were attics and cellars.[40]

Finally, on September 3, 1941, mass gassing was tried for the first time with Zyklon B granules[41] in Death Block 11, and specifically in a corridor of its basement.[42] Other sources have fixed the experiment as having taken place on September 15. Hoss, in Appendix I of his autobiography, wrote that the extermination of the Jews began as early as September 1941 or possibly not until January 1942; he did not remember exactly. Regardless, the former *kommandant* stated that the result of Fritzsch's original experiment with Zyklon B was that the prisoners were killed instantly.

But according to the Commission of the Polish Government, it was Gerhard Palitzsch, the *Rapportfuhrer*, who, wearing a mask, threw the contents of cans of Zyklon through the open door, which was then slammed shut. The next afternoon, Palitzsch, again wearing a mask, opened the door and saw that many of the prisoners were still alive. More Zyklon was added and the door shut until the following evening. This time all the prisoners were asphyxiated,[43]

Such operations, however, could no longer be carried out in Block 11, which had to be ventilated for at least two days after each session. The mortuary of the crematorium[44] next to the hospital block was chosen instead. The gassing was then carried out through openings in the ceiling and the doors, one at each end of the room, and made gas-tight.

During the month of October 1941, following Himmler's recent orders, a zone of 40 square kilometres was cleared of its Polish inhabitants, and the construction of the greater complex was started, according to plans, on the marshland of Brzezinka (Birkenau), three kilometres from the Auschwitz *Stammlager*. Eventually the entire camp, as mentioned earlier, was divided into three areas: the original Auschwitz I-*Stammlager* to the southeast; Auschwitz II-Birkenau; and Auschwitz III-Subcamp to the northwest.[45]

The same month, several cargoes of Soviet prisoners were moved from Lansdorf to Auschwitz. The number of POWs at the time thus reached a total of 13,775, more than two-thirds of whom perished between October and March 1942—supposedly from heart failure, according to the SS *Totenbuch*!

Eventually the prisoners filled 263 huts; their total reached 120,000 in Birkenau, and two years later, 140,000.

According to Hoss, one of the first, if not the very first, transport of Jews was from Beuthen, on February 15, 1942. From then on, Auschwitz-Birkenau became a Jewish camp, a collecting place for Jews on a greater scale than anything ever heard. The first consignment was earmarked for immediate extermination. Then there followed cargoes—which continued without stop until the end of the war—from the Jewish Department of the Reich Security Office (RSHA). On March 26, 999 Slovak Jewesses together with 999 prisoners from Ravensbruck arrived; on the 28th, 718 Jewesses also from Slovakia, and on the 30th, 1,112 Jews from Paris.

The question of how to cremate these people remained. In the Auschwitz mother-camp, the mortuary served as the gas chamber. Hoss designated it as a multi-room bunker. There were five rooms, wrote the *kommandant*, and after half an hour "the dead bodies were taken out and brought to the pits in small trolleys which ran on rails."

During the summer of 1942, Hoss went on to explain, the transports increased and "a further extermination building" had to be erected on the future site of Crematoria III and IV (Hoss' numbering). "Two huts near Bunker I and three near Bunker II were built, in which the victims undressed." Other sources have stated that the two bunkers in Birkenau were actually former peasant dwellings which had been equipped for the extermination process. Once gassed, the bodies were dumped into mass graves. This continued until the end of the summer, "when we started to burn them at first on wood pyres bearing 2,000 corpses, and later in pits together with bodies previously buried." Finally, by the end of November 1942, all mass graves, filled with some 107,000 corpses, had been emptied. This was in response to orders from Himmler, after his visit to the camp in July: "the ashes were to be disposed of in such a way that it would be impossible at some future time to calculate the number of corpses burnt."

It is interesting to note at this juncture, for Ernst Zundel's education on the subject of the Holocaust, that "originally all the Jews transported to Auschwitz on the authority of Eichmann's office were, in accordance with orders of the *Reichsfuhrer* SS to be *destroyed without exception*."

As Hoss also explained, it had become "apparent during the first cremation in the open air that, in the long run, it would not be possible to continue in this manner."

Until the new crematoria could be installed and since all the inmates were doomed anyway, on July 8, Himmler placed the camp at Professor Karl Clauberg's disposal for his experiments on humans and animals (probably making no distinction between the two). These experiments were of the greatest importance since they were designed to find a method of sterilization which, when applied to non-Germans, would result in these people's biological extinction.[46] In his letter of June 7, Dr. Clauberg had promised the *Reichsfuhrer* that *one* properly trained surgeon working in a suitably equipped surgery with perhaps ten medical assistants "will probably be in a position to sterilize several hundred or even 1,000 persons in the course of one day."

Let there be no doubt in anyone's mind about these and other doctors in Auschwitz-Birkenau. They were grotesque criminals whose activities consisted of selecting prisoners and patients for the gas chambers, killing some of them by injections, practising sterilization and other experiments on living prisoners, and supervising or witnessing the gassing of millions of individuals, and the flogging, shooting and hanging of others.

Sterilization of men by X rays was also contemplated and Dr. Clauberg and his colleague, Dr. Johann Gebel, carried out their experiments in Auschwitz in Block 10, while Horst Schumann performed in Birkenau. When, for one reason or another, it happened that some victims were not fit to stand the torture to which they were subjected, they were sent to the gas chambers.[47]

At this time, it was about nine months since Heydrich had been appointed by Hitler as Acting *Protector* of Moravia and Bohemia. This post had given the SS *Obergruppenfuhrer*—the Hangman, as he was to be called—the opportunity to initiate a bloody wave of terror in the country and to crush resistance. On May 27, 1942, however, the *Protector* had fallen mortally wounded when a grenade was thrown at his car. He died a few days later in Prague, on June 4.[48]

More than ever was mass extermination the order of the day. First there was the immediate retaliation by the SS when 152 Jews were executed in Berlin and 3,000 removed from Theresienstadt and taken to the death factories in Poland. Early that summer, Himmler confirmed the mass killing of the Jews. On July 28, he wrote to Gottlob Berger, Chief of the SS Main Office, that the Jews in the occupied Eastern territories must be cleared away. "The implementation of the very hard order has been placed on my shoulders by the Fuhrer. No one can release me from this responsibility in any case. So I forbid all interference."

On August 3, 1942, the decision was made to install two large crematoria, Nos. I and II (Hoss' numbering), together with gas chambers, which were built by a firm of Erfurt. They became operational in the spring of 1943 when, under pretence of fighting an epidemic of typhus, 747 invalids and even convalescents were taken from the Revier and sent to Birkenau to be gassed. The construction of smaller crematoria, Nos. III and IV, soon followed.[49]

Speedy killing, of course, was the reason why these four units had been built, for the small crematorium already in operation in the mother-camp and the transformed bunkers in Birkenau could not cope with the demand for body burning.

A problem which could not be solved as easily was the stench of burning flesh. It carried many miles away where people began to talk, among them the members of the nearby German Air Defence Service, who complained about the fires, visible at night.[50]

"Later," wrote Fania Fenelon, "we learned that the cause of those flames had been a ditch filled with corpses of gassed Hungarians which had been sprinkled with gasoline and set alight. In the morning, the sky was still glimmering; they had burned all night."[51]

"Inside our block," recalled another inmate, Kitty Hart, "the air became so black and foul we opened a window which only made it worse.... [And] this time it was the screaming of thousands in agony quite different from the muffled retching and howling of those hit by gas.... [The prisoners were being roasted alive]... It was true...."[52]

In the spring of 1943, when Crematoria II, III, IV and V[53]—plan numbering in Birkenau—were installed, this situation was bound to change. The last two units, IV and V,[54] were located near a pond to which the ashes from both units were transported by means of a narrow gauge railway. They were then dumped into the pond.[55]

The women who lived in Auschwitz, in Blocks 1 to 10 surrounded by a wall, were first transported to Birkenau on August 16, 1942, in B Ia, enlarged a year later to sector b.

In June 1944, a branch line from Auschwitz Station to Birkenau had been constructed. Passing through the main entrance to the camp and running as far as Crematoria II and III, the tracks separated the women's camp B I from the larger men's camp B II. Between the two were raised two electrically charged wire fences between which ran the railroad ramp with three platforms where the convoys were unloaded and the newcomers assembled before being marched to their deaths or their "accommodations."[56]

This was the situation in the summer of 1944, but for the previous two years, trains had stopped at the siding outside Auschwitz Station and the prisoners had been marched or taken by truck to the camp.

Between February and April 1942, the first consignments of Gypsies from several countries arrived in Birkenau. Twenty-one thousand eventually passed through camp B IIe (adjacent to the men's), to which they were assigned. When on July 17 and 18, 1942, Himmler visited the camp for the second and last time—Hoss reminisced—the SS *Reichsfuhrer* saw the overcrowded quarters, the unsatisfactory hygienic conditions, the hospital barracks filled with the sick, and the ward for infectious diseases. He saw children suffering from *noma*, a disease which had always filled the *kommandant* with horror, as it resembled leprosy...the wasted little bodies, the big holes in the cheeks, the slow decay of living organisms.[57] The death rate was naturally very high. "I have seen everything," said Himmler, "and I have seen enough of the deficiencies and difficulties and I have heard enough of them from you. I can, however, do nothing to alter them. You will have to manage as best you can." This, of course, was what Hoss had been doing all along. Himmler continued:

> We are now in the middle of a war and we must learn to think in terms of war. The actions, which I have ordered the security police to carry out, will not be stopped under any circumstances, least of all because of the lack of accommodation and so on, which I have been shown. Eichmann's program will continue to be carried out and will be intensified month by month. You must see to it that swift progress is made with the building of Birkenau. The gypsies are to be destroyed. The Jews who are unfit for work are to be destroyed with the same ruthlessness. Soon the labour camps at the armaments factories will absorb the first large contingents of able-bodied Jews, and that will give you some breathing space again. Armaments factories will also be built in Auschwitz camp, so prepare yourselves for that. Kammler will give you far-reaching support in matters connected with their construction.
> The agricultural experiments will be intensively

pursued, for the results are urgently required.

I have seen your work and the results you have achieved, and I am satisfied and thank you for your services. I promote you to *Obersturmbannfuhrer!*

The planned killing of the Gypsies, however, did not begin until the night of July 31-August 1, 1944, when almost 3,500 disappeared into the ovens. Then, only a few weeks later, all men, women and children were driven to the crematorium in columns of five. "The gypsies offered resistance and hence the shouting heard all over Birkenau. The noise continued throughout the night, but in the morning the gypsy camp was empty."[58]

In the summer of 1943, the "quarantine" camp for men in B IIa was established. It was not, as may appear, intended for early detection of diseases. Selections were made and thousands of prisoners were moved on to the gas chambers, thus making room in the camp for daily newcomers. Many of the men were beaten and kicked, ordered to kneel down, and had a revolver put to their heads. The game of the SS men was then to force the prisoners to get up and run and, at this point only, the guards would fire at them.

Ludwick Ragewski, a survivor, recalled that the persecutors pounced upon the "quarantined" prisoners. Then "for hours, we had to run, jump, crawl, turn round while kneeling on the gravel and sharp pebbles. Weaker prisoners collapsed, older and stouter men fainted, blood rushed to the temples. Hearts burst due to excessive strain and exhaustion, particularly so as we had had nothing to eat since we were arrested."[59]

Besides the three camp divisions already mentioned, there were three more.[60] A Families' Camp, Thereseinstadt in B IIb was opened to Jewish families who arrived from Teresina in September 1943 and, in short order, there were further cargoes until May 1944. These people were eventually liquidated in the gas chambers and burned on

March 9, July 11 and 12 of that year, 1944.

There was also a special camp for Hungarian Jewish women in B IIc. By June 1944, their numbers reached 20,000; most also ended in the gas chambers after the healthy ones were transported to German factories.

Finally, next to the B II men's camp, separated by a road that led to Crematorium No. V, was another sector, B III, called *Mexico*, which, though unfinished, was used to house 15,000 women, mostly Hungarian Jewesses who lived in the worst possible conditions until the time of their liquidation. The bunks were not finished, and the women lay on the concrete floor "almost naked, grey with dirt and exhausted."[61] A few of these women were transported to Germany; the others, the old, the weak and the sick, and those considered unfit for work were, of course, led to the gas chambers.

Selections of young and old in the barracks and the hospital huts, though frequent and yielding large contingents for the gas chambers, were somewhat secondary. In actuality, the main selections had already been performed during the daily arrivals of the *cattle* transports, on the ramp beside the tracks.[62]

It was then that a large number of newcomers in the *Stammlager*—the elderly, the weak, the sick, the crippled, the ones obviously unfit for work—were singled out for immediate death, generally by a doctor, sometimes an SS officer. Only the slave prisoners, who would work in a nearby factory, were recorded in the camp register. As it was retrieved, this register showed that over 450,000 prisoners had been listed, of whom 340,000 were to perish due to malnutrition, exhaustion, punishment, and ill-treatment inflicted in the "quarantine" huts. Those who survived were given labour assignments and eventually they died too, of the same causes.

Hoss has described briefly what happened as the trains, mostly crowded with Jews, pulled in alongside the ramp:

The vans were unloaded one after the other. After
depositing their baggage, the Jews had to pass
individually in front of an SS doctor, who decided on
their physical fitness as they marched past him. Those
capable of employment were immediately taken into
the camp in small groups. Taking an average of all the
transports, between 25 and 30% were found fit for
work, but this figure, for Greek Jews, for example, was
only 15%.[63]

Other witnesses have narrated even more dramatically
how these selections were performed in two columns: one
on the right, which would be marched to "quarantine," the
other on the left, which would be escorted directly to the gas
chambers. "The doors of the railway carriages were open,"
wrote Fania Fenelon,[64]

and out of them tumbled men, women and children.
Few got up. Others came out shrieking, leaping over
the dead. The transports, it seemed, took several days,
standing on sidings to give priority to military convoys.
These deportees had been traveling for twelve days;
twelve days without air, food or water.... The SS
soldiers grouped the survivors five by five.... Graf
Bobby[65]... separated those who were to enter the hell
of the camps from those who were to make a hasty
entrance to paradise. What a Noble metier!
[In the midst of the crowd] a young man, entirely
naked, was surging and prancing outside the open door
of a carriage.... The SS, from the humblest to the
highest were having fun, Graf Bobby among them....
The procession of victims filed slowly past.... When
they had disappeared in the direction of the ramp
which led to the gas chambers the madman was alone
with the dead from the carriages; and while the
prisoners, in their striped rags, piled them onto the
trolleys, he laughed and clapped his hands and capered
grotesquely. The empty carriages slowly backed away
and new ones arrived at the platform.

Another witness on the SS side was Dr. Johann Paul Kremer who was assigned to Auschwitz in August 1942, to substitute for a colleague who was sick. A few days later, on September 2, at 3 p.m., he attended for the first time a *Sonderaktion*. "Compared with it," he wrote in his diary,[66] "Dante's Inferno seems almost a comedy. No wonder Auschwitz is called an extermination camp. . . ."

Three days later, Kremer watched another selection operation carried out on women, and he thought it a most horrible spectacle. "Thilo," he added in his diary, "the troop's doctor, was right this morning to tell me we are the 'world's anus.' "

On September 9, he noted that, in his capacity as camp doctor, he attended corporal punishment inflicted upon eight prisoners, followed by a capital execution with small calibre guns. In the evening, Kremer was for the fourth time witness to a *Sonderaktion*. On October 12, again in the evening, although he had a fever following vaccination against typhoid, he attended another *aktion*—the tenth one—performed on 1,600 Dutchmen. On this occasion a terrible scene took place near the last bunker.

Five days later, on the 17th, he was present at corporal punishment sessions followed by eleven executions, and on the 18th, though a cold Sunday morning, he witnessed "impressive scenes with three women who beseeched us to spare them." Kremer's busiest day seems to have been November 8, when he watched three more *Sonderaktionen* —followed by more carnage on the 12th, 13th and 14th.

Though Kremer did not describe these selections, punishments and killings in great detail, it appears obvious that not all were carried out on the ramp upon the arrival of the prisoners. At the same time, he concerned himself with writing in his diary about the good food he enjoyed and filled himself with—"over-baked brochet as much as we liked; excellent coffee, delicious beer"—and, all the while, adding references to excisions of "living human material: liver, spleen and pancreas," but failing to mention what else he did with these anatomical specimens. In fact, the prisoners' organs were studied to find out what changes had occurred in the human body as a consequence of starvation.

Cruelty and sadism were displayed when punishments were meted out and at execution time.[67] Flogging and starvation and the use of dogs[68] were some of the terrorist methods practised on the prisoners. More vicious penalties were suffered in Hut No. 11, known as the Death Hut, in which the basement and the courtyard (separated from the rest of the camp by a high wall) formed a prison called the Bunker.[69] Crucifixions were carried out in that courtyard or in the attic of the block. Prisoners were hanged by a chain or a rope; their twisted arms tied behind. The regular, completely dark cells in the Bunker were called *Stelhzelle*, meaning that the punished "animals" could only stand. The cells were entered by small openings close to the ground and secured by an iron grating and a wooden door.[70] In those cells, which were 90 x 90 cms., four prisoners were locked in for several nights and left standing, the only posture the tiny cells allowed. Sure enough, they slowly suffocated since the inflow of air through an opening 5 cms. in diameter could not suffice inasmuch as even this hole was covered outside by an 18 x 18 cms. sheet of metal.

If prisoners survived, one can imagine how they emerged from those cells after several days of martyrdom. Death by starvation was even harsher since the doomed were shut in a dungeon,[71] and removed only when it had been made quite certain that all prisoners were dead.

In addition to crucifixions, executions by firing squad were also performed in the courtyard of Death Block 11, against what came to be known as the Black Wall. Twenty thousand men and women perished there. They were forced to undress before being led into the courtyard, the women always going first.[72]

The ground floor of Block 11 was where male and female civilians were kept imprisoned while they awaited the verdict of the Gestapo Police Summary Court in Katowice. Summary indeed! In two to three hours, this court would pronounce more or less 200 death sentences. Added to these victims were the prisoners selected in the camp during the roll call, and escorted to the Death Wall for execution by a firing squad or, as it was decided later, by an SS man shooting each victim in the back of the neck. In 1941, such selections occurred every time a prisoner escaped; ten men or more who belonged in the same barrack were then led to the dungeon where they perished from starvation.

An ex-prisoner whose testimony is quoted in the *Auschwitz Museum Guide-Book*[73] has narrated his personal experience with 38 of his companions in cell No. 20 of the infamous Block 11. They soon suffered from lack of air. After some time, the narrator recalled, "The prisoners lost consciousness and in the morning, when the door was opened at 5 o'clock, we had to be dragged in the corridor and laid there. We were stark naked. . . . Only nineteen had survived and six out of the nineteen had to be carried immediately to the hospital where four of them died."

Penal companies—*Strafkompanien*—also existed in the camp. They were, so to speak, pseudo-work squads to which prisoners "guilty of transgressing the order and discipline" were sent to be assigned to the hardest jobs all day long. At his trial, Rudolf Hoss reminisced about how prisoners came back from their work site: "Some were brought in carts," he said. "Those were the corpses of killed prisoners. Others were brought in wheelbarrows. Those unable to walk in march step had to be supported by the stronger men who also carried half-dead prisoners on their shoulders, using special appliances for the purpose."

Eventually few, if any, of the punished men survived the regimen. The women, too, who had transgressed the regulations, were assigned to penal companies. In their case, they were made to work immersed in water, removing rushes from the fishponds in the village of Budy near Birkenau. A mutiny finally broke out in autumn 1942, which only brought havoc. SS retaliation was prompt and efficient as Hoss testified at his trial. The French Jewesses, who had been the leaders of the mutiny, "were killed with axes and poles; some had their heads completely severed, others found death as they threw themselves from the windows of upper storeys." Thus, approximately 90 women prisoners perished as a result of the mutiny, and six so-called functionaries, who had participated in the bloodbath, were put to eternal rest by phenol injections. To complete the SS repression, their Political Section conducted an investigation (as they did in all such cases) and, during interrogation, tortured a number of prisoners under suspicion. Fingernails were pulled off, breasts and genital organs were pricked with needles, water was poured through funnels down their throats causing suffocation. These tricks of the trade were combined with beating all the while; many victims died there and then, and those who survived were shot, hanged or sent to penal companies where death would end their moral and physical sufferings.

Hanging was carried out primarily on portable gallows erected on the parade ground in front of the kitchen. There the executions would take place during the evening roll call so that the other inmates would attend the killing of their comrades.[74]

Extermination, the main purpose of Himmler and his henchmen, also operated in the hospital installed partly in Block 19, and in Blocks 20, 21 and 28.[75] Overcrowded, as it always was, the "hospital" was an antechamber to the crematorium rather than a place where patients were treated to recover. Selections were made regularly and the selected were either sent directly in large numbers to the gas chambers[76] or, if their numbers were small, killed by phenol injections into the heart—a quick and clean procedure. In addition to these deaths, several hundred additional patients were also murdered daily. They died in the lazarets, notably during epidemics, and thus cremation statistics were raised even higher. The latter included women who died of infection after childbirth; newborn infants died as well. If any survived, they were killed forthwith.

The whole procedure of extermination—first, the selection, the breaking up of families, then the herding to the "baths," the undressing, the screams, the shattering and heart-rending scenes involving children, and so on—all has been described at length by Hoss. Then, he went on to say, "the bodies had to be dragged to the pits or to the crematoria.... The fires in the pits had to be stoked, the surplus fat drained off, and the mountain of burning corpses constantly turned over so that the draught might fan the flames.... I had to see everything, I had to watch hour after hour, by day and by night, the removal and burning of the bodies, the extraction of teeth, the cutting of hair, the whole grisly interminable business. I had to stand for hours on end in the ghastly stench, while the mass graves were being opened and the bodies dragged out and burned...."

Since the aim of this book is to research how and to what extent systematic extermination of human beings was carried out by the friends of Ernst Zundel and Douglas Christie, details regarding the prisoners' lives and the work they were forced to do have generally been omitted. Still, readers should not ever forget that "the hands of the camp clock were mercilessly... measuring out the prisoners' span of life; from morning bell to evening bell, from one dish of soup to the next, from the first roll-call to the one at which the prisoners' corpses would be counted for the last time."[77]

Roll call is mentioned here again because it soon became one of the horrendous nightmares of the prisoners. At first there were three roll calls every day, then two, and toward the end, the SS did with only one in the evening after work time. It would seldom last less than an hour.

On July 6, 1940, when operations at the Auschwitz camp were not quite organized yet, it lasted nineteen hours: from 7 p.m. through the whole night until 2 p.m. the next day, prisoners had had to remain standing or yielding on bending knees where they stood.

One of the survivors narrated in her book[78] that "dying women were carried out [of the barracks] and laid upon the ground to be counted. Inert, human figures stretched out on the wet, muddy ground and covered with blankets, dirtied with the mud arrested the eyes of healthy prisoners, newcomers to the camp.... It is impossible to avert one's eyes—everywhere, in front of other barracks, similar sights are to be seen...."

Daily work, of course, was another painful trial for as long as the enslaved could stand it—that is, until death. It is important also to keep in mind that almost the entire camp of Birkenau was built by inmates brought in "herds" from various German-occupied countries. The ground had to be levelled using an enormous roller at which a gang of ten to fifteen men pushed and pulled.[79] The land had to be drained, which meant working in water and mud, and the soil had to be dug up for long stretches and to a certain depth. It was a back-breaking job, as was the loading and moving of wagons of rocks, gravel, dirt, steel rods and cement. "We used to draw fifteen or more wagons a day," a survivor testified. "Everything had to be done double quick, and should anyone fall down exhausted he would be beaten and kicked by the SS men and the capos." If the slave-prisoners had not been needed for the development of the complex and the factories, there is little doubt that Himmler and Eichmann would have found it more expeditious to stop the convoys on the very steps of the crematoria and, dispensing with the selections, send the crowds directly to the gas chambers and the ovens, as was the fate of those unfit for work.

But a cheap and abundant labour force was necessary to proceed with the building of new industries and the operating of those which already existed. One of these, already mentioned, was I.G. Farbenindustries' Buna factory designed to produce synthetic rubber and petrol. It was built at Monowice. The slaves who were put to work there[80] had to cover a distance of some five kilometres from the camp to the factory and back for the evening roll call, which lasted two hours. "Under such conditions," said Dr. Bertold E., "it was impossible to survive three to four months; after that period the men died of exhaustion and overwork.... About 500 to 600 patients came to the surgery each day.... There were cases of severe beatings at work,[81]

and every day about ten persons were brought dead or
half-dead; the latter expired soon after...." As a matter of
fact, in a period of only three years, about 30,000 prisoners
perished at building the Buna factory and at working in
other plants.

Here, then, was another facet of Hitler's extermination
program of Jews.

As was stated earlier, during the middle of May 1944,
Eichmann's great deportation drive from Hungary was
started and developed with staggering speed. Sometimes as
many as five trains packed to a total of 14,000 people
arrived at Auschwitz-Birkenau in a single day.

Hoss, who had been transferred at the end of November
1943 to the political section of the Economic-Administra-
tion Head Office (WVHA) in Berlin, where he was chief of
the DI Department of Concentration Camps Inspection,
had been replaced at Auschwitz by his predecessor in the
Camps Inspectorate, Arthur Liebehenschel. But, upon the
exceptional occasion of the Hungarian Jews' slaughter,
Hoss hurried back to the camp on May 8 to ensure that the
installations were ready to meet the pace of Eichmann's
deportation.

It is said that on three occasions Hoss travelled to
Budapest to ascertain what number of Jews he might
expect. He and Eichmann finally agreed on a schedule of
two trains one day and three the next.

Although Eichmann's *Kommando* was eventually dissolved on September 29—the Hungarian flow having ended
in the middle of the month—by July 11, Edmund
Veesenmayer figured out that 437,402 Jews had been
deported and done away with.

The country was then considered free of Jews,[82] but on
October 17, as the Red Army was marching on Budapest, a
new government of the Nazi Arrow Cross Party replaced
Horthy's, and a fresh chase of Jews was started. At once,
Eichmann, the angel of death, was back; he wanted to

march 50,000 Jews out of Budapest. Three days later, wasting no time, he ordered that the Jews get ready within the hour. But only in November did the march begin.

A survivor, Aviva Fleishmann, testified in Jerusalem in 1961 what the march turned out to be: people dying by the thousands. Kurt Becher, head of the economic staff of the *Waffen* SS in Budapest, dared say the march was clear murder. On November 12, 27,000 people were taken away and Eichmann was still planning to have 40,000 follow. He managed to get a few trains from Vienna, and when he could obtain no more, he had people set out on foot again.[83]

That same month, however, Himmler ordered the stoppage of all further camp extermination and summoned Eichmann to Berlin: "If you have killed Jews till now," he told him, "and I order you to spare them, I wish to hear from you whether you will carry out this order or not."[84]

Flabbergasted and petrified, Eichmann could only answer in the affirmative. According to Dr. Rudolf Kastner's deposition in Nuremberg, Himmler's instructions to stop the gassing of Jews were released on November 25, 1944, when the *Reichsfuhrer* also ordered all gas chambers and crematoria in Auschwitz to be dynamited.

Under the circumstances, as the Red Army was closing in on the capital, this military development at the last moment saved a small part of the Hungarian Jewry from Eichmann's clutches. On January 17, 1945, Budapest was liberated and there remained 100,000 Jews in the city. It was the only ghetto that had escaped total annihilation.

Question: Was the secrecy of the gigantic program of the "final solution" as tightly kept as Hitler and Himmler had wanted it to be?

First it should be borne in mind that it was Hitler who had imposed the seal of secrecy "before leaking out the truth a little at a time to his own people. Eventually the time would be ripe for revelations that would tie all Germans to their own fate.[85] . . . Complicity in his crusade to cleanse Europe of Jewry would make it a national mission and rouse the people to greater efforts and sacrifices."[86]

Except for those who were in on the secret of Hitler's and Himmler's program, not many knew about Auschwitz and other killing centres.

> These were all in Poland and each was surrounded by a barren stretch several miles wide posted with notices that trespassers would be shot at sight. To ensure secrecy, the process from deportation to murder was not only executed speedily but done under a smoke screen of euphemisms: the over-all operation was referred to as "special treatment"; collectively the centres were described as the "East"; individual installations were called labour concentration transit or PW camps; and gas chambers and crematorium units were "bathhouses" and "corpse cellars."[87]

Therefore, the *Reichsfuhrer* denied vehemently that Jews were being executed in mass numbers.

The denial, however, must have been hardly credible to many Germans, for on February 15, 1943, after Rommel had suffered a severe defeat at El Alamein and the Allies had landed in North Africa, and while the battle of Stalingrad had been fought and lost, Goebbels addressed an audience in Dusseldorf on the theme of whether the people wanted total war. He argued that international Jewry behind the Russians endangered Western civilization through a victory over Germany. But the clubfoot Nazi propagandist promised that his country would retaliate with "total and radical extermination and elimination of the Jews." Retaliate! It was already more than ten years that Hitler and his henchmen had been persecuting and assassinating Jews.

In point of fact, Felix Kersten, Himmler's masseur, mentioned in his memoirs what his patient had confided to him. For months and years, Himmler had said, Goebbels had been exciting the Fuhrer to exterminate the Jews by radical means, and finally gained the upper hand, Then, in the summer of 1940, the Fuhrer ordered that the Jews be exterminated by degrees. He gave his task to me. That was the one and only time I contradicted the Fuhrer. He was at his headquarters in France. I told him: "The SS are ready to fight and die from myself down to the last man, but don't give us a mission like this!" The Fuhrer became furious and said: "Himmler, you are being disobedient! What is the meaning of this? This is an order; I take the responsibility of it." So I had no other recourse. Understand me, Kersten, and I hope that History will understand me also.[88]

More than two years later, after the Allied landing in North Africa, the Fuhrer ordered that the action against the Jews be intensified. Hitler asked for the actual figures of the extermination program in progress and it was Korherr, Himmler's inspector of statistics who (in 1943) after more than two months of compilation, produced a sixteen-page report, abridged to six pages, which revealed that "since 1933, that is during the first decade of National Socialism, European Judaism had already decreased by almost one half."[89] (This official admission Ernst Zundel will not easily swallow!)

Hence, it was hardly possible that in upper circles or down to the man in the street, and even more certainly those closest to Hitler, no one knew what was happening, especially since Goebbels made public the annihilation in progress. If some individuals really did not know, or pretended not to know, they must still have had doubts and guessed what was going on.

As Hans Frank said to Dr. Gilbert at the time of the Nuremberg trial:

Don't let anyone tell you he had no idea. Everyone sensed that there was something horribly wrong with the system, even if we didn't know all the details. We didn't want to know! It was too comfortable to live on the system, to support our families in royal style, and to believe that it was all right.[90]

"This was the man," Toland reflected, "who had recently told his subordinates that they were all accomplices in the elimination of the Jews which, disagreeable as it might be, was necessary in the interests of Europe."[91]

Indeed, in a secret conversation on June 19, 1943, Hitler had instructed his SS double to proceed with the deportation to the East "regardless of any unrest it might cause during the next three or four months." It must be carried out, he added, "in an all-embracing way." He admitted later to Borman that, having purged Germany of the Jewish poison, the operation for Germany "has been an essential process of disinfection, which we have prosecuted to its ultimate limit without which we should ourselves have been asphyxiated and destroyed."

He had warned the Jews, he said, "that if they precipitated another war, they would not be spared and that I would exterminate the vermin throughout Europe, and this time once and for all," and since the Jews "retorted with a declaration of war . . . well, we have lanced the Jewish abscess; and the world of the future will be eternally grateful to us."

In his talk it appears that Hitler had taken little, if any, notice of Himmler's recent drawback on April 27, when the *Reichsfuhrer* had had to yield to the pressure of industrialists who insisted that mass murder be slowed down, so as to leave the fittest Jews and Russian prisoners to continue working in weapon factories—until starvation and exhaustion finished them off.

On that same day, Himmler sent his directive to Glucks, who passed on the instructions whereby only the mentally sick could be selected for Aktion 14 F 13, while all other prisoners were to be excepted from this action. "*Requests for fuel for the purpose [of cremating] were now unnecessary*"[92] (emphasis added).

Six weeks later, Hitler having brushed aside or simply ignored Himmler's decision, the *Reichsfuhrer* who, on August 28, had become Minister of the Interior, could now forget about his previous orders to Glucks, and on October 4, 1943, at Posen, Himmler addressed his generals of whom he was still the Commander-in-Chief. "We Germans," he told them, "who are the only people in the world who have a decent attitude towards animals, will also assume a decent attitude towards these human animals." (He was referring to Russians.)

> But it is a crime against our own blood to worry about them and give them ideas. I want to talk to you openly on a very grave matter. Among ourselves it should be mentioned quite frankly, and yet we will never speak of it publicly...I mean the clearing out of the Jews, the extermination of the Jewish race. It's one of those things it is easy to talk about...Most of you must know what it means when 100 corpses are lying side by side or 500 or 1,000...That is what has made us hard. This is a page of *glory* in our history which has never been written and is never to be written. We have taken from them what wealth they had. I have issued a strict order that this wealth should, as a matter of course, be handed over to the Reich without reserve. We have taken none of it for ourselves. Whoever takes so much as a mark of it is a dead man...Because we have exterminated a bactirium we do not want in the end to be infected and die of it.[93]

On the 6th it was the *Gauleiters* and *Reichsleiters* he spoke to. He asked them "only to hear" what he was going to tell them "and never talk." When the question arose as to what should be done with women and children, he said he just adopted a clear solution. He did not feel justified in exterminating the men while giving the children the chance "to grow up to avenge themselves on our sons and grandchildren." They, too, had to die. "The hard decision had to be taken: this people must disappear from the face of the earth.... It was carried out, I think I can say, without our men and leaders suffering the slightest damage to spirit or soul.... You now know what is what and you must keep it to yourselves."[94]

The reader cannot but face the facts. The planned extermination of the Jews may have been at the outset one of the most guarded secrets in the Reich, but in short time it became widely known. The daily killing, gassing and burning of thousands of people in all parts of Eastern Europe until one third of the Jews were consumed could not, of course, pass unnoticed and be kept a secret. In the army and government circles and even moreso among the executioners, it was *secret de polichinelle*—an open secret. However, Albert Speer, Minister of Munitions, has claimed he did not know about the annihilation of the Jews. Since he attended Himmler's conference at Posen on October 6, 1943, where the *Reichsfuhrer* made no secret whatever of the program of extermination and confiscation of property, Speer's denial that he knew nothing about it is unacceptable. At one point in his speech, Himmler even addressed "Comrade Speer," as he called him, saying that "of course all this has nothing to do with him."

Speer later affirmed that he spoke first at the meeting and left immediately after his own speech, leaving Himmler to take over. He did not hear what the *Reichsfuhrer* had to say.[95]

As Toland remarked: "One particular horrifying aspect of Hitler's Final Solution had recently come to an apocalyptical ending." The author was referring to the Warsaw ghetto which, certainly, could never be regarded as a secret. The ghetto had numbered 400,000 Jews when it was established; then, between 1940 and 1942, over 300,000 were deported to various concentration and extermination camps. Of those left in the ghetto, a few thousand succumbed to epidemics, undernourishment and exhaustion, and a number of others, who cannot be counted, were killed through blasting. However, after he had obeyed

Himmler's orders of February 16, 1943, Major General Stroop in charge of the operation proudly wrote in his report: "a proved total of 56,065" Jews were eliminated.

In April and May, therefore, more than 56,000 people had just been wiped out. They had been killed, commented Willi Frischauer, like rats in the sewers. "Smoked out, burnt out, blasted, they were hounded day and night by men armed with the most modern weapons and by army engineers equipped with explosives, always eager to put fire to a fuse." But Stroop thought only of the sacrifices which his men made in this horrific action. "For the Fuhrer and their country, the following fell in the battle for the destruction of Jews and bandits in the former Jewish residential area of Warsaw. They gave their utmost, their lives. We shall never forget them. . . ." And how was that? asked Frischauer. "How many SS men fell for Fuhrer and Fatherland while murdering 56,000 human beings? Stroop's list includes fifteen names. Repeat: fifteen names!"[96]

The Polish Commission which investigated German war crimes in Poland, in part X of their report, commented upon Stroop's twelve page account to Himmler, the title page in Gothic letters announcing: "There is no Jewish residence quarter left in Warsaw," and the twelfth page, dated May 16, 1943, bearing the SS general's signature.

When the proud executioner was arrested by the American Military Police, he was found carrying an album of 33 photographs which have been reproduced by the Polish Commission as supporting documents to the two first parts of Stroop's report.[97]

In the next six months, after the obliteration of the Warsaw ghetto until the end of the year 1943, the *Wehrmacht* suffered defeat upon defeat as the Russians pushed them back, in some places as much as 400 kilometres. But Hitler did not neglect his beloved "final solution." It just had to be speeded up and, on January 26, 1944, again in Posen, Himmler delivered another of his speeches to an audience of 260 high-ranking officers of the army and the navy, and assured them that the Jewish question had been solved. In the following weeks, he shamelessly told another group of navy officers that he had ordered women and children killed, and repeated to the generals at Sonthafen that the Jewish question had been solved in Germany as well as throughout the occupied territories.

All such talk proved that the program to assassinate millions of human beings had been carried out as planned and was continuing. There was no further mention of any secret to safeguard.

Chapter III
SURVIVORS
ON THE WITNESS STAND

Every survivor of a concentration camp has his or her own personal experiences, but all their stories bear the same tragic imprint of the cruelty and atrocities perpetrated by their SS guards.

Their clothes in tatters, the lack of hygiene, the malnutrition and dehydration, their skeletal condition, the camp routine of the roll calls, their distress and despair, the brutal scenes they witnessed, the daily death of inmates in their barracks, the shots they heard, in some cases the hangings they saw, the odor of burned flesh and hair which nauseated them, and the chimneys of the crematoria which they saw spewing smoke and fire—all are recurrent horrors with minor variations.

The dreadful picture and the emotional tone of their testimonies hardly vary at all. This is why I decided to limit my selection to two such contributions, to avoid unnecessary repetition. The narratives I chose are those of Odd Nansen, a Norwegian, and Dr. Miklos Nyiszli, a Hungarian physician.

There is, however, one outstanding testimony of two Czechoslovakian political prisoners who survived the Auschwitz apocalypse which deserves a very special mention. The two men, Ota Kraus of Prague, arrested in April 1940, and Erich Kulka of Vsetin, arrested in June 1939, had both been incarcerated successively in three concentration camps, and were eventually transferred to

Auschwitz where they arrived on November 4, 1942. By this time, they had become inseparable friends. They managed to be allowed to work as locksmiths in Birkenau. During two years, they collected information which eventually was passed through resistance groups to their homeland. In their workshop, at the southern end of the men's camp B IId, they kept a record of the reports which they received from participating prisoners. They hid documents and plans in "the double walls of [their] hut, under the anvil and among tools. [They] had cameras and even a radio set." All that SS search squads ever found was a pair of radio headphones.

Kraus and Kulka were determined to preserve the evidence they had collected in the form of reports, plans and documents. In 1945, the rich and incriminating collection served the two locksmiths in their writing of an illustrated book, *The Death Factory*, which is a masterful and vivid account of how the greatest extermination camps of Auschwitz-Birkenau operated and of the atrocities that were carried on during four years by a crowd of SS criminal-minded sadists.

Ernst Zundel would hate its convincing tone, since it is based on the many stories of inmates which the authors recorded and included in their book. These tragic experiences of prisoners who survived, added to the technical details which Kraus and Kulka revealed, make their publication an exceptionally high quality contribution to the history of Auschwitz-Birkenau. For the serious student of Nazi war crimes, there is no part of the authors' 284-page narrative which should be skipped over. The events that they and their companions lived through in the hell of the two camps cannot be summarized. I urge every interested party to read, without fail, the authors' grisly story of one of the darkest dramas in the history of the Nazis' crimes against humanity.

I will now return to Odd Nansen's diary,[1] written secretly during his incarceration, and to Dr. Nyiszli's narrative, which he wrote in 1946. I will quote at length from these two invaluable sources throughout this chapter.

On October 4, 1943, Nansen, who had been arrested in Norway, was to be evacuated to Sachsenhausen with other prisoners. As the train was about to leave Stettin, he wrote that it was impossible to find room for 53 men in his cattle car. "We tried every method of sardine-packing," he added, "but there were always ten sardines over."

October 6: We were in the cattle cars, tired and stiff after a night and a day without sleep or rest. The train stopped at a station with a jerk. A board said: Oranienburg. [Then] the train jerked us back and forth half a dozen times.... The whole train moved again. It didn't stop until we reached another station...Sachsenhausen...some distance from Oranienburg. There, we were ordered out.

October 11: Outside and between the huts are gardens of flowers and little railings all along the path.... It looks well kept and idyllic, and a "visitor" never gets a glimpse of the fact that it only serves as a frame for the most unbounded filth, the worst hatching ground for lice and bacteria. White sepulchers they are. How many have ended their lives in them it's impossible to say.... The every day reality is so violent and deadening and brutal. Some say that 40,000 have died here, some 30,000, some less.... My number is 72,060. There are [now] about 17,000 prisoners in this camp. About 10,000 are on loan to other camps and places of work, so, all told, the figure of those present on the records in Sachsenhausen should be over 25,000.... The Ukrainians, especially, are the camp's pariah caste and their condition is appalling. Accordingly they die in crowds.... There are people here who have been "inside" since 1933. Ten or twelve years in a German prison or concentration camp!

October 14: Some time ago a transport of prisoners one day reached the camp. As usual they were counted

and line up on the parade ground just outside the main
entrance. There were two men extra. The two men were
posted at the main entrance under the windows of the
gate house. They stood there all the rest of the day, and
no one gave them another thought. Then came evening
roll call, with counting. These two men were still superfluous. Still the figure wouldn't come right. And German figures *must* and *shall* be right. A few revolver
shots from a window in the gate house worked out the
sum. The figure was right again, the two were carried
away, they had ceased to be superfluous in this world.

November 11: Yesterday I was talking to a Jew.
There actually are a few of them alive in the camp. This
one is named Keil [a watchmaker who had been in
Norway as a German refugee in 1936]. He came here
from Auschwitz in Poland. An extermination camp of
the worst type. What he told me about that camp was
so horrible, so incomprehensible in ghastliness that it
defies all description. [Very few of the Norwegian Jews
sent there were still alive.] About 25 out of 1,200 was
his estimate.... Most of them were gassed. Whole
transports went straight into the gas chamber and
thence into the crematory. Men, women and children
of all ages, from every corner of Europe and every
social class. There were five crematories in the camp,
and they were going day and night—and had been for
several years. Keil's story paralyzed me. [Nansen
asked, by name, about people he knew who had been
sent to Auschwitz.] They had all died in the gas
chamber.... And all, all the others! Keil himself had
been spared because he was a watchmaker. They
needed watchmakers.[2] All the rest of them, dead, all
dead. Starved to death, beaten to death, worked to
death or sent in the gas chamber. Keil estimated that
three or four million Jews had been killed in Auschwitz
and in Lublin during these last few years. And he
thought at least as many Poles had gone the same

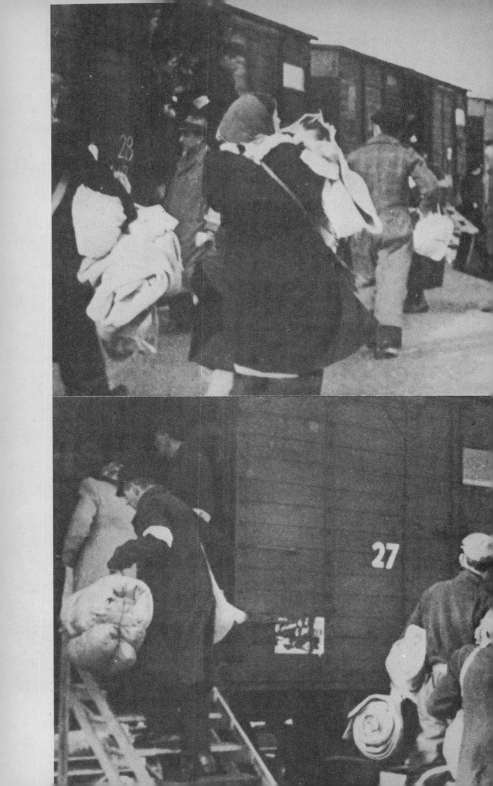

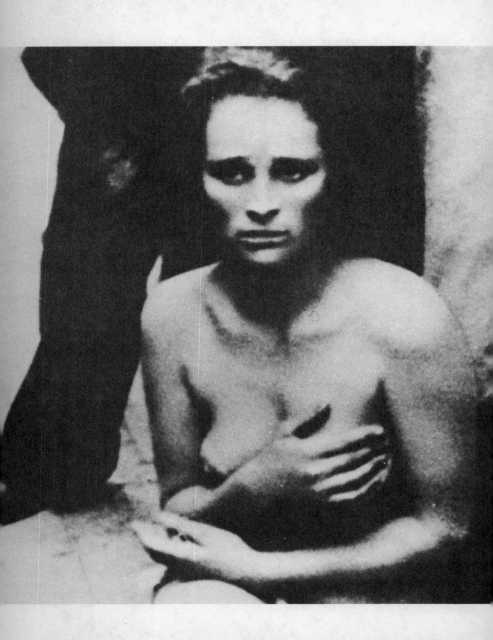

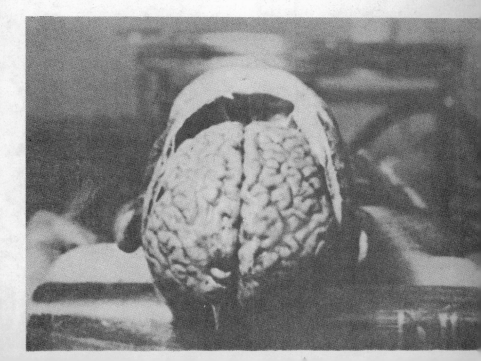

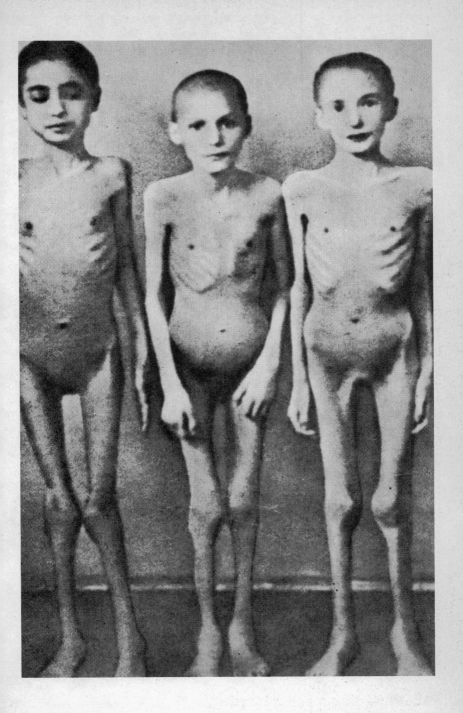

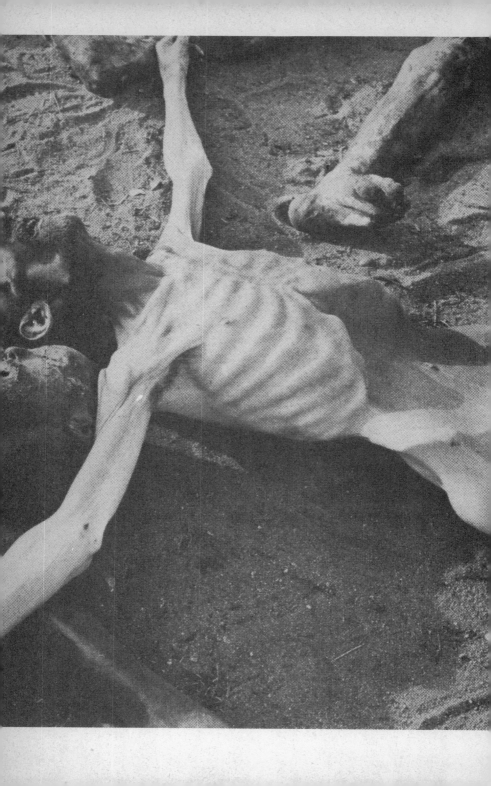

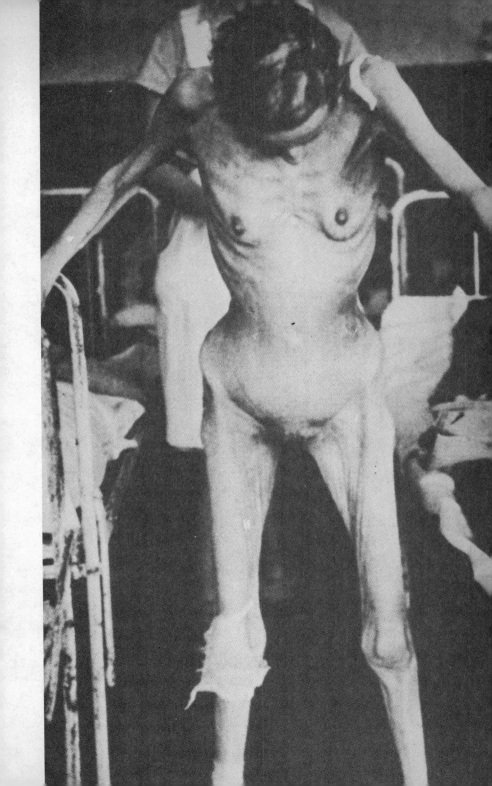

way—and hundreds of thousands of Russians and Ukrainian prisoners as well.

November 29: This time we got a little more peace to listen to the ghastly stories of Lublin, Auschwitz, Warsaw, and other towns and camps. Beside the drama of horror thus unfolded, all the other horrors, atrocities, and massacres we know of in the whole history of mankind go, as it were, for nothing. It's impossible to form any picture of the evil revealed here; human comprehension and imagination fall short. One can "follow" up to a point, imagine thousands of Jews, young and old, being sent out in the death transports, see them marching in endless columns, day and night, week after week, month after month, yes, year after year, into annihilation. And yet what one can imagine is still assuredly nothing but a pale reflection of the reality. How those unhappy millions must have longed to die! They must have looked on the gas chambers as a sheer deliverance from the scenes of horror outside. Why that was an easy death! But it wasn't granted to all; hundreds of thousands of the strongest and best...had first to be exploited—their strength had first to be made use of in the death gangs, moving corpses, burning, hanging! And it was their own people they were moving, burning, and hanging—their own!

December 6: Everyone knows what a death transport is—*ein Todestransport*. People who are to be extirpated....The prisoners who could not be saved ...incurably ill, people on whom the SS could not expect to make any "profit" in this camp. For the camp is also run as a business....As to whether this death transport will ever get to Lublin at all, or was ever meant to go so far, opinions differ. Some hold that they will merely be sent straight into the gas chambers "round the corner" in camp. Others maintain that the transport of 600 men was to leave today or in the immediate future. One can't avoid the idea that they may intend to liquidate the whole camp by degrees in this way. Perhaps we're all to go off in transports and have our forearms marked (our respective numbers) with copying ink.

January 2, 1944: Joel told me yesterday about the transport of a thousand men that left here some time ago. The death transport! They had had nothing to eat on the way and had never been let out of the trucks in which they were packed. When they got to Lublin, the trucks were driven into a hall, the whole of which was put under gas. All perished. Joel had heard the story from one of the SS guards who accompanied the transport.

January 26 and February 7: It's wet and windy just now; horribly raw, cold weather; typical Sachsen-hausen....It's biting cold, and we're frozen to the bone. But now as always we have to console ourselves with the reflection that we're better off than so many people.

Mass killings had, indeed, begun in Auschwitz.

In Bruno Bettelheim's foreword to Dr. Miklos Nyiszli's account of his horrible experience in Hoss' camp, he wrote: "We would prefer to think that it never happened; we'd like to dismiss the story of the German extermination camps [as a whole]....What was new, unique, terrifying was that millions like lemmings, marched themselves to their own death."

On duty at the time of Dr. Nyiszli's arrival at the camp, in May 1944, was the 12th *Sonderkommando*, a specially qualified and privileged (so to speak) group of prisoners who worked exclusively in the crematoria. It was more specifically a commando of 853 living dead who survived only four months from the time they were assigned to the job; at the end of those four months they were liquidated by a new group. There would be no one to tell what had been going on in the death factory. No account of life in the *KZ* (*Katzet* or concentration camp) would ever reveal in detail the conditions of the crematoria because their gates were simply the gates of death.

On the very first page of Dr. Nyiszli's book, *Auschwitz,* which he wrote in 1946, he said that his work "relates the darkest days in the history of mankind, drawn in accordance with reality, and without the slightest exaggeration, in my capacity as an eyewitness and involuntary participant in the work of Auschwitz crematorium in whose fires millions of fathers, mothers and children have disappeared. . . . I lived through these horrors which were beyond all imagining."

One evening in May, he was part of the first group of over a million Hungarian Jews condemned to death to arrive in Auschwitz. As his train, filled to over capacity, pulled along the ramp and the doors of the box cars were opened, "one object," he wrote, "immediately caught my eye: an immense square chimney built of red bricks tapering towards the summit. . . . I was especially struck by the enormous tongues of flames rising between the lightning rods, set at angles on the square tops of the chimney. I tried to imagine what hellish cooking would require such a tremendous fire: the factory was a crematorium."

As he caught sight of two other chimneys spewing the same flames, "my nose, then my throat were filled with the nauseating odor of burning flesh and scorched hair."

From the beginning, therefore, he knew what to expect. One man on the platform was Dr. Mengele, doctor-in-chief of Auschwitz-Birkenau, who performed "selections" of the prisoners as the latter were assembled into two groups: the left column consisting of the aged, the crippled, the feeble, women, and children under fourteen. Those too sick to walk, the aged and the insane, however, were loaded into Red Cross vans. A few moments later, all those people would be shoved through the doors into the nearest crematorium from which there never was any return.

The men of the right column would go into the barracks

which, on either side, lined the main road of the camp.
Meanwhile, the heavy baggage from the train's 40 box cars
was unloaded by men clothed in prison garb. In each
barrack, 800 to 1,000 prisoners were crammed in
superimposed compartments.[3] Every day selections would
take place there, as in the hospital barracks, and hundreds
of dead prisoners were loaded onto trucks to be transported
to the crematoria, only a few hundred yards away.

The merciless SS commanders ruled over each camp
section. They arrived at 7:00 a.m., a time when the roll
call—one of the most inhumane parts of the *KZ*
program—had ended. The inmates had already vacated the
barracks at 3:00 a.m.; the dead—five to ten prisoners
daily—had to be present physically, standing stark naked,
and supported by two living men until the muster was over.
Such was the routine because the dead had to be accounted
for until they were taken away in wheelbarrows by the
transportation *Kommando*.

The reader must be reminded that the Auschwitz *KZ* was
not a work camp but the largest extermination camp the
Third Reich built. The healthiest individual would collapse
of hunger, filth, blows and inhuman labours in three to four
weeks. Some prisoners were hanged or hanged themselves;
others threw themselves against the high-tension wires to
electrocute themselves, or they could have been pushed
against the fences. Both kinds of death were common. The
corpses, some bearing the letters Z and S (*Zur Sektion*) on
their chests, were then loaded onto "hearses," of sorts, and
transported to the camp morgue, where Dr. Nyiszli would
handle them in his capacity as pathologist. Later, another
truck would pick them up, 40 to 50 a day, and move them to
a crematorium.

As mentioned earlier, women, children and the ill had
been liquidated, burned upon arrival. Relatives and friends
of members of the subaltern medical corps working in the
hospital had met the same fate.

In the hospital itself were the living dead, breathing
skeletons, dehydrated, emaciated, their lips cracked, their

faces swollen, plagued with incurable dysentery. Their bodies were covered with enormous, repulsive running sores and suppurating ulcers. Such were the *KZ*'s sick.

Within the barbed wire enclosures was the famous 4,500-person Gypsy camp. Naked, dark-skinned children ran and played while women and half-naked men chatted and watched. Although they were themselves regarded as an inferior race, their job was to police the neighbouring Jewish camp and barracks. There, the Gypsies exercised their authority with vigorous cruelty.

Auschwitz had a stadium, but except on Sundays, the vast field lay quiet and empty. A barbed wire fence separated it from number I Crematorium which never ceased spewing tongues of fire. One would not dare approach it, however, for the watchtower machine guns sprayed the field without warning to frighten away anyone who might enter the no man's land.

Line-ups of 200 or more men were held in the crematorium courtyard. This crematorium worked, as the others, on a 24-hour schedule. The personnel on duty were known as the *Sonderkommando*.[4] These prisoners were well fed and given civilian clothes, but they were never to leave the grounds. Every four months, they were liquidated because they knew too much. This explains why no member of this group has been able to tell the world what went on behind the camp walls.

Few people ever realized how vast the exterminating *KZ* was, but when Rudolf Hoss testified in Nuremberg, he said it held 140,000 prisoners when filled to capacity. They died in a very short time; in fact, the majority died the very day they arrived. Trains steamed in daily and the death toll kept increasing.

Soon after Dr. Nyiszli entered the camp as a Hungarian "deportee," he visited a crematorium with Mengele, and was shown what looked to him like an exact replica of any large city's institute of pathology. Paralyzed with fright as he realized he was on death's path, Dr. Nyiszli now understood why he had been given civilian clothes. He was

wearing the "uniform" of the *Sonderkommando*—the
Kommando of the living dead. He felt he was one of them.
Mengele assigned him to do laboratory and anatomical
work, as well as the medical care of all SS personnel—who
numbered about 120 men—and some 860 *Sonderkommando*. In addition, he had to visit the sick once or twice a
day. To perform these duties, he could circulate in the camp
and among the four crematoria without a pass, from 7 a.m.
to 7 p.m.

At this point in his account, Dr. Nyiszli wrote:

We [he, his wife and daughter] had already been separated for a week. Where could they be, lost in the enormous mass, anonymous like all those swallowed by
this gigantic prison? Had my daughter been able to stay
with her mother, or had they already been separated?
What had happened to my aged parents, whose last
years I had tried to make more pleasant? What had
become of my beloved younger sister whom I had
raised practically as my own child after our father had
fallen ill? It had been such a pleasure to love and
help them. I had no doubt about their fate. They
were certainly en route to one of the forty-car trains
that would bring them here to the Jewish ramp of the
Auschwitz extermination camp. With one mechanical
wave of his hand, Dr. Mengele would direct my parents
into the left-hand column. And my sister would also
join that column, for even if she were ordered into the
right-handed column, she would surely beg, on bended
knees, for permission to go with our mother. So they
would let her go, and she, with tears in her eyes, would
shower them with thanks.[5]

When Dr. Nyiszli visited the *Sonderkommando* accommodations, he noticed that they enjoyed another privilege.
They were allowed to possess books, whereas anyone else in
the *KZ* caught reading was punished with twenty days of
solitary confinement in a sort of large sentry box with just

enough room to stand in, unless, of course, he died from the blows dealt him beforehand. Dr. Nyiszli spoke to the personnel whom he ministered to and he learned from them the history of the crematoria.

> Tens of thousands of prisoners had built them of stone and concrete, finishing them in the middle of an extremely rigorous winter. Every stone was stained with their blood. They had worked day and night often without food or drink, dressed in mere tatters, so that these infernal death factories, whose victims they became, might be finished in time. Since then four years had passed. Countless thousands had since climbed down from the box cars and crossed the threshold of the crematori. The present *Sonderkommando* was the twelfth to bear the name.[6]

The day after that entry in his "eyewitness account," Dr. Nyiszli observed from his window the arrival of another very long train, and the usual routine which ensued.

> The doors were slid open and the box cars spilled out thousands and thousands of the chosen people of Israel. Line-up and selection took scarcely half an hour. The left-hand column moved slowly away.... The sounds of rapid footsteps came from the furnace room of the crematorium; they were preparing to welcome the new convoy. The throb of the motors began. They had just set the enormous ventilators going to fan the flames in order to obtain the desired degree in the ovens. Fifteen ventilators were going simultaneously, one beside each oven. The incineration room was about 500 feet long; it was a bright, white-washed room with a concrete floor and barred windows. Each of the fifteen ovens was housed in a red brick structure. Immense iron doors well polished and gleaming, ominously lined the length of the wall. In one or six minutes the convoy reached the gate, whose swing-doors opened inwards.

No one who entered there would ever return "to tell the tale."

Still in the distance, the column advanced with slow, weary steps, the children clinging to their mothers' skirts, the babies in their fathers' arms. "The deportees were quick to notice the water faucets used for sprinkling the grass that were arranged about the courtyard," and having had nothing to drink for five days or more, they rushed to the faucets and quenched their thirst.

At the end of the cinder path they followed were some twelve steps leading underground, to the bath and disinfecting room. It was about 200 yards long. Its walls were whitewashed and it was brightly lit. On benches and coat hangers, the doomed would have to leave behind their clothes and their shoes, "sorely needed by the Third Reich."[7]

There were 3,000 people now stark naked, men and women, old and young, and infants. The elderly, the crippled and the insane had to be helped by the men of a special *Sonderkommando* squad. When the "herd" was ready, they had to walk into a second well-lighted room, in whose centre "at thirty yard intervals columns rose from the concrete floor to the ceiling. They were not supporting columns, but square sheet-iron pipes, the sides of which contained numerous perforations, like a wire lattice."

Upon a hoarse command, the SS and the *Sonderkommando* would leave the room, the doors would swing shut and, from outside, the lights in the fateful place would be switched off.

At that very instant, a deluxe model car, furnished by the International Red Cross,[8] would pull up in the courtyard. An SS officer, accompanying a Deputy Health Service man carrying four green sheet-iron canisters, would step out. In the lawn, just in front of that man, a line of short concrete pipes was jutting out of the soil every 30 yards. The officer, wearing a gas mask, had only to lift the lid of each pipe and pour in the contents of a can of Zyklon granules. The gas that it produced escaped through the perforated columns inside the death chamber, and within five minutes everybody was dead. The faked Red Cross car could then leave; the two officers had just killed 3,000 innocent people.

Afterwards, the ventilators were switched on to evacuate the gas. Because the fumes lingered for two or more hours, the *Sonderkommando* were forced to wear gas masks when they entered. What they saw through the goggled apparatus was a horrible spectacle.

> The bodies were not lying here and there throughout the room, but piled in a mass to the ceiling...the victims [having trampled] one another in a frantic effort to escape the gas [rising from the base of the columns]. What a struggle for life it must have been! Nevertheless, it was merely a matter of two or three minutes respite...I noticed that the bodies of the women, the children and the aged were at the bottom of the pile; at the top, the strongest. Their bodies... covered with scratches and bruises from the struggle which had set them against each other, were often interlaced. Blood oozed from their noses and mouths; their faces, bloated and blue, were so deformed as to be almost unrecognizable....The Sonderkommando squad, outfitted with large rubber boots, lined up around the hill of bodies and flooded it with powerful jets of water. [The process cleared away the feces which accompanied the victims' suffocation.] Each body was befouled and had to be washed.

Once the "bathing" was completed, the separation of the welter of bodies was carried out. It was a very hard job for the *Sonderkommando* who

> knotted thongs around the wrists, which were clenched in a viselike grip, and [thus]...they dragged the slippery bodies to the elevators in the next room. Four good-sized elevators were functioning. [Each] loaded 20 to 25 corpses....The elevator stopped at the crema-

torium incineration room, where large sliding doors
opened automatically. The kommando who operated
the trailers was ready and waiting. Again straps were
fixed to the wrists of the dead and they were dragged
onto specially constructed chutes which unloaded them
in front of the furnaces.[9]

Dr. Mengele sent millions of people to their death merely
because, according to German racial theory, they were
inferior beings and therefore detrimental to mankind.
Allegedly, the immediate objective of the criminal doctor's
experiments was the increased reproduction of the German
race. The final objective was the production of pure
Germans in numbers sufficient to replace Czechs,
Hungarians and Poles, all of whom were condemned to be
destroyed. Thus the medical pathology reports of Dr.
Nyiszli, which were carefully checked by Mengele, were
forwarded to the Institute of Biological Racial and
Evolutionary Research at Berlin-Dahlan, one of the most
famous scientific institutes of its kind in the world.

In the course of his work, Dr. Nyiszli discovered one of
the monstrous secrets of the Third Reich's medical science.
This was a procedure for injecting chloroform into the left
ventricle of the heart: the coagulating blood would be
deposited on the valves and cause instantaneous death due
to heart failure. Dr. Nyiszli made this discovery when he
performed the dissection of one set of twins whose corpses
Mengele had sent him to be examined.[10] If Mengele had
suspected that his pathologist had discovered the secret of
his injections, he would have sent "ten doctors in the name
of the political SS to attest to my death."

One evening when it was already late and growing dark,
Dr. Nyiszli heard scream upon scream originating from the
place adjoining the dissecting room. He used this as a
storeroom for corpses, keeping them there till it was time
for their dissection, and then returning them after the
autopsy to be sent away for cremation. After what he had

heard, he was prepared for something extraordinary. He entered the room and glanced around.

> A terrifying scene gradually unfolded: before me were sprawled the naked bodies of seventy women; curled up, bathed in their own blood and in the blood of their neighbours, they lay in utter disarray about the room ...I discovered to my horror that not all the victims were dead. Some were still breathing, moving their arms or legs slowly; with glazed eyes, they tried to raise their bloody heads. I lifted two, three heads of those alive, and suddenly realized that, besides death by gas and chloroform injections, there was a third way of killing here: a bullet in the back of the neck.... It appeared that in some instances the [soft lead] bullet had deviated slightly; thus death had not always been instantaneous.

As Dr. Nyiszli glanced in the direction of the crematoria, he noticed that No. I was not working, but the chimneys of Nos. II, III and IV were spewing flame and smoke. "Business as usual."[11]

For Dr. Nyiszli, medical visits meant making the rounds of those four crematoria in which an SS might feign illness to get a short respite from his exhausting and nerve-racking labours. Members of the *Sonderkommando* also had a tendency to acquire nervous disorders. They worked with corpses all the time; it was mandatory for them to wash twice a day, in beautiful, new ten-man showers. Day after day, they handled thousands of corpses, dragging them to the crematory ovens where they were loaded into the incineration cases. The result was, not surprisingly, acute nervous depression. Dr. Nyiszli was reminded again that the future of these men was tightly circumscribed by time. At the end of the fatal four month period a company of SS appeared. The entire *Sonderkommando* was herded into the crematorium's rear courtyard. There was a long machine-gun blast to kill those hundreds of men; half an hour later, a new *Sonder* squad arrived to undress their dead companions. An hour later, only a heap of ashes remained of the first squad.[12]

The No. II Crematorium was separated from No. I by a path through some fields, and by the Jewish unloading platforms along the railroad tracks. The only difference noticed by Dr. Nyiszli was that the space corresponding to his dissection room in No. I was used as a gold foundry in the other. It actually handled material acquired in all four crematoria. All the gold teeth and bridgework were melted down. The gold settings for jewelry, gold coins and gold cigarette cases were taken there after three goldsmiths had separated these items from others, like precious stones and metals, all of which had been removed from the trunks, suitcases, clothes and bodies of the dead. Every day the foundry produced 65 to 75 pounds of pure gold in cylinders of 140 grams. The *Sonderkommando* also took their gold in to be refined and, somehow, many managed to retrieve it in cylinder form. As Dr. Nyiszli observed, to be condemned to death, and yet forced to perform the kinds of jobs they were responsible for, was enough to break body and soul of the strongest, and to drive many to the brink of insanity. Fortunately, their gold could buy them useful goods, which made life easier for them. Smuggled cigarettes, brandy, butter, eggs and ham could be exchanged for the 140 gram "coins."[13]

Dr. Nyiszli also visited the two other crematoria—Nos. III and IV. In the former, besides the Greeks and Poles who composed the majority of the *Kommando*, there were already about 100 Hungarian deportees. Number four *Kommando* consisted largely of Poles and Frenchmen.[14]

"In all these death factories," Dr. Nyiszli reported, "work was in full swing. From the Jewish unloading platform. . .the victims spilled to their death with maniacal fury. Horrified I noted with what order and robot-like precision the murders were perpetrated as if these factories were here for all eternity. . . ."

There was also a pyre in operation in the camp. It was located 500-600 yards from No. IV Crematorium, directly behind the small birch forest of Birkenau, in a clearing surrounded by pines. This was outside the *KZ*'s electric barbed wire fence, between two lines of guards. One day, Dr. Nyiszli was ordered to go there to collect all medicines and eyeglasses which had been gathered there.[15]

Everyone who arrived at Auschwitz could see the thick twisting spiral of smoke, visible from any point in the *KZ*, from the moment they first descended from the box cars and lined up for selection. It was visible at every hour of the day and night. By day, it covered the sky above Birkenau with a thick cloud; by night it lighted the area with a hellish glow. Dr. Nyiszli and two helpers he had taken with him finally reached a clearing, in the middle of which was a thatched-roof house. (The Reich had expropriated the entire village of Birkenau near Auschwitz to establish the *KZ* there. All houses, with that one exception, had been demolished.) It was now used as an undressing room for those on their way to the pyre. There lay their shabby clothes, their eyeglasses, their shoes. The pyre was used for the "surplus"—to handle those for whom there was no room in the four crematoria. The worst kind of death awaited them. Behind the house, enormous columns of smoke rose skyward and diffused the odor of broiled flesh and burning hair. In the courtyard, between the gate and the house, Dr. Nyiszli saw a terrified crowd of about 5,000 souls; on all sides, thick cordons of SS held their police dogs by the leash. The prisoners were led 300 to 400 at a time into the undressing room. Once they had undressed, under a rain of truncheon blows, they left by the door at the opposite side of the house. Immediately, a *Sonder* man seized their arms, and steered them between the double row of SS, who lined the twisting path which ran for 50 yards to the pyre. The pyre itself was 50 yards long, six yards wide and three yards deep. It was a welter of burning bodies. SS soldiers stood at five-yard intervals along the pathway side of the ditch and awaited the victims. At the end of the pathway, two *Sonder* men pushed or dragged the victims along for fifteen to twenty yards into position before the SS. Their cries of terror covered the sounds of the shots. Fifty yards farther was another ditch, another pyre, and there the massacre was repeated. One *Oberscharfuhrer*, by the name of Molle, was in charge of the SS butchers. He was, as Dr. Nyiszli watched him, the most diabolic and hardened assassin he had ever seen. Sometimes, those who had not been killed outright were thrown alive into the flames. Molle did not waste time!

There were a number of adolescents among the condemned who instinctively tried to resist, with a strength born of despair. If Molle happened to witness such a scene, he took his gun, fired from a distance of as much as 40 to 50 yards, and the struggling human target fell dead in the arms of the *Sonder* man who was dragging him towards the pyre. If Molle was dissatisfied with a *Sonderkommando* man's work, he would aim for the arms without warning.

When the two pyres operated simultaneously, the output was 5,000 to 6,000 dead a day, slightly greater than the crematorium's, but here death was even more terrible, for one was murdered twice, first by a bullet in the back of the neck, then by fire. After seeing death by gas, by chloroform injections, and a bullet in the neck, Dr. Nyiszli now became aware of this fourth combined method.[16]

The next day, there was something new. The *KZ* had been put in strict "quarantine." No one could leave the barracks. SS soldiers and their police dogs were out in full force. They were going to liquidate the Czech camp—15,000 Jews deported from the Theresienstadt ghetto. Upon their arrival, they had not even been selected; nor were they put to work. Thus they had lived for two years, but at Auschwitz it was never a question of whether you would live or die, but merely a matter of *when* you would die. In the Czech camp, both the children and the aged had greatly weakened during their two-year ordeal: the children's bodies were mere skin and bones, and the elderly prisoners were so weak they could scarcely walk.

Rations had eventually been suppressed altogether, and hunger had reduced the prisoners to raving, moaning maniacs. Diarrhea, dysentery and typhus had begun their deadly work. Fifty to 60 deaths a day were normal. Their last days were spent in terrible suffering until they finally died. Now what remained of the "herd"—12,000—were assembled. Their cries of terror, as they were loaded onto the waiting vans, were appalling to hear, for after two years in the *KZ* they had no illusions about what lay in store for them. Fifteen hundred able-bodied men and women were chosen along with eight physicians. The rest were sent to Nos. II and III Crematoria. "On the following day," Dr. Nyiszli ended his narrative, "the Czech camp was silent and deserted. I saw a truck loaded with ashes leave the crematorium and head towards the Vistula."[17]

Another camp, Camp C, close to the Czech one, was composed of Hungarian Jewish women, often as many as 60,000 at a time, in spite of daily shipments to distant camps. When one of the inmates came down with scarlet fever, Dr. Mengele ordered the barrack quarantined, along with those on either side of it. They were there scarcely twelve hours. At dusk, all the inmates were herded on trucks and driven to the crematorium. Such were Mengele's efficacious methods to prevent the spread of contagious diseases. In SS medical language, it was called an intensive battle against the spread of infection, but the results were always one or two truckloads of ashes.

The images of horror varied from place to place. In another camp, the women's *"FKL"—Frauenkonzentrationslager*—thousands and thousands of prisoners had their heads shaved, and wore tattered clothes. Everywhere Dr. Nyiszli looked, he saw nothing but a vast network of barbed wire, concrete pillars and signs forbidding entrance and exit. "The *KZ* was nothing but barbed wire; the whole of Germany was encompassed in barbed wire, itself an enormous *KZ*."[18]

From Nansen's Journal:

June 27, 1944: A Ukrainian boy of 19 was hanged before the gateway at evening roll call last night. Before being hanged he got fifty blows, the first 20 of which were dealt by two of his comrades,...two Ukrainian boys from the youth block, chosen haphazard. They were forced on this hangman's job by threats of twenty-five if they didn't do it, or didn't do it properly. Both had their faces punched after they'd began, for not hitting hard enough.... The Ukrainian boy had been employed in the shoe factory. There he had taken two leather bags and cut shoes soles out of them. For which he was now to have fifty blows and then be hanged.... The punishment began... I could see the rubber hose swing through the air, and after the first blow we heard a hoarse, muffled scream; then came a dead silence, one heard nothing but the "thuds" each time the rubber hose sank into his flesh.... The last thirty blows [were] dealt by the Schlager. There are several of them besides the hangman, who has a full-time job with daily hangings and executions. [The flogging over, the boy was hanged.] ...Those who were close by and saw it all say that the boy's neck hadn't broken properly in falling, and it took five minutes for him to die.... Hanging would surely have been enough. Therefore, the flogging must have been an outcome of the purest sadism, of a craving for the sight of pain, the display of power, the exercise of hate!

July 13: Last Friday we had another hanging.... A young lad, I think a Pole. We're getting used to it now. That was the fifth hanging since we arrived. Transports are going off, too. All the sick Jews who have been "discharged" from the watchmaking shop because they are sick were sent off yesterday to Auschwitz in Poland, which means quite certainly to the gas chambers.

Dr. Nyiszli had been Mengele's assistant as a pathologist for more than three months now. And he filled other duties as a physician making regular morning rounds. "All four crematoria were working at full blast," he wrote.

> Last night they had burned the Greek Jews from the Mediterranean island of Corfu.... The victims had been kept for 27 days without food or water, first in launches, then in sealed box cars. When they arrived at the Auschwitz unloading platform the doors were unlocked, but no one got out and lined up for selection. Half of them were already dead, and the other half in a coma. The entire convoy, without exception, was sent to No. II Crematorium. Work was accelerated during the night, so that by morning, all that remained of the convoy was a pile of dirty, disheveled clothes in the crematorium courtyard.... Glancing upward, I noticed that the four lightning rods placed at the corners of the crematorium chimneys were twisted and bent, the result of the previous night's high temperature.

At the entrance of the camp, a sign over the gate exhorted the prisoners: "Freedom through work." Here, said Dr. Nyiszli, is a concrete example of what those words really meant: "One day a line of box cars stopped at the Auschwitz unloading platform. The doors slid open and 300 prisoners climbed down. Their skin was a lemon yellow colour, and they were emaciated beyond all description."

"Three months ago," they told him, "we were shipped away from Auschwitz to work in a factory that manufactures sulphuric acid. When we left, there were 3,000 of us, but many died of various and sundry illnesses. Now only 300 are left, and we're all suffering from sulphuric poisoning."

Not for long! They were told they were being sent back for a cure to a rest camp. Half an hour later, Dr. Nyiszli saw their blood-spattered bodies lying in front of the crematorium ovens. "Freedom through work!"

Dr. Nyiszli had yet another horrible experience. On one particular day, 3,000 dead piled up in Crematorium No. I, where he had his dissection room. The *Sonderkommando* men were busy; the gas chambers had to be cleared for the arrival of a new convoy which had been announced. Suddenly the chief of the *Kommando* rushed in and asked the doctor to come quickly: "We just found a girl alive at the bottom of the pile of corpses!" Moments later he was standing at the entrance of the chamber. "Against the wall, half covered with other bodies I saw a girl in the throes of a death rattle, her body seized with convulsions. The gas kommando men around me were in a state of panic. Nothing like this had ever happened in the course of their horrible career." When Dr. Nyiszli had administered three intravenous injections, the girl, almost a child, reacted swiftly. "Her pulse became perceptible....I waited impatiently....Within a few minutes she was going to regain consciousness; her circulation began to bring colour back into her cheeks, and her delicate face became human again."

In the gas chamber, Dr. Nyiszli speculated further: "Pressed close against the wall, she had waited, her heart frozen, for what was going to happen....The lights had gone out....Something had stung her eyes, seized her throat, suffocated her. She had fainted."

After Dr. Nyiszli's intervention, she recovered gradually though feeling exhausted. "The kommando gave her a bowl of hot broth which she drank voraciously....I told her that she should try to get some sleep."

> What could one do with a young girl in the crematorium? I knew the past history of the place: no one had ever come out of here alive, either from the convoys or from the Sonderkommando....[When *Oberscharfuhrer* Mussfeld arrived to supervise the work that had been done] even before we told him, he had seen the girl stretched out on the bench....This

was the man I had to deal with, the man I had to talk
into allowing a single life to be spared. I calmly related
the terrible case we found ourselves confronted
with....I asked him to do something for the child....
One solution would have been to put her in front of the
crematorium gate. A kommando of women always
worked there. She could have slipped in among them
and accompanied them back to the camp barracks after
they had finished work....But Mussfeld thought a
young girl of sixteen would in all naivete tell the first
person she met where she had just come from, what she
had seen and what she had lived through. The news
would spread like wild fire, and we would all be forced
to pay for it with our lives. "There is no way of getting
around it," he said; "the child will have to die." Half
an hour later the young girl was led, or rather carried
into the furnace room hallway, and there Mussfeld
sent another in his place to do his job. A bullet in the
back of the neck.[19]

There was also the daily contingent of 70 to 80 women
who were selected in the hospital barracks to be liquidated.
Sooner or later, what difference did it make! They were
fully aware of the fate awaiting them, yet when the truck
entered the courtyard, the walls resounded with their
screams and cries. They knew that at the foot of the
crematory ovens all hope of escape dissolved. The staccato
of revolvers and the screams were muffled by the time Dr.
Nyiszli heard them.

One evening, the funereal routine changed. The prisoners
led into the courtyard were extremely calm. Selected in the
hospitals, they were all seriously ill, too weak to scream or
even to climb down from the raised platform of the truck.
Naturally the SS began to shout at them. As no one moved,
the driver finally started the motor and slowly the truck's
immense dump began to rise, till suddenly it spilled the
"occupants on to the ground, a writhing, slipping,
frantically gasping mass." As the bodies reached the

concrete and they bumped against each other, a horrible collective cry of pain burst forth. The sick were then stripped of their clothes, which were piled up on the spot, and the victims were led into the crematorium rooms. Mussfeld was the happy killer of the day. Standing near the ovens, wearing rubber gloves, he held his weapon with a steady hand. One by one the bodies fell, each yielding his place to the next in line. Half an hour later, the 80 bloody corpses had all been cremated.

Dr. Nyiszli has written that afterwards, when the killer asked him for a physical check-up, he found the man had a slightly high pulse rate. No doubt it was the result of his recent job, but Mussfeld protested. "Your diagnosis is incorrect," he said. "It doesn't bother me any more to kill 100 men than it does to kill 5. If I'm upset, it's merely because I drink too much." He was another of the Master Race.

After the Czech camp, when it was the Gypsies' turn to be annihilated, the 4,500 of them were also "quarantined" in their camp, just long enough for the guards with their police dogs to chase the inhabitants out of their barracks. It was a large group to handle, so to allay their fears and avoid any resistance or delays, they were given rations of bread and salami. The trick worked to perfection. "Everything went off as planned," writes Nyiszli. "Throughout the night the chimneys of Nos. I and II Crematoria sent flames roaring skyward. Next day the Gypsy camp lay silent and deserted."

These people were not Jews, but Catholic Gypsies from Germany and Austria. By morning, their bodies had been transformed into a pile of silvery ashes. On Mengele's orders, however, the bodies of twelve sets of twins had not been consigned to the flames. They were later stretched on the concrete floor of the morgue, and it would be Dr. Nyiszli's job to dissect them and report his findings to Dr. Mengele.[20]

The elimination of debilitated prisoners of the C camp was soon to follow. Mengele could no longer feed them;

they would be liquidated during the next two weeks. Dr. Nyiszli was deeply worried because he knew that C camp housed not only thousands of his compatriots but also his wife and daughter. Because two convoys of 3,000 prisoners were due to be sent from C camp to Germany's war plants, those people who were going to work in the factories would in fact stay alive. Dr. Nyiszli had been lucky enough (he said to the *Oberscharfuhrer* in the camp) to track his family down with Dr. Mengele's permission, and the *Ober* promised to help him. Both the wife and the daughter had to be selected for one of the convoys. Dr. Nyiszli explained to them that the situation demanded that they leave. Two days later, when he took warm clothes and food to his wife, she told him that everything had worked as planned. Both she and their daughter had been accepted even without the *Ober*'s help. They left and were then "far from the path leading to the funeral pyres."[21]

Mengele's liquidation of C camp was carried out after the convoys to Germany had steamed out of Auschwitz.

> Every evening, fifty trucks brought the victims, 4,000 at a time, to the crematorium...each bearing a human cargo of eighty women who either filled the air with their screams or sat mute, paralyzed with fear. In slow succession the trucks rolled up and dumped the women, who had already been stripped of their clothes, at the top of the stairway leading down into the gas chamber. From there they were quickly pushed below....They were no longer capable of putting up any resistance. They were herded passively into the gas chamber....For their life had lost all meaning and purpose....The C camp inmates had lived for four months in the shadow of the crematorium gate; it took ten days for all of them to pass through it. Forty-five thousand tormented bodies rendered up their souls there.[22]

The 12th *Sonderkommando*, which operated in Ausch-

witz and to which Dr. Nyiszli actually belonged, was
awaiting the final blow.[23] "Day after day," he wrote,
"week after week, month after month, terror had hovered
over our heads, suspended by the thinnest of threads. And
now, in a day or two, it would descend bringing with it
instantaneous death, leaving in its wake only a pile of
silvery ashes. We were ready for it. Hourly we awaited the
arrival of our SS executioners."

In a conversation with those he called his comrades, the
doctor found out that their liquidation would not take place
before the following day or perhaps the day after. "But
careful plans had been made for the 860 members of the
kommando to try and force their way out of the camp. The
break was scheduled for that night." The dramatic events
of that night have been recounted by Dr. Nyiszli, and are
too detailed to be repeated here. In a nutshell, a long and
real fight ensued in which, of course, the SS got the better
of the situation. In the last part of the struggle, "for about
ten minutes the fighting was [still] heavy on both sides.
Loud machine-gun fire from the watchtowers mingled with
the lesser blasts of the sub-machine guns, and, interspersed,
could be heard the explosion of hand grenades and
dynamite. Then as suddenly as it had begun, everything
became quiet."

The prisoners were surrounded and, under a rain of
blows, were eventually assembled on their bellies in the
courtyard. Two more groups of *Sonderkommando* men
were rounded up and made to lie down next to the others.
"A hail of kicks and blows from the guards' clubs fell on
our heads, shoulders and backs. I could feel the warm blood
trickling down my face."

A moment later, Mengele arrived. Dr. Nyiszli explained
that he was busy dissecting a cadaver when he was arrested
following an explosion. Mengele ordered him to go wash up
and return to his work. His three assistants followed him.
"We had gone no more than twenty steps when a burst of
machine-guns sounded behind us. The Sonderkommando's
life was over."[24]

Dr. Nyiszli thought there had been a traitor among the *Kommando*. In the afternoon he went out to see exactly what had happened. He saw his comrades naked, lying in long rows, in front of the cremation ovens. They must have been brought back in pushcarts from the spot where they had fallen; that is, from Nos. II and III Crematoria to be cremated in No. I. The cremation was to be handled now by 30 new, hastily recruited *Sonder* men. Dr. Nyiszli was told that twelve of his comrades were still missing. Of the others, all but seven were dead. There were himself, his three associates, and the engineer in charge of the dynamos and ventilators, the head chauffeur, and a jack-of-all-trades helper assigned to the SS personnel. It was this man who assured Dr. Nyiszli that there had been no traitors among the *Kommando*.[25]

It was certain that the No. III Crematorium roof had been blown off. Four drums of gasoline had exploded, reducing the building to rubble and burying the *Sonder* men inside. A few who escaped with their lives tried to carry on the fight, but the SS machine-guns quickly mowed them down. In a few moments, the explosion from No. III Crematorium caused the men at work in No. I to leave their posts, and the SS guards moved in. One of the guards arrived just in time to see the booted feet of one of his colleagues disappear into the oven. A bloody fight ensued. The survival of the prisoners was becoming so precarious that twelve of them fled across the Vistula River—only to be recaptured on the far bank. Thus, no one succeeded in escaping to tell the world the full story of the hellish prison. All in all, 853 prisoners (plus 70 SS) were killed, No. III Crematorium was burned down and No. IV was knocked out of service.[26]

The balance sheet was still not closed. The next day, October 7, 1944, as Dr. Nyiszli went to work, he had to pass by the incineration room. There he discovered that the cremation of his comrades had been completed—at midnight, actually. Thirty new *Sonder* men, stricken with the tragedy they had witnessed on the day of their arrival, were sitting or lying in silence on the beds of the dead. But life was soon to resume its "normal" course again. On that same day, Dr. Nyiszli was visited by Mengele, "the fiendish physician of Auschwitz [who] made me cut open the bodies of the freshly murdered people, whose flesh was also used for the cultivation of bacteria in an electric incubator."

Mengele had just attended the arrival of the inhabitants from the Riga ghetto. He had not made any selection, but simply sent the whole "herd" to the left. Nos. I and II Crematoria, as well as the immense pyre, were still in full operation. To cope with the fresh influx, the ranks of the new, 13th *Sonderkommando*, were increased to 460 men.

By this time, in the fall of 1944, only 70,000 souls of the original half a million who had worked in the Litzmann-stadt ghetto were continuing to arrive in Auschwitz in "herds" of 10,000. "Persecuted and tortured, physically and morally broken by five years of ghetto life, bowed by the knowledge of their accused race's tragic destiny, aged by forced labour, they [were] completely apathetic." On the ramp, 95 per cent of them were sent to the left and marched directly to the crematorium. By the end of the week, the liquidation of the Litzmannstadt ghetto would be completed.

In the late afternoon of October 7, after the first hecatomb, Mengele arrived and listened to Dr. Nyiszli's report concerning "both in vivo and post-mortem obser-vations" he had made on the victims.[27] This time the bodies were not to be cremated; they were to be prepared and their skeletons sent to the Anthropological Museum in Berlin. The best method was to boil the bodies in water until the flesh could easily be stripped from the bones. Dr. Nyiszli reported that he tested the bodies after five hours and found that the flesh would come off easily enough. The fire was put out and the containers allowed to cool until dusk. Then a *Sonder* man came running to Dr. Nyiszli, requesting that he hurry, for Poles were eating the meat in the casks! And indeed Dr. Nyiszli witnessed a scene which he had never seen before in all his life.

Thinking it was meat cooking for the *Sonderkommando*,

a few Poles had sniffed at it, fished out a few pieces of the human flesh not covered with skin and begun to eat. When two men of the *Sonder* told them what it was they were eating, sick, horrified and paralyzed, they stopped their banquet abruptly. Eventually, the two skeletons were wrapped in large sacks of strong paper and forwarded to Berlin, marked: "Urgent. National Defence."[28]

"On All Saints' Day, a deadly silence brooded over Auschwitz. The cold concrete steps descended and dissolved into darkness. These same steps where four million people, guilty of no crime, had bade life good-bye and descended to their death, knowing that even in death their tormented bodies would not be granted the sanctuary of a grave."[29] But there was no respite. Another convoy had been announced, from the Theresienstadt ghetto in Czechoslovakia, and the motors of the big ventilators in the crematorium purred once again and reawakened the furnace flames.

The ghetto housed 60,000 Jews from Austria, Holland and Czechoslovakia itself. Apparently they had been well-treated, says Nyiszli, so that the Reich could brandish "the reports of the International Red Cross which had the effect of qualifying as evil slander the rumors going round concerning the horrors of the KZ and the crematoria. But now, on the eve of the collapse, the Third Reich ceased to worry any longer about opinion." The time had come to exterminate the population of the ghetto. In Auschwitz, therefore,

> 20,000 men, fully flush of their youth, died in the gas chambers and were incinerated in the crematory ovens. It took 48 hours to exterminate them all.... Two weeks later, still more deportee trains began arriving in endless succession at the Jewish ramp. 20,000 women and children scrambled out of the box cars. There was no selection. All were directed to the left...and were marched to the gas chambers and the ovens where their husbands and fathers had preceded them.[30]

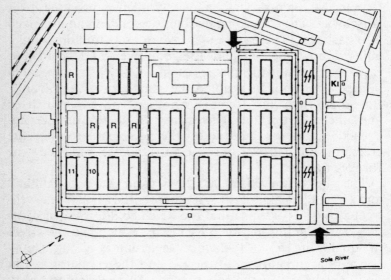

Plan of Auschwitz I.
K: Crematory I; R: camp hospital barracks; 10: barracks where pseudo-medical experiments were conducted; 11: "death barracks." The rest of the barracks inside the barbed wire were prisoners' residences.

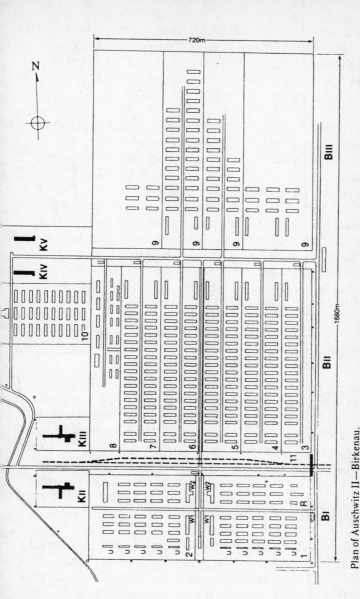

Plan of Auschwitz II—Birkenau.

1 and 2: The women's camp. 3: Men's quarantine camp. 4: Family camp for Czech Jews. 5 and 6: The men's camp. 7: Family camp for Gypsies. 8: Hospital in men's camp. 9: Under construction; known as "Mexico." 10: Storehouses of plundered effects; known as "Canada." K: Crematories and gas chambers. 11: Rail platform; site of "selections" for gas chamber. R: Hospital barracks in women's camp. W1: Kitchens. W2: Bathhouses; place to get water in women's camp. U: Washrooms and toilets without running water. Continuous lines around sections = electrically charged barbed wire.

On November 13, 1944, Nansen writes:

> A transport of a thousand Jews arrived here [at Sachsenhausen] from Auschwitz, among them two Norwegians. [One, Wolfberg, a friend of Nansen's, told of his observations at Auschwitz. Nansen goes on to summarize them.] I believe it will be hard for posterity, indeed for other people at all to grasp the depth of the suffering and horror of which Auschwitz has been the frame. Still less will it be possible to understand those who survived it. That they can remain human beings, think and feel and be like human beings.... All of them were in rags and tatters, like all who come here—all *Zugangere*.... But none of them looked exactly doomed; they weren't walking skeletons.... The explanation is a simple one; all who were so far gone, died or were killed in the gas chambers. These were the survivors, the pick of serviceable hands whom they can go on exploiting a while longer, in workshops and other working places, *for victory*!

Nansen's entry of November 16 relates further observations of Wolfberg's.

> There seems to be little doubt that practically all the Norwegian Jews are dead...it may be a whole thousand.... Many saw death as a deliverance when they could not stand it any more. The youngest of the Kaplan boys, Konrad...had a job on the ramp, that is on the platform where the railway cars drew up to the crematory buildings, with their tragic loads of people mostly condemned to death. Transport after transport from Hungary, from Slovakia, Bohemia, Moravia, Germany, Belgium, Holland, Norway, France, Yugoslavia, the Ukraine, with thousands upon thousands more Jews came rolling into that ramp. When the trucks had been emptied, the Jews were lined up five and five on the ramp and a selection was made. All the

healthy and able-bodied were picked out; the rest were for the "baths." All the small children went into the "bath." Every woman with a child in her arms went the same way, and all the old and feeble. This was known to all who worked on the ramp, but the poor creatures who arrived with the transport had no suspicion of it.[31]

When those who were to die had been separated from those who were to live, the death cortege moved off to the crematories. These contained, besides the gas chambers and the furnaces, which could burn forty-eight corpses at a time, a big dressing room where they were taken on the pretext that they were to have a bath. They undressed without suspicion and went into the "bath" which was next door. There, gas came out of the showers instead of water.... The road from the bath to the furnace was short. The process has been going on several years without a break, and in spite of that, the five crematoria have been inadequate. They also had to burn corpses out in the open...The whole process—stoking, moving corpses and all—was of course attended by the prisoners themselves. No SS man soiled his hands with such dirty work as Jew-killing....When [Wolfberg] asked me if I thought any of them would come through this alive and get back home after the war, to tell the truth I didn't know what to answer, for there is no denying it would be queer and inconsistent to leave such witnesses alive to tell posterity and the world what has been going on.

The day before yesterday 700 Jews arrived here from Yugoslavia. They were Hungarian Jews and were all in soldiers' uniforms, or their remains. They had been on the march for ten weeks all the way from the Yugoslavian frontier, and had scarcely any clothes or shoes left. They were in a miserable conditon; many had died on the way; they had dead bodies with them, too, and several died on the parade ground where they had to stand for most of the night after their arrival here.

They had wrapped their legs, arms and bodies in paper and sacks picked up the roadside, to keep warm....

Dr. Nyiszli recounts developments in Auschwitz:

On November 17, [1944]...an order reached the Kommandant of the camp that it was now forbidden to kill any more prisoners. There were no more violent deaths in the KZ...but the bloody past had to be hidden, the crematoria had to be demolished, the pyre ditches filled in, and any witness to or participant in the horrors that had been perpetrated had to disappear. It did not take long.

In the afternoon, the men of the Sonderkommando were called out to assemble. "With sinking hearts we headed for the crematorium courtyard where a group of well armed SS already encircled a group of Kommando men". When the last stragglers had joined the ranks, the men were led into No. II Crematorium room, the SS guards remaining outside. "The doors were shut and the windows covered with heavy iron bars, completely thwarting any possibility of escape. Our comrades from No. II were also present and a few minutes later...the Kommando from No. IV was sent in. Later the heavy doors were swung open and the Oberscharfuhrer Steinberg accompanied by the two guards, entered and ordered the doctors to leave: *"Arzte heraus!"*

Dr. Nyiszli, his colleagues and his lab assistant were then told to return to their rooms. "The following morning," Dr. Nyiszli goes on to narrate, "a five-truck convoy arrived in the crematorium courtyard and dumped out its cargo of bodies, those of the old Sonderkommando. A new group of thirty men carried them to the incineration room where they were laid out in front of the ovens. Terrible burn scars covered their bodies. Their faces and clothing were so charred that it was all but impossible to identify them, especially since their tattoo numbers had disappeared.... During the night our comrades had been taken into a nearby forest and killed by flame throwers! That we, four, were still alive did not by any means signify that they wanted to spare us, but simply that we were still indispensable to them. In allowing us to remain alive, Dr. Mengele had merely granted us another reprieve.''[32]

Soon Mengele announced that by superior orders Auschwitz would be completely destroyed. The "institution," that is Nos. I and II Crematoria, was to be demolished first; No. III had already been blown up during the October revolt. Only No. IV (where the dissection room was transferred to) would be kept in operation to dispose of the hospital's dead. Jews had built the infamous *KZ*; Jews would now start to tear it down.

Ten days later (around the end of November), Dr. Nyiszli learned from Mussfeld that they would soon die. "Our guards were going to disappear with us.... 'It's all over,' added the drunken SS. 'The Russians are barely 40 kilometres from Auschwitz. The whole of Germany is in exodus on the highways. Everyone is leaving the frontier areas to seek refuge in the West.'''

Odd Nansen takes up the narrative:

> One big transport after another is arriving in camp from Auschwitz, from other camps in Poland, from camps in Germany, and "evacuated" Jews by thousands from Hungary. 2,600 Jews arrived the other day from Budapest. The transport hadn't taken more than three days. Eighty died on the way, and when they got here they were left starving out in the cold most of the night...None had a drop of water for three days. Food, they had brought from home.
> ...If one goes through one of the Schonungsblocken ...one keeps on seeing living skeletons....The other

evening I was talking to an old Pole.... He was sixty-seven, but looked 97; bones, sinews, and skin apart, I'll wager his flesh and stomach didn't weigh five kilos.... He was a Polish peasant from the Warsaw district, and had been "evacuated" here, starving and suffering; of the rest of his family, children and wife, he knew nothing. They had lost each other during the "evacuation." Now he had *Durchfall* and couldn't eat. He had already gone out, was no longer a man, only a poor, suffering, still living creature waiting for peace. There are hundreds and thousands like him—innocent, harmless, suffering human beings.

December 18:... The Jewish builder from Budapest who was in the march from South Serbia to the German frontier has told me details about that 840-kilometer trek. After crossing the frontier into Hungary, the guard of Hungarian soldiers and their officers disappeared, and only SS were left. "When we reached [an abandoned] brickwork, we were completely worn out with hunger, thirst and exertion. Twenty-five names were called out by a Scharfuhrer. These 25 were taken away, and we heard shots from tommy guns. They shot at them until none was left standing; then they came in and fetched more.... They were human beings like us...they had wives and children. Used for target practice! Nearly 2,000 men were killed that night. We were all expecting our turn and felt certain we were all to die. But then they suddenly stopped, and the next day the march continued; we were now only a thousand odd. A number had died of overstrain or had been shot because they couldn't keep going.... In southern Hungary, the roads were filled with Swabians who were being evacuated—and with our own SS soldiers and their transport trucks.... The Swabians, women, children and men, struck us with rope ends and abused us the whole time as the cause of their calamity. The SS men, who were also Swabians, drove us on with whips and firearms; those who couldn't go on were shot and left in the ditch. [In a certain town the "herd" was asked what they would like: *either* food *or* drink.]...We agreed to choose water. Our tongues were sticking to our palates. Thirst was really the worst of all....We drank like animals and fell sick. I drank three liters. From that moment the "natural" deaths began.

"[The next day the prisoners were given food, in the form of a live cow.] We slaughtered it, and as there were no cooking vessels but an empty gas tank, we got that open and boiled the meat in it. Then I saw for the first time that men are animals. They didn't eat like men, they hurled themselves upon the kill like wild beasts, and scraped and clawed the flesh from the bones with their hands and teeth. It was an appalling sight. I shall never forget it. Nearly a thousand men, dead beat and half mad with hunger, in a shambles full of blood, slime, and bits of entrails and filth, hurling themselves on and rending in pieces the quarters of a cow boiled in a gas tank. The meat tasted horrible, saturated as it was with gas, and of course we fell sicker than before. But still it was food....Then we had to go on...[In the countryside] a favourite sport with the SS was to order a number of us up into the trees, ten or twelve at a time. They had to climb up high, sit on the branches, and sing Jewish songs. As they sang they were shot down like birds, and the shooting didn't stop until none was left on the branches. Thus our days went by for almost three months; then we reached the German frontier."

In Auschwitz on New Year's Day, 1945, "Brown Toni," a large van that was used to transport prisoners, brought in 100 Christian Poles, left and came back with 100 women, also Polish Christians. They had committed, so Dr. Nyiszli was told, "minor slips and infractions of the law turned into fabulous, trumped-up charges." Since there was no longer any *Sonder* man on the site, SS guards led the prisoners, naked, to the *Ober*'s revolver. The same SS squad carried out the cremation.[33]

Far away, in New York, on January 14, 1945, three and a half months before the end of the war, the famous writer in exile Thomas Mann addressed the German people in a broadcast. He asked them whether they had any notion "of their country conditioned to brutality through a monstrous dictature...of the horrible crimes committed in your name?"

Did they know what Majdanek was, that extraordinary camp near Lublin in Poland? "It isn't," said Mann, "an ordinary concentration camp, but a gigantic death machine. There is an enormous stone building topped by a factory chimney; it is the greatest crematorium in the world.... More than half a million Europeans, men, women and children of all ages have been asphyxiated in its gas chambers and incinerated at a daily rhythm of 1,400. Night and day smoked the chimney, and the death factory worked full swing."

Thomas Mann added that the delegates of Swiss institutions for the safeguard of humanity visited Auschwitz and Birkenau, and there they saw what no human being could have imagined. In a period of two years, from April 15, 1942, till April 15, 1944, those two extermination camps have destroyed 1,715,000 Jews. Mann asks, "Where do I hold those figures from?... Your compatriots did not fail to put their accountants to work. That macabre file has [already] been found with hundreds of thousands of passports and identity papers made out in 22 European countries...."

These figures would not have surprised Dr. Nyiszli, had he been able to hear them in Auschwitz, the hated and hellish camp he was about to flee. In Chapter 36 of his book, he describes how he was awakened at midnight on January 17, and how he promptly found that the crematorium's heavy gate was open. The SS had disappeared. Now it was Dr. Nyiszli and his companions' turn to take the road toward Birkenau, only two kilometres from the crematorium. "Immense flames glowed along the horizon there. It was probably the KZ burning." The path that led through the little forest of Birkenau was the one which millions had walked on their way to death. Now the doctor and his colleagues reached the *KZ* gate where they joined a crowd of 3,000 prisoners who were gathered there, waiting to leave. "It was about one o'clock in the morning. The last SS had left the camp. He closed the iron gates and cut off the lights from the main switchboard, located near the entrance. The enormous cemetery of European Judaism, Birkenau, sank into darkness. My eyes lingered for a long while on the barbed wires of the camp and the rows of barracks that stood out against the night. Farewell cemetery of millions, cemetery without a single grave!"[34]

It was goodbye forever to Auschwitz.

That same day, in the women's camp, "news of the proposed evacuation spread rapidly." Olga Lengyel recounts how "a dense crowd pressed against the barbed wire which separated the men's camp from the women's. Husbands, lovers, friends called goodbye, wondering whether they would ever see each other again.... Across the wires they cried out addresses of rendezvous where they might meet after the war. It was forbidden to have writing materials, so one had to memorize these precious bits of information.

"The wildest rumours were rampant. Some affirmed that we would all be put to death on the road. Others declared that the Russians would be here in a few hours, and that we must wait for them there.

"...During that morning the Germans assembled us in the *Lagerstrasse*[35] in columns of five. They made us wait an hour or two in spite of the bitter cold. Then they sent us back to the barracks.

"In the afternoon a new camp commander arrived escorted by a large entourage. At once a severe selection followed. The sick were sent back into their barracks; [some] tried to slip into the groups that were leaving. But the SS always without pity pursued them with sticks and with revolver shots."

Lengyel had to give up her hospital rounds "to take my place in the ranks again.... When I rejoined my group, I saw a long line begin to march in the men's camp on the other side of the barbed wire. I glanced over the vast area of Birkenau. Before Camps F, D, C, and B II, vast piles of paper were burning.[36] The Germans were destroying every record of their crimes.... A few minutes later, an inmate hurried up. 'Get ready, quickly! We shall probably leave right after the men.' "

After Olga Lengyel and her companions had rushed to the warehouse to get some food for the journey, "...I hurried [back] to the barracks and settled my affairs. My parcel was ready; my blanket was rolled and knotted at both ends like a soldier's pack.... Thirty guards stood at the gates. Before letting us out, they examined us one by one under a pocket flashlight, in what became another selection. Those who were judged to be too old or too feeble were driven back into the camp. Once we were outside the camp, we had to line up, as always, in columns of five.... The whole convoy was to consist of six thousand women.

"The SS closed the gates. An order was barked. Our column was under way. Was it possible! We were leaving Birkenau still alive!... Now everything was plunged into darkness, and only burning embers, where the crematory records were being incinerated, feebly lighted the barracks, the miradors, and the barbed-wire fences.... The SS hurried us along, and the lights grew dimmer and dimmer. Birkenau, the greatest slaughterhouse in human history, was little by little disappearing from view... We were herded along Auschwitz road. It was freezing cold, and the air knifed through our rags."[37]

Odd Nansen relates events of late winter and spring 1945:

> January 26-29: The evacuees from the east [because of the Russian advance] are constantly streaming toward Berlin. They arrive on foot or by train. The cars are opened, and stiffened corpses roll out. Mothers, children, old people frozen to death as they sit with their heads in their hands or hunched up in corners.... Yesterday morning [January 28] a transport of half-dead men left the camp. 1,000 sick people, all of them the wretchedest and feeblest muselmen[38] that could be exhibited, chosen from the Revier, the Schonungs-blocken, and the Tub. Many died at the gate of the Revier, where they had to line up in frost and snow, half naked, to be called over. They dropped dead in advance. Most of them had been taken straight out of their beds.... [The survivors] are literally nothing but bones, skin and sinews. All have the same expression on their faces, that is if one can talk of expressions and faces, for they are nothing but skulls, death's-heads, like those that are painted on the death placards along the electric fences around the camp.... What an abyss of resignation and suffering stares out on you, without a word, without a sound.... And in this dance of death, criminals are playing their game, swindlers, thugs, bank robbers, pickpockets, cheats. Most of them, raised to positions of authority in camp, have a free hand within this community. They steal the food out of starving mouths, the clothes off bodies that are freezing to death.
>
> February 6: Yesterday 225 Jews went to the gas chambers. It was a transport from Liberose.... It's predicted that all the Jews are to be gradually extirpated. The crematory is busy day and night. The crematorium gang, 25 Jews, are on shift work. The previous gang has been liquidated; of course they knew

too much. These Jews will doubtless go the same way, when they have done their job.

February 9: Activity in the crematorium is undiminished; the burning goes on day and night....We are always hearing of Jews and muselmen going into the gas chamber.

March 22: [At the Neuengamme concentration camp, where Nansen and other prisoners had been evacuated], the first thing to do was to secure a place in the sty....The whole yard was pretty much an open sewer, which stank even worse than the inside of the huts. Although the weather was dry and had been for a long time, puddles filled the holes in the concrete, and the grooves and cracks. What they were puddles of, the smell betrayed, and the condition of the gully holes and the drain they were supposed to lead to, was beyond all doubt. The filth was everywhere, in thick layers; it was worse than a pigsty. The hut was the stall where the beasts were kept at night, the courtyard the outer sty.

March 24:...There is already typhus in the camp. The dungheaps lie open, sewage and filth are afloat everywhere. Lousy, sick and dying muselmen drag themselves around and hang begging on the barbed-wire fences round our yards. One has a sense of wading in and swallowing bacteria and bacilli. Every day 100 or 150 men are dying in the camp, which contains 8,000 prisoners altogether, or possibly 12,000. The figure varies, for fresh transports keep arriving, and also transports are going out all the time. Several of the chaps have been in the crematory cellar, looking at enormous piles of muselmen corpses, more than the furnace can burn. Also there's a fuel shortage. Shooting and hanging, too, go on here continually.

March 25: ...One sight I saw yesterday is in my mind the whole time...the sight of hundreds of corpses piled on top of one another in the mortuary, as high as houses...I wanted to see. It was appalling. There might have been 300 or 400 corpses. Not

ordinary corpses; these were 300 or 400 skeletons;...
they weren't human beings—so small and miserable.
The numbers, the overwhelming numbers, I suppose,
completely throw out one's sense of scale. But the faces
and those ghastly hundreds of pairs of staring eyes,
those gaping mouths and distorted features—they were
human. Those human beings who had lived, suffered
and died. And all those hundreds were only three days'
harvest! They were piled on top of each other with all
their heads, or rather skulls, the same way. The bodies
took up no more space than the heads, so they lay flat.
For there were only bones left, covered with skin. Some
were bloody, with running sores and discoloured
bruises where they had been struck, others pale as wax.

March 28: [Describing a two-story brick building,
the Schonungsblock]...The misery passed all bounds
and baffled all conception. In every bed there were
three or four, indeed sometimes five or six men. It
sounds incredible but I saw them. Certainly they were
lying on top of each other, but most of them were
nothing but skeletons and didn't take up much room.
And they lay quiet: they hadn't the strength to move.
They were there to die!—and many were already dead!
The whole interior of the building was one inferno, a
waiting room of death worse than could be conjured up
in the wildest fantasies....Some had tuberculosis,
others dysentery and typhus, others open wounds and
running venereal diseases and all conceivable and
inconceivable sufferings of every kind....They re-
lieved themselves where they lay. One can imagine
what the bunks (in three tiers) looked like, and the
bunks below. The straw was antique, and the blankets
hadn't been shaken, let alone washed, for years; they
lay on the bunks like stiff cakes of filth. On the floors
and up the walls the dirt lay in thick, hard layers, and
when one entered the building the stench that met one
was imaginable. In the passages, the washroom, in
the of the staircase, inside the wards, and in the

beds, corpses lay around. And now these people were to clear out to make room for more Norwegians in the camp. And we were to move in after them. The SS intended us to move into the house and get into the muselmen's beds just as they were. Into the cakes of ordure and the filth, into the same straw that has lain in the bunks for years, collecting every known species of bacterium and bacillus and every variety of human excrement! Here we have German *Sauberkeit* in a nutshell; that's what it is. The covers must be smooth and the edges flush like rulers—in a row, there must be nothing on the blankets, nothing under the beds; what the blankets are concealing, though it were a dump heap, is of no interest, provided it's as smooth as a dance floor. Yes, even if there are corpses under the blankets, rotting away, that's quite in order so long as they are invisible. I mention this last because in the cleaning that followed, dead bodies actually were found, hidden in the straw of the bunks. Their bedmates "kept" the bodies there so as to get an extra helping of soup or an extra bread ration.

The results of the Nazis' unspeakable crimes struck the advancing American and British soldiers full in the face as they "opened the gates of concentration camps, and saw the gas chambers and ovens, looking in horror at the huddled masses of skeletal inmates clad in lice-infested rags and riddled with typhus. The Nazis had once disposed of the bodies of those they murdered in the camps. . . .Allied bulldozers now had to shovel mounds of corpses into mass graves."[39]

Chapter IV
THE HOLOCAUST HYDRA

The torture and extermination camps were initiated by the SS apparatus. Their men ran the camps, imposing deliberate and efficient torture on a rising scale of intensity, beginning with the lash and continuing through electro-shocks, the crushing of sexual organs, burning with a soldering torch, hanging by the armpits, and asphyxiation by plunging the victim's head into cold water until he was about to pass out.

As Rebecca West justly reflected, "The Nazi apparatus had so openly aimed at the commission of violence and the preaching of race hatred that no man could have joined them without criminal intent. In other words, SS men, who are here at the pillory, were not only obeying orders blindly, they had joined because they liked the job: torturing and killing, gassing and burning."[1]

Propelled by the "final solution," these torture camps, which had been used since 1933 as a method of political terrorization to break opponents of Nazi ideology, were turned into abattoirs.[2] How this transformation was carried out has been shown in the preceding pages.

From 1940 onward, the Jew was doomed. When they arrived at the slaughterhouse, Jews were openly told that, for them, there was no way out except through "those chimneys." Those annihilation camps—*Vernichtungslager* —"welcomed" Jews only; other camps received Jews and non-Jews alike (partisans, hostages, gays, members of

159

Resistance groups, Communists and other political enemies). So-called labour camps were in reality no different
from death camps. Finally, the Nazis operated a number of
transit camps. One was in a village next to Belsen. Another
was Theresienstadt, designed for the immediate deportation
of the Jews from Bohemia and Moravia, a territory of
which Heydrich was the protector from September 27,
1941, until his death in Prague on June 4, 1942.

Heydrich and Eichmann, as outlined above, decided to
use Theresienstadt as a centre of deportation to the east. On
January 20, 1942, at Wannsee, Heydrich announced that
the city was to be a ghetto for "old and privileged Jews"
but, as Eichmann explained to the police chiefs involved,
this deceptive appellation was meant as a public relations
sop to world opinion. When Red Cross inspectors showed
up, the camp was turned upside down, a survivor testified in
Jerusalem, to ensure that it was perceived as a paradise. But
in fact, the hunger was awful; there was no water; hygiene
was non-existent; and people fought for potato peelings
soaked in dirt. The death rate was appalling. In October
1942, a record month, the figure was over 3,000. Yet, the
crematorium was also working full blast, as people were
now streaming in from all over Europe, especially Prague,
Vienna, Berlin, Brno and Frankfurt. The roll of prisoners
thus swelled to 60,000, but altogether 141,000 passed the
gates of the camp, 33,500 of whom died and 88,000 were
deported to the east.

Inside the camp, death penalties were imposed for such
offences as "breach of censorship regulations." Sixteen
Jews were hanged for this crime in March 1942, when
Eichmann declared it to be a capital offence. "But I wrote
only to my grandmother," protested one of the convicts
before his execution.[3]

The second camp mentioned above was Bergen-Belsen, a
"foreigners' camp" established in the summer of 1943.
"Tens of thousands were placed in a camp built for

several thousands," testified Dr. Josef Melkmann in Jerusalem. "The sanitary conditions were indescribable. There was one lavatory always out of order for a hut of 400 people....Dead people lay outside on the paths of the camp....Women fought in the gutter for food refuse.... There were fourteen cases of cannibalism...."

On the day of liberation, May 25, 1945, the camp still contained 52,000 inmates, 27,000 of whom died of exhaustion and starvation during subsequent weeks.

Eighteen days after liberation, Dr. Mordechai Chen, a captain in the British Medical Corps, could not believe his eyes: "Heaps of corpses were all around. I knew that ordinary human beings would hardly believe such things had ever existed, and I was sure that in ten years certainly nobody would believe it, and we ourselves might not believe that we had ever seen it."[4]

In the General Government, the ghettos had given way to huge labour camps in order to squeeze the last ounce of strength and energy from the able-bodied Jews, while sending all others to destruction. The sadistic pattern did not change, and killing through labour was rewarded with official blessings in writing from superiors.[5]

Cruelty and terror, at the farthest rim of the imagination, were part of the SS credo, and were common practice. The Jewish child was an object of particular venom. At Jerusalem, Noah Zabludowicz testified: "Once I saw an SS officer in Ciechanow politely asking a Jewish mother in the street to let him try to appease her crying child. With incredulity in her eyes and with trembling hands, the woman delivered the infant, whereupon the Nazi smashed the baby's small head on the sharp edge of the curbstone. The mother did not even have time to cry out. At that moment I thought God had hidden his face from the human race."

Another witness, Dr. Buzminsky, had a similar, terrifying story to tell the judges. On one occasion, he had

seen an SS officer accost a woman who had come too near a
fence separating the ghetto from the non-Jewish part of the
town. She was carrying an emaciated infant about a year
old, and when the SS officer drew his pistol to shoot her,
the woman fell on her knees and pleaded with him to spare
the child. "'Shoot only me!' she begged. The officer
snatched the infant away, shot the woman twice and then
putting the child's leg under his foot, tore the baby in two
like a rag."

The indictment of SS officers after the war during their
trial in Nuremberg reflected the magnitude of their repeated
crimes. Testimony at the trials indicated that they had
mercilessly destroyed children, killing them at the same time
as their parents or separately, in hospitals or in children's
homes, "burying the living in the graves, throwing them
into flames, stabbing them with bayonets, poisoning them,
conducting experiments upon them, taking their blood for
the use of the German army, throwing them into prison and
Gestapo torture chambers and concentration camps where
they died from hunger, torture and epidemic diseases."

It was estimated that of the six million Jews who had been
massacred, a million were small children!

There were many other camps, of course, in which the
Nazis employed more direct, business-like methods of
killing Jews rather than simply exposing them to disease and
starvation.

For almost three years, the area around Lublin became
one of Europe's busiest transportation centres, with trains
following each other in close succession, arriving day and
night at small stations now jolted out of their customary
slumber. Arriving trains were full to the bursting point with
men, women and children. It was the end of the road for
them. The return cargo, as the engineers reversed the trains,
consisted only of the clothing, shoes and belongings of
those who had arrived a short time before. Thus at Sobibor,
Belzec, Treblinka, where the trains unloaded, the victims

were instantly exterminated, and their clothing and baggage shipped back, looking like a "Canada" store on wheels. (At Auschwitz, "Canada" was the name given to the mounds of all belongings taken from the inmates.)

The killing procedure was merely the last phase of the process. But to a newcomer, the railway station looked like any other. Everything seemed normal (except for the puzzling stench in the air and the heavy overhanging smoke). Soon the prisoners were led to "the baths," where they were told to breathe deeply—to facilitate the disinfection procedure.[6]

Chelmno (Kulmhof in German) was no exception. This extermination camp, 40 miles from Lodz, was actually the first to be completed. It became operational on December 8, 1941, a full six weeks before the Wannsee Conference. It functioned until October 1944. There, the so-called "disinfection vehicles" were actually mobile gas vans; the "disinfecting" agent was deadly carbon monoxide emitted in the engine's exhaust. The SS men's ruse was to distribute towels and bars of ersatz soap for use in the "showers" installed in these vans. As soon as the desired number of people were packed inside, the doors were locked and exhaust gases pumped into the seated compartment. In the last phase of the procedure, the vans drove off in the direction of the nearby forest, where the corpses were dumped.

In December 1941, Belzec near Lublin was readied and, in three months' time, it was put to use as a human death camp. It was so efficient that 600,000 Jews were soon put to death; there were no survivors. Also near Lublin was the labour camp of Majdanek, which had been established at the end of 1940, and was transformed into an annihilation site in 1942.

The construction of the Sobibor camp, apparently the last one to be built, was not started until March 1942. It is in this camp that Himmler attended a "ceremony whose primeval barbarism makes it unique in the annals of Nazi terror.... Three hundred young Jewish women picked for their beauty were gassed'' in the *Reichsfuhrer's* honor "while he stood like a Teutonic Moloch watching with calm, sovereign approval.''[7]

Among the renowned abattoirs was Treblinka, 50 miles from Warsaw. It had been a labour camp since 1941, and then was renovated to handle all of the functions of mass annihilation demanded by Eichmann's program. In the second half of 1941, buildings in this camp were camouflaged; the construction of others was carried out in the spring of 1942, and completed in the middle of July. Gas chambers were installed in brick buildings. First, three chambers were operational, but by autumn of the same year a second building was completed, comprising ten gas chambers.

With this new installation and the one in operation in Majdanek, Himmler, who in autumn of 1942 had just met SS Leader Globocnik in Lublin, hoped to speed up the destruction of the Jewish population of Poland. The Polish Government Commission, which investigated those camps after the war, stated that late in April 1942, the erection of the gas chambers was completed in Treblinka, but the general massacres were performed by means of steam.[8]

The Polish Commission reported that by the summer there were two railway transports of Jews daily, and there were days of much higher efficiency. In fact, Treblinka may well have outdone the pace of Auschwitz. "Since a string of twenty cars arrived at the platform every half hour," wrote Jean-Francois Steiner, "the Lalka[9] system made it possible to process fully twelve trains of twenty cars each, or four convoys, or twenty-four thousand persons, between seven o'clock in the morning and one fifteen in the afternoon."

When the trains arrived from Poland, scores of Jews were found dead. The sight was no different from that at Auschwitz or other camps. The remaining prisoners were killed by the exhaust gas produced by motors installed in the annex of the building. The gas was delivered to the chambers through pipes whose outlets were fixed into the ceilings. Two thousand people in thirteen chambers would be killed simultaneously.

As for the sick, the infirm and the old, their deaths were expedited by a shot at the back of the head, since they were unable to follow the other prisoners herded to the undressing room and to the gas chambers.

SS *Obersturmbannfuhrer* Eichmann intensified the consignments to Treblinka in the period from August 1942 to the middle of December, and from the middle of January to the middle of May 1943. From this date, the number of transports began to decrease somewhat.

On August 2, 1943, after several postponements, the inmates broke out in an armed mutiny; several SS were killed, buildings were set on fire. The purpose of this carefully planned uprising was to enable some of the prisoners to get out of the camp in sufficiently large numbers so that at least *one* man would survive and thus be able to tell the world the story of Treblinka and the reason behind the tragedy of the mutineers' deaths.

About 600 of them escaped into the nearby forests but in the year that followed—until the Red Army reached the region—most of the escapees were killed by units of the Gestapo and the *Wehrmacht*, which were tracking them down, as well as by Polish peasants. Only 40 *Treblinkanese* were finally rescued, and their story of the hell-camp told and heard.

One of the documents produced by the Russian prosecution in Nuremberg was a statement from a Warsaw carpenter, Jacob Vernik, who had been an inmate at Treblinka. "I have lost all my family," he declared. "I have myself led them to death, built the gas chambers in which they were murdered. I am afraid of everything. I fear that everything that I have seen is written on my face. An old and broken life is a heavy burden, but I must carry on and live to tell the world what German crimes and barbarism I saw."

In November 1943, what remained of the camp at Treblinka was liquidated, the gas chambers destroyed and all the incriminating documents burned.[10] Nonetheless, the record speaks for itself: The Treblinka extermination camp swallowed up about 800,000 human beings, most of them Jews. The ashes resting in Polish soil are the only remains of the victims of the mad SS. Before the mutiny, when bodies were exhumed to be burned, the ashes were screened and reburned before being mixed with sand, and the mixture was shovelled back into the empty graves. "On top," J.F. Steiner recounted, "grass was planted and white gravel paths were laid out. Wooden benches were set up as in a public park. Every trace of Treblinka's function was disappearing." And, indeed, it disappeared completely when the land was ploughed at the time the camp was liquidated.[11]

In other camps, the Jews were confronted with the same standard procedure. Upon their arrival, the 10 per cent who looked the fittest were selected for work; the remainder were consigned to the gas chambers. There, the Jews were packed in, one person per square foot. The gassing lasted from ten to 30 minutes. In Belzec, according to an eye-witness,[12] it took 32 minutes until "finally all were dead, like pillars of basalt, still erect, not having any space to fall." To make room for the next load, the bodies were tossed out immediately, "blue, wet with sweat and urine, the legs covered with feces and menstrual blood."

Later, the bodies were burned either in the open air or in the crematoria. Initially, the bodies were buried and then, before the crematoria were operational, they were burned in heaps. But afterwards, to conceal all traces of the crimes, the bodies from the first period of extermination were exhumed, counted and also burned. J.F. Steiner described how the action was carried out in Treblinka's Camp No. 2.[13] "To the left yawned an immense ditch and moving around it were three excavators, mechanical giants which jerkily plunged their long jointed arms to the bottom of the pestilential pit and lifted them more slowly, loaded with dismembered bodies.... Each long steel arm ended in a monstrous set of jaws which closed gradually as they rose, inexorably eliminating anything that was too long, severing heads, torsos and limbs, which fell heavily into the ditch. After that the mechanical arm would describe a large circle, pause, shudder, and brutally open its jaws, hurling to the ground its cargo of damned.

"A few dozen yards away, immense bonfires roared. As the flames reached them, the faces of the dead suddenly came back to life. They twisted and grimaced as if contorted by unbearable pain. The liquid fat and lymph that were suddenly exuded covered their faces with a kind of sweat that further reinforced the impression of life and intense suffering. Under the effect of the heat the belly of a pregnant woman burst like an over-ripe fruit, expelling the foetus, which went up in flames...."

In the middle of 1943, a special multi-unit "Death Brigade 1005" was organized and entrusted with the job of locating former mass graves, digging up the bodies and burning them up to obliterate any trace of the past actions of the *Einsatzgruppen*. The brigade was put under the command of SS Colonel Paul Blobel who belonged to *Einsatzgruppe* C. All the graves were reopened, the bodies piled up, counted and burned. When bones were found, they were pulverized in grinding machines; the ashes were dispersed, blanketing the graves; saplings were planted on the sites. The whole macabre work took the brigade almost two years to complete and involved the exhumation of more than two million corpses.

At his trial on November 2, 1947, Blobel testified that in the cemetery at Kiev he attended the opening of a tomb 165 feet long, 9 feet wide and 6½ feet deep. When the grave was opened, the bodies were sprinkled with a combustible and burned during two days. "I was careful to see," he said, "that the grave turned cherry red right down to the bottom. In this way, all traces were destroyed."

There were exact records of each grave's location and the number of people in it. Dr. Leon Wells, a prosecution witness at Eichmann's trial in Jerusalem in 1961, actually took part in one of the ghastly operations. Hausner writes, "[Wells] reached the grave where, thirteen months earlier, the slave-labour group he belonged to at the time had been shot and buried while *he* managed to escape. Caught once more, he now helped to open the grave. But only 181 bodies were found, instead of 182 the records indicated. 'We dug for three days in search of my own body,' said Dr. Wells, 'before we were ordered to give up and move on.' If Dr. Wells had indicated that his was the body they were searching for he would have certainly been shot on the spot—if only to make the records tally.''[14]

Auschwitz-Birkenau, of course, took the record in terms of horror. Fifteen square miles of territory between the rivers Vistula and Sola were evacuated to accommodate a colossal industrial complex beside the camp whose main purpose was death. The Master Race, armed to the teeth, courageously liquidated three and a half million unarmed civilians there in the three years of its operation.

Typically, upon arrival of the convoys, all but those singled out as being fit for work were sent straight to the crematoria; in each of the 46 ovens,[15] a minimum of three bodies could be burned in twenty minutes. But these people were not accounted for in the camp's register. Their personal cards were removed and stamped SB—*Sonderbehandlung*—(special treatment), intended to imply that the death was not unnatural, though indeed it was. As for those who were starved, shot, hanged, whipped to death or inoculated with phenol or some other deadly chemical, they were listed in the record as having succumbed to pneumonia, heart failure or dysentery.

A survivor, Yehiel Dinur, who wrote under a pen name, K. Zetnik (KZ, pronounced Katzet, a slang name for concentration camp), said in Jerusalem that his pseudonym was no pen name. ''I do not regard myself as a writer of literature. My writings are the chronicles of the planet Auschwitz. I was there for about two years. Time does not run there as it does here on earth. Every fraction of a second there passes on a different scale of time. The inhabitants of this planet had no names; they had no parents; they were not born there and they did not beget children. They breathed according to the laws of nature. They did not live nor did they die according to the laws of this world. Their name was 'Number.....Katzetnik.'"

The author felt that he should continue to bear the name K. Zetnik "so long as the world has not been roused, after this crucifixion of a nation, to wipe out this evil, as it was once roused after the crucifixion of one person."[16]

Apart from the *Transportjuden*, the Jewish cargoes which were for immediate or early destruction, there were also detained prisoners—*Schutzhaeftlinge*—sent to Auschwitz for criminal offences. They were not subjected to the immediate right-left selection process, but they were gassed anyway when they had served their sentences and had been subjected to the SS men's cruelties.

To conclude with the figures of the death camps: these statistics are only approximate. At Auschwitz, the largest mass-killing installation, many transports of deportees went directly from the detraining ramps to the gas chambers and were never statistically registered. Most victims were Jews, but there were also Gypsies and thousands of others who were gassed. The SS obituary list reaches a total of 5,370,000 victims. Transformed into cinders in the crematoria were:

    2,000,000 in Auschwitz
    1,380,000 in Majdanek
      800,000 in Treblinka
      600,000 in Belzec
      340,000 in Chelmo
      250,000 in Sobibor[17]

As far as Auschwitz-Birkenau is concerned, two million dead is an underestimate that Hoss later corrected in his signed affidavit of April 5, 1946. One must also take into consideration the three official surveys in which the overall total of persons executed (by gassing and cremation, shooting, flogging, burning in pits, hanging, starvation and inoculation) is, in fact, given as four million.[18]

Chapter V
THE HOLOCAUST IN FIGURES

In Appendix A of *The War against the Jews—1933-1945* (pp. 357-401), Lucy S. Dawidowicz outlines, by country, the fate of the Jews in Hitler's Europe. Only a sampling of her findings will be quoted here—some of the figures have been cited earlier.

In 1940, German Jews began to be deported into the General Government of Poland. At the same time, however, 7,500 from Baden and the Palatinate were dumped into France. A year later, in October 1941, there were extensive deportations to Lodz, Warsaw, Lublin, and as far east as Riga and Minsk, where the Jews were herded into ghettos. "Privileged" Jews—40,000 of them—were sent to Theresienstadt, formerly a Czech garrison town. By the end of 1942, a total of 150,000 Jews had been deported from Germany and Austria. In 1943, after another 20,000 were swept out of Berlin, the city could be declared "free" of Jews.

Theresienstadt was not only a ghetto but also a model transit camp from which Czech Jews were transported to the death camps in Poland. Some 55,000 of them, from the Protectorate of Bohemia and Moravia, eventually ended in Auschwitz and other extermination camps, as described above.

In August 1940, Eichmann's representative for the Reich Security Main Office, SS *Hauptsturmfuhrer* Dieter Wisliceny, arrived in Bratislava in Slovakia as an adviser on

Jewish affairs. Soon Jews were declared subject to forced labour and they were evicted from specified towns and districts. Plans for deportation, however, were not initiated until late 1941. In March 1942, five assembly points for deportees were organized, and during six months Jews were herded from these to the extermination camps. At this time, only 25,000 Jews remained in Slovakia. After three additional transports during September and October, 58,000 Jews in all had been deported—mostly to Auschwitz. Then, following the Slovak national uprising in 1944, there were other dragnet operations until no more than 5,000 Jews remained in hiding in the country.

In Hungary, the virtual occupation by the Germans in March 1944 and the installation of the pro-German Sztojay government drastically transformed the situation of the Hungarian Jews. "On March 19, the very day of the German take-over, Eichmann himself came to Budapest with a battery of SS officers in charge of the Jewish affairs. Eichmann ordered the Jewish community to appear for a conference the next day, when they were told to establish a *Judenrat*, which would carry out German orders." Drastic other measures followed. Then Eichmann organized the deportation of Jews by dividing Hungary into six zones. Further, "with the participation of a Sondereinsatz-kommando [special duty commando] that Eichmann had brought from Mauthausen, and with the help of the Hungarian police, the Germans began to round up the Jews, concentrating them within the designated areas and deporting them in rapid order. By June 7, Zones I and II (Carpathians and Transylvania) had been cleared of nearly 290,000 Jews. By June 30, over 92,000 from Zones III and IV (Northern Hungary and Southern Hungary east of the Danube) had fallen into the net. Seven days later, over 437,000 Jews, including 50,000 from Budapest, were also deported to Auschwitz."

After the German coup of October 1944, the Jews again fell into Nazi hands. On October 26, 35,000 Jewish men and women were rounded up, but since Auschwitz was then being liquidated, these Jews were used as slave labourers. There was no means of transportation however, and so the Germans marched 27,000 of them on a terrible trek of over 100 miles to Austria.

About 160,000 Jews had remained in Budapest where they were either subjected to terror and murder at the hands of the Arrow Cross or were forced to endure cold, hunger and disease. All in all, over 450,000 Jews—70 per cent of them from Greater Hungary—were either deported and then murdered, or they died under German occupation.

Poland was another viper's nest. Before the outbreak of war, there were about 3.3 million Polish Jews, almost 10 per cent of the country's population. With the German occupation, the Jews were isolated from the Poles. In accordance with Heydrich's instructions to the leaders of the *Einsatzgruppen* on September 21, 1939, the Jews were expelled from most of the incorporated territories, except for Lodz.

In the General Government, Jews were expelled from small communities and forced to make their way to the large cities. About 300,000 Jews then fled into Soviet-occupied Poland. This flight precipitated a series of ordinances from Governor Hans Frank, whose purpose was to isolate the Jews from the Poles, and then subject them to "special treatment." Among other measures, they were allotted smaller food rations than the rest of the Polish population. They were subjected to arbitrary terror and violence; most synagogues were destroyed and thousands of Jews were killed at random.

This first period of German occupation lasted six months; then the ghettoization began. After the war, it was estimated that at least half a million Jews died as a result of the German policy of annihilation from "natural causes" and random terror.

The third stage of the plan began "at the end of 1941 when the death camps became operational." In December, Jews started to be moved from the Wartheland to Chelmno. "In March 1942, the Jews of Lublin began to be deported to

Belzec. From July to September, over 300,000 Jews were deported from Warsaw to Treblinka.'' Another order from Himmler resulted in all Jewish workers being replaced by Poles. At the same time, he ordered the destruction of all ghettos by the end of the year. The actual process, however, took longer; only in March 1943 was the Cracow ghetto liquidated. And it took all of April to carry out the complete destruction of the Warsaw ghetto. In June, Lwow's disappeared; the Lodz ghetto lasted until August 1944 when the last 70,000 workers were deported. By the war's end, more than 3,000,000 Polish Jews had been killed.

The Soviet Union was not spared the SS dementia. With the German invasion of the USSR on June 22, 1941, the *Einsatzgruppen* arrived to round up Jews and murder thousands upon thousands of them in mass shootings at execution pits. Soon the German civilian administration set up ghettos in a number of cities for the remaining Jewish population, except where massacres proceeded so rapidly that ghettos were hardly needed. In Kiev, for example, in September 1941, more than 33,000 Jews were shot in two days at a ravine in outlying Babi Yar. By the end of October 1941, German statistics showed that a quarter of a million Jews had been slaughtered systematically in the Baltic and White Russia.

In sum, Jewish deaths amounted to over one million, perhaps as high as 1.3 million. In the Baltic, about 90 per cent of the Jews were killed; in White Russia about 66 per cent; and in the Ukraine about 60 per cent of the Jews were annihilated. Losses in Russia proper were about 100,000.

No one can establish with certainty the exact number of Jews murdered in the course of the "final solution." The earliest estimate, made at the Nuremberg trials in 1945, was that 5.7 million Jews were killed. It has been shown by subsequent censuses and statistical analyses to have been remarkably accurate. The 1959 census in the Soviet Union confirmed the staggering Jewish losses during World War II. According to Lucy Dawidowicz's overall figures, 5,933,900 Jews—that is, 67 per cent of the original population—were annihilated. The countries with the largest death toll (included in the above total) are:

Poland: 3,000,000 dead (90 per cent of the Jewish population;

SSR Ukraine: 900,000 dead (60 per cent); and

Hungary: 450,000 dead (70 per cent).

As well, Germany and Austria and the Baltic countries lost 90 per cent of their Jewish population; the Protectorate 89 per cent; Slovakia 83 per cent.[1]

The annihilation included murders of various kinds, chiefly: by gassing and cremation; by the *Einsatzgruppen*'s techniques; by all other methods resorted to in the extermination camps—shooting, hanging, burning in pits, flogging, starvation, poison inoculation and pseudo-scientific "experimentation."

In *The Destruction of the European Jews*, Raul Hilberg provides a double column chart detailing the size of the Jewish population of Europe in 1939 and 1945. The difference between the columns represents the number who perished: 5,397,000.

Gerald Reitlinger, in *The Final Solution*, suggests a "low" and a "high" estimate, country by country, of the Jewish losses from 1939 to 1945. His total ranges from 4,194,200 to 4,581,200. He asks the reader to consider his figures as conjectural but he provides a statistical analysis in the appendix (see pp. 489-501).

The balance sheet of extermination computed by Jacob Lestchinsky for the American Jewish Congress showed a total of 5,957,000 Jewish deaths.[2]

Another estimate is given by Martin Gilbert in his *Atlas of the Holocaust*.[3] His figures, based on surviving records, total 5,758,720. His map shows that the Nazis' fury swept across every country, from Norway and Finland in North Europe, to as far south as Libya.

Gilbert also warns that such a total can never be complete

since "thousands of infants and babies were murdered. . . before their birth could be recorded for any statistical purpose." Besides, there were other victims, "especially in the remoter villages of Poland [who] were 'added' to the deportation trains which left larger localities without any numerical register being made of their existence or fate. For several hundred Jewish communities throughout Europe, the most that the historical research of more than 35 years has been able to record is some phrase such as: 'the fate of this community is unknown.' "

To the round figure of 6,000,000 Jewish victims must be added 4,000,000 other prisoners whom the Nazis detained and murdered in the 1,000 concentration and labour camps, set up by the German state throughout Europe. Thus, the total number of civilians of all nationalities put to death in Himmler's camps and by the *Einsatzgruppen* reached 10,000,000. This staggering figure, and the savagery it stands for, will remain irreversibly burned into history, representing the lowest pit on the graph of human civilization.

Chapter VI
THE LAST HORSEMAN

Of the bloody quartet—Hitler, Himmler, Heydrich and Eichmann—only Eichmann survived the war. Reinhard Heydrich was killed in June 1942. Hitler and Himmler had cowardly committed suicide—not out of regret or shame, but to escape punishment. All three had orchestrated the score of the "final solution" which Adolf Eichmann performed masterfully.

Finally, in 1961, in a courtroom in Jerusalem, Adolf Eichmann was seated alone in a bullet-proof cubicle, on trial for the crimes he had perpetrated. When the chief prosecutor, Gideon Hausner, stood up to present his case to the court, he pondered how he would speak for six million dead. Earlier, the presiding judge had read the fifteen-point indictment to the accused, and fifteen times the latter repeated the well-known formula adopted by the war criminals in Nuremberg: "In the sense of the indictment—not guilty."

Moments later, Hausner spoke: "As I stand here before you, Judges of Israel, to lead the prosecution of Adolf Eichmann, I do not stand alone. With me, in this place and at this hour, stand six million accusers. But they cannot rise to their feet and point an accusing finger toward the man who sits in the glass dock, and cry 'I accuse.' For their ashes are piled up in the hills of Auschwitz and in the fields of Treblinka, or washed away by the rivers of Poland; their graves are scattered over the length and breadth of Europe...."

The description of the "final solution" followed. It had risen, said the prosecutor, "to a dreadful climax in the murder of a million and a half Jewish children whose blood was spilt water throughout Europe when they were separated by force from their mothers who tried to hide them, torn to pieces before their parents' eyes, their little heads smashed against the walls."

When Hausner presented the 76 recorded tapes of the interrogation of the accused by Chief Inspector Less, the court heard Eichmann's voice, first proclaiming that he was "only a minor transport officer," and then offering to hang himself in public "for expiation."

Then the prosecution witnesses took the stand. Instantly the audience, aghast, was plunged into the war years and the story of the mass persecution in Poland. These were overwhelming and shocking narratives which could have been voiced by any one of the millions who had been slaughtered.

Judge Beisky, when testifying about the horrors of the Plazow labour camp, which he had seen, recalled that one day all the children were told to step aside. "There was a great commotion in the camp. Mothers rushed forward, crying and shouting. They felt that their children were being sent away. Then two things happened at once. Machine guns were mounted and loaded for action. The other thing was the sounding of lullabies over the loudspeakers.... Thus the children were carried away to the tunes of lullabies, and their mothers, half-paralyzed with fear and half-fooled, stopped in their tracks."

As the hearing continued, the prosecutor completed the evidence of the events in Poland, submitting over 370 exhibits—a number that was soon to increase fourfold. The documents (submitted together with the oral testimony) were of crucial importance, for it was through them that it was possible to link Eichmann legally with the unravelling atrocities.

The evidence of two other witnesses added a great deal to the picture. Justice Musmanno, an American judge of the Supreme Court of Pennsylvania, had been one of the judges at Nuremberg. For seven months he had presided over the trial of the *Einsatzgruppen*.

The other witness was Dean Heinrich Karl Grueber, a German pastor from Berlin. He had organized a bureau to assist the Jews in hiding and to help them escape from Germany. He would go to Eichmann to plead for them. Eventually, Eichmann had him jailed and sent to a concentration camp, where his teeth were knocked out and also, he developed heart disease. But he had survived and now he and Justice Musmanno were in Jerusalem to testify. It was, said Hausner, "as if the long slumbering human conscience were speaking at last, expressing its grief and shame at what had happened."

Dean Grueber proved that Eichmann was a powerful figure who made independent decisions. He described an occasion when he was admitted to Eichmann's office to plead for the Jews. "I never had the impression that he had to consult his superiors on these matters. . . . It was he who took the decisions. . . . He always spoke in the first person, using the word 'I.' 'I order, I instruct, I cannot. . .' I do not remember that he ever said he would have to contact a higher authority."

Dr. Servatius, Eichmann's defender, cross-examined the witness to little avail, and when he turned to Justice Musmanno, he fared even worse. In Nuremberg, Musmanno had heard everybody, including Goring, mention Eichmann as one of the few responsible for all that had happened to the Jews. Responding to a question from Dr. Servatius, Musmanno stated that Goring did not refer to Eichmann as a small official. "On the contrary, he made it very clear that Eichmann was all powerful on the question of the extermination of the Jews. He went into that at great length: that Eichmann had practically unlimited power to declare who was to be killed."

In Auschwitz, the exterminations went on and on. Then,

on his official inspection in the summer of 1942, Himmler informed Hoss that Eichmann's program would be intensified even more month by month. Soon Eichmann himself arrived at Auschwitz with a further order stating that gold teeth were to be removed from the corpses, and hair cut from women.[1]

At the time of the Nuremberg trial, Hoss testified that 2.5 million men, women and children had been destroyed, but Goring dismissed it all as mere propaganda talk because it was "technically impossible," he said, to kill so many people within the time Hoss had specified.[2] Professor Gilbert, a psychologist from Long Island University who was now testifying for the prosecution in Jerusalem, had assisted as an expert at Nuremberg. He had asked the question: "Was it technically impossible?" The former commander at Auschwitz, Hoss, then gave his handwritten reply on the same page of prison stationery on which Professor Gilbert had worded his question, set out the main technical details of the extermination machinery, and made his calculation which tallied with the figure he had mentioned. That single sheet of paper, entered as a court exhibit in Jerusalem, is the "final solution" in a nutshell, and on it Eichmann's name appears three times in full prominence: "once as the delivering authority, which sent the Jews to the camps; second, as the commanding authority which issued instructions on the fate of the deportees; third, as the registering authority, which alone kept all statistical records of the annihilation." (Hausner)

Next the prosecutor moved to the subject of the death camps, a topic which took him four days, that is, eight sessions. Millions had died and Hausner found it imperative to present the events in some detail. In particular, a report by Dr. Kurt Gerstein[3] was entered as another exhibit; it gave a vivid description of the Belzec camp where 600,000 Jews had been put to death, leaving no survivors.

More dramatic evidence followed as the prosecution showed an hour-long film about Auschwitz. "There was much in this film," said Hausner, "to give concrete shape to the preceding eight weeks of evidence." It included, for example, sequences showing open pits and the prisoners standing naked at the brink of these excavations, their faces full of incredulity and horror, and then the shooting and the victims falling into their graves.

At another point, the camera panned heaps of naked bodies—corpses. "It was revolting to see naked bodies piled up like plucked slaughtered chickens. Among the dead wandered the so-called 'Muselmans,' morbid dried-out creatures completely apathetic to their surroundings."

Eventually, the last of 112 witnesses took the stand. He was a Tel Aviv lawyer, A. Hoter-Ishai, who had served with the Jewish Brigade which had fought with the British Army during the war. He described the rehabilitation work undertaken by the Jewish Brigades with the survivors they found as they entered the camps. "With this description of the Shield of David," said Hausner, "coming to the blood-soaked soil of Europe to rescue the saved remnant of a people, I closed the evidence."

When the defence lawyer, Dr. Servatius, took over, he argued that documents would prove—once the defence had shown them in their proper light—that responsibility for extermination lay on the shoulders of the political leaders of the country. As for Eichmann, his visits to the camp had been only for the purpose of "looking, observing and reporting without comment." Otherwise, he was nothing more than a dispatcher. "I had only railway timetables to take care there [Hungary] and even this only marginally. Everything was done by my superiors, Winkelmann and Veesenmayer.[4] I had only to report and to inform my superiors...."

He added that he did not initiate the march from Budapest nor did he have a hand in its implementation. In any case, he had no trucks at his disposal,[5] and therefore he could not have carried out this or any other deportation.

To conclude his direct examination, Eichmann then read

a statement he had prepared. He insisted again that there could not be any legal guilt attached to what he had done. The guilt lay with those who had ordered these acts and who had claimed his obedience. (This was Dr. Servatius' thesis.) Good leadership was a matter of luck, said the accused. He had to obey. The alternative was suicide. He admitted he had maintained contact with Hoss and had visited Auschwitz four or five times, but he insisted that he was a receiver, not a giver, of orders. "I was the man who demanded more trains. I was not authorized to decide the speed and the tempo of the transports. This was the discretion of my superiors, as is evident from the documents."

A few moments later, the prosecutor pointed out to the accused that in his autobiography, Hoss had also described himself as "a cog in the wheel of the great extermination machine created by the Third Reich." Well, since Eichmann had seen the camp *kommandant* killing Jews, what did he think of Hoss? Hausner realized the accused was trying to wriggle out of responsibility, so he suggested that Eichmann did not consider Hoss to be a murderer. "I did not say that," the accused protested. But he added that he would write a book which would "call the thing by its proper name." The presiding judge told him it was the accused's duty to say what he intended to write. Eichmann said: "I declare that I regard the murder of the Jews as one of the greatest crimes in human history." He had just put his neck into the noose.

When the court came to deliver its judgment, on December 11, 1961, it was at once made clear that "it is not necessary to recapitulate in Jerusalem, fifteen years after Nuremberg, the grounds for the legal rule of the 'crime against humanity,' for these terms are written in blood, in torrents of blood of the Jewish people which were shed."

In analyzing the evidence, "the court pointed out that Eichmann had been singled out as a recipient of the *Einsatzgruppen* from June 1941." Henceforth, he had contacts with the units and, from spring 1942, the accused was active in connection with the issuing of operational directives to these units. Hundreds of thousands—perhaps a million—Jews were shot[6] by them, but this alone could not have achieved the "final solution" which meant the extermination of millions. That required an additional method for more efficient mass killings, and also a *tidier* way for those who actually dealt in the business of murder. In short, the system of mass killing by means of gas.[7]

In the eyes of the court, the introduction of gas killings as a *cleaner* and more efficient method of killing than mass shooting was a matter that "undoubtedly occupied the attention of the accused as early as the end of the summer and the beginning of autumn of 1941." The method had been discussed toward the end of October between Dr. Erhard Wetzel, a senior official of the Ministry for the Eastern Territories, Colonel Victor Brack of Hitler's Chancellery, and SS Lieutenant-Colonel Eichmann. They then decided to use gassing in the execution of the Jews.

The judgment which was read in court also referred to a certain letter of Wetzel's in which Eichmann was mentioned as having given his blessing to the use of gas as an extermination method. The documents—i.e., the written outline and the final draft of the letter—were written in an official office of the German Reich, and the court did not doubt their formal authenticity. . . Thus it was proved that the accused expressed the consent of the RSHA (*Reichssicherheitshauptampt*)—the National Security Office—to the use of gas vans in October, 1941, as a substitute for the execution of Jews by shooting."

At this juncture, "all the testimonies and affidavits produced in court pointed to the accused's strong and influential position in the RSHA and was incompatible with the tendency of the accused to represent himself as having been devoid of any initiative or influence from 1941 onward." The court, thus, rejected absolutely the accused's version that he was nothing more than a *small cog* in the extermination process.

For example, the deportation of Poles was not merely a resettlement. Far from it. The plan laid down by Heydrich on November 21, 1939, clearly envisaged a sinister scheme: two waves of deportation, 1939-1940 and 1942-1943, of about half a million people. In these deportations and the following exterminations, Eichmann was certainly no small cog.

In regard to the last and decisive stage of the "final solution," the court claimed that "all acts perpetrated during the implementation of the program are to be regarded as one single whole...The criminal intent was continuous and embraced all activities, until the whole operation had been completed...The accused's criminal responsibility [therefore] is to be decided upon accordingly ...Hence the accused will be convicted of the general crime of the Final Solution in all its forms, as an accomplice to the commitment of a crime, and his conviction will extend to all the many acts forming part of that crime, both the acts in which he took an active part in his own section, as well as the acts committed by his accomplices to the crime in other sections of the same front."

The court also acknowledged that Eichmann was merciless in all his actions. "He admitted, on cross-examination, that he pursued the 'Hungarian deal' for reasons of utility and not as a rescue operation...Blind obedience could never have brought him to commit the crime which he committed with such efficiency and devotion as he evinced, were it not for his zealous belief that he was thereby fulfilling an important national mission. No single case brought to our notice has revealed the accused as showing any sign of human feelings in his dealing in Jewish affairs...In all his activities the accused displayed indefatigable energy verging on overeagerness toward advancing the Final Solution both in his general decision and in his treatment of individual cases of Jews who wished to escape death."

Eichmann was convicted on all fifteen counts of the indictment. The prosecutor's duty now was to ask for the penalty imposed by law. This, Hausner formulated: "By the enormity of his crime, Eichmann has excluded himself from the society of human beings...he has shaken off moral restraints, and has given gratification to the basest society. Such a creature has denied himself the right to walk among human beings, and human society is enjoined to spew him out...I pray the court to award the wicked man facing it the penalty that a human and civilized agency is capable of meting out...There stands before you a murderer of a people, an enemy of mankind, one who has shed the blood of the innocent. I pray you to judge that this man deserves the capital punishment of death."

The accused was now called upon to say his last words. He had become involved in misdeeds against his will, he claimed. "It was not I who persecuted the Jews with avidity and fervour; that was done by the government. The whole persecution could only have been carried out by a government, never by me...As I have already stated, it was the ruling circles, to whose ranks I did not belong, who issued the orders...Legally I am innocent...The witnesses here have been most untruthful. While the summing up of the testimonies and documents by the court may, at first sight, seem convincing, it is in fact deceptive and misleading...No one came to me and reproached me for my activity in the performance of my duties...Today, of my own free will, I would ask the Jewish people for pardon and I would confess that I am bowed down with shame at the thought of the iniquities committed against the Jews and the injustices done to them, but in the light of the grounds given in the judgment this would, in all probability, be construed as hypocrisy. I am not the monster I am made out to be. I am the victim of a misconception."

In his own words, Eichmann had just espoused what his attorney, Dr. Servatius, had told the court: "that it must be borne in mind that the accused did not act according to his own initiative but according to the will of others, who were the leaders of the state...It is fitting that the judge who strives for the highest justice should, in his judgment, let mercy predominate." But had mercy been shown to the Jews?

The judgment was postponed until the next day, December 15, 1961; the session lasted only sixteen minutes. "This court," said the presiding judge, "sentences Adolf Eichmann to death for the crimes against the Jewish people, the crimes against humanity and the war crimes of which he has been found guilty."

In a 59-page written appeal, Dr. Servatius could attack only the judgment of the lower court. It was now the duty of the Appellate Tribunal to study the accused's plea; they convened three months later, on March 22, 1962.

Meanwhile, Hausner had had the opportunity of looking through the huge volume of mail that his office had received. "We feel better now that the story has been told to the world" was a reaction of many of the survivors who had experienced a kind of emotional catharsis as a result of the trial.

The prison authorities had also received many messages for Eichmann. On the one hand, threats, and on the other, the Chicago Division of the Nazi party cabled their birthday greeting to Eichmann, and assured him that he had "set an example for us to follow." Obviously those men in the United States felt that the remaining six million Jews still alive in the world were now to be gassed as Eichmann's victims had been destroyed! Their Nazi hatred had not abated, nor had their taste for cruelties, atrocities and murder.

An earlier message of encouragement had been sent to Eichmann, months before, by the Arab press, printed in the *Jerusalem Times* of April 24, 1961: "Find consolation in the fact that this trial will one day lead to the liquidation of the remaining six million."[8] Perhaps momentarily, a few of those who, like Ernst Zundel, denied that the "final solution" had ever taken place, felt that they were quite wrong, that six million Jews had really been annihilated and that six million more, for good measure, should follow in the ovens. This must have been a consolation to SS Lieutenant-Colonel Adolf Eichmann.

Among other angry messages there was one, from Winnipeg, Manitoba, which, quite concise and significant, summarized what millions of people thought: "Drop dead!"

Eichmann had vainly appealed. The justices rejected his defence, finding that he had carried out the extermination orders with genuine zeal and devotion. "As a matter of fact, the appellant did not receive orders from above; it was he who was the high and mighty one, he who was the commander in all that pertained to Jewish affairs. He ordered and commanded, not only without orders from his superiors in the hierarchy of the service, but also, at times, in absolute conflict with these orders... It is clear that the *idea* of the Final Solution was not his own but the Fuhrer's. Yet that idea might not have assumed so satanic and infernal an expression—in the blood of millions of tortured and martyred Jews—but for the thorough planning, the zeal, the fanatical enthusiasm and the insatiable blood thirstiness of the appellant and those who did his bidding. We do not here minimize by even an iota the terrible guilt that rests on the heads of many, many others."

On May 31, 1962, close to midnight, Eichmann was led to the gallows. His body was cremated in the predawn hours of June 1, and his ashes placed aboard a police boat which headed out to sea. When it was well beyond the three-mile limit, the pilot cut the boat's engines. The vessel glided for a while over the swell and then Arieh Nir, the Prisons Commissioner, tossed the ashes overboard.[9]

At long last, Adolf Eichmann discovered for himself what the "final solution" was.

CONCLUSION

At the outset of this book, it was stated that in the early seventies, Richard Verrall, alias Harwood, released a brochure, *Did Six Million Really Die?*, which Ernst Zundel found so inspiring that he published it in Toronto.

Zundel shared the author's view that there had never been a Holocaust under the Nazi regime during the 1939-1945 war years. The burden of proof of this claim rested on Zundel, but while using Harwood's methods and distortions of the truth, neither Zundel nor his lawyer succeeded in convincing the Toronto court, the jurors or the public. Counsel and client, following in Harwood's footsteps, failed to undermine the mountainous accumulation of evidence, much of it taken from the files, the *Totenbuchen* and the archives of their beloved friends and assassins, the Nazi culprits themselves.

In their audaciousness, Zundel and his lawyer retreated behind a claim of freedom of expression. This neo-Nazi and his defender invoked "historical truth" only to distort it and to deny the implementation of the "final solution."

Zundel made a number of absurd claims in court. It is entirely likely, though, that he is less of a fool than he appears and that he expected *almost* no one to take him seriously. Seeing himself as a politician whose cause is everywhere reviled, he is prepared to mount any soapbox in order to find one or two new adherents, to slowly build a

movement which will ultimately complete the job begun
with the first Holocaust, which Zundel knows full well
existed—but imperfectly. He and his lawyer expected the
court, the listeners and the public to believe:

1. Hitler never delivered any speeches calling for the
persecution and annihilation of the Jews, not even well
before the beginning of World War II.
2. No pogrom, such as that of *Kristallnacht*, in November 1938, ever took place.
3. Himmler and Heydrich never issued any directive to
implement the Fuhrer's orders, in particular, the opening of
ghettos, concentration and extermination camps in Germany
and conquered territory.
4. Eichmann, the so-called specialist in Jewish questions,
never directed or organized the transportation, emigration
and eventual deportation of Jews to such camps, and never
saw to it that the extermination of those people be carried
out in the field by the *Einsatzgruppen*, and in gas vans and
chambers of the abattoirs.
5. Goebbels, in his diaries, never mentioned Hitler's
"final solution," or revealed in his speeches, that he fully
approved of the Fuhrer's program.
6. Hans Frank, head of the General Government in
Poland, never took part in the implementation of his crimes
against humanity and never controlled or speeded up the
extermination of the Jews in his territory. (Yet, this was the
man who admitted to the Nuremberg Court: "We have
fought against Jewry; we have fought against it for years
and we have allowed ourselves to make utterances and my
own diary has become a witness against me in this
connection—utterances which are terrible...A thousand
years will pass and the guilt of Germany will not be
released.")[1]
7. Rudolf Hoss, Josef Kramer, Christian Wirth and
Odilo Globocnik never witnessed SS cruelties in torture
sessions and never ordered or participated in such practices,
and that their admissions and confessions are mere lies.

Again, following Harwood's vicious document, Ernst Zundel and his counsel were eager to deny before the Toronto Court:

1. The verbal testimonies of survivors of the Holocaust; the official military and civilian investigators' findings; statements of German and other witnesses to the rounding-up of Jews, deportations, torturing, shooting, hanging and gassing, as well as the piling-up of corpses[2] before mass burial.

2. The deposition in Nuremberg by Schirach von Baldur, leader of the German Youth, in which he admitted that Hitler's racial policy was a crime which led to disaster for five million Jews and for all Germans. Asked by his counsel what Auschwitz meant to him, he said it was the greatest and most devilish mass murder of history, a crime shameful to every German.

3. The findings of the Nuremberg judges, in their own words, "based on a mass of incontrovertible evidence including very extensive documentation obtained from Nazi sources, the authenticity of which was undeniable." Also, in the passages which referred to the persecution of the Jews by the Nazis, the judges stated that "it has been proved in the greatest detail before the Tribunal. It is a record of consistent and systematic inhumanity on the greatest scale."[3]

The defence pleas had stressed that the accused had not known of the crimes, that they were committed "in secret." This was a preposterous claim and the prosecutors rejected it wholly. The British chief prosecutor, Sir Hartley Shawcross, put more emphasis than his colleagues on the question of the accused's responsibility. He said that a minister or an executive in the Nazi state which in the course of six years had transported 7,000,000 people—men, women and children—to labour camps, exterminated 275,000 of their own citizens—aged or mentally infirm—and annihilated in the gas chambers or otherwise a total of at least 12,000,000 people—these leaders, Nazi ministers and executives could not have remained ignorant or innocent of those crimes. The vast amount of evidence that the Allies had gathered was not ignored at Nuremberg, but what the prosecution concentrated on were the actual words and statements under the signatures of the defendants themselves.

Prosecuting Justice Jackson was also skeptical of the defendants' claim that "they had been without authority, without knowledge, without influence, without importance."If that were the case, they constituted a ridiculous composite picture of Hitler's government! Pointing to Hitler's number two man, Goring, who claimed he had not even suspected that there was any extermination program, Jackson reminded him that there was ample documentary proof that Goring himself had signed decree upon decree implementing the plan. (Goring made a face at this!)

Yet the ex-marshal, his colleagues and accomplices in the dock had been granted a hearing by the Tribunal, the right to a defence, "the kind of trial which they, in the days of their pomp and power, never gave to any man."

4. Albert Speer's affidavit, signed in Munich on June 15, 1977, after his prison term: "Hatred of the Jews was Hitler's motor and central point, perhaps even the very element which motivated him. The German people, the German greatness, the Empire, they all meant nothing to him in the last analysis. For this reason he wished in the final sentence of his testament* to fixate us Germans, even after the apocalyptic downfall, in a miserable hatred of the Jews." Hitler had also stressed in his will: "It is not true that I or anybody else in Germany wanted war in 1939. It was desired and provoked exclusively by these international statesmen who were either of Jewish origin or agents of Jewish interest."[4]

5. The trial documents of Rudolf Hoss and other

*"Above all, I enjoin the government and the people to uphold the racial laws to the limit and to resist mercilessly international Jewry, the poisoner of all nations."

butchers in Poland and elsewhere.[5]

6. The records of the trial, conviction and execution of Adolf Eichmann in Jerusalem.

7. The thousands upon thousands of photographs and film strips which were taken by soldiers, civilians, American senators, members of the Red Cross, and American, British, French, Polish and Russian official commissions of investigation; including photographs taken even by SS men themselves, and later retrieved.

8. The tragic narratives of survivors, and the works of hundreds of researchers and historians—based on archival documents, official records, speeches, reports, decrees and surveys.

9. The demographic censuses compiled after the war which were compared with pre-war figures, indicating the monstrous scope of the Holocaust.

Nevertheless, neo-Nazi Zundel made it clear to the public, his readers, jurors, journalists and judge that all of this evidence (and more, which has not been listed here) was merely fabricated and false. All the recorded testimonies and figures were dismissed as plain lies.

To cite further evidence, Leon Poliakov quotes Lobsack in the *Danziger Vorposten*[6] of May 13, 1944: "After the dragnet and assassination of the Jews in 1939-1942 the Jewish population of Poland has been neutralized, and the same may be said right now for Hungary. By this action five million Jews have been eliminated in those two countries." Poliakov continues:

The extermination policy thus became a matter of common knowledge and enough information filtered through a thousand channels for a location of the murder camps and the methods of execution to become notorious....Only those who did not wish to know might continue to pretend ignorance. During a dramatic session at one of the Nuremberg trials, a highly qualified witness, SS General Bach-Zelewsky, who was head of the anti-partisan campaign of the German armies during the war, insisted on clarifying the matter.

"Nobody," he said to the judges, "wants to be in a position of having known anything. I want to establish the truth here, regardless of whether it hurts or helps me.... Of all the German generals I am perhaps the one who travelled most all over Europe during the war [fulfilling his duties].... I talked to hundreds of generals and thousands of officers of all categories, and it is a fact that extermination began on the first day of the war. This is the truth; anything else is a lie and a euphemism.... And anyone who travelled knew from the beginning that the Jews were being exterminated in a way that at first was not systematic. Later, when the Russian campaign began, the extermination of Judaism was an explicit part of the aim."[7]

To Ernst Zundel, this candid deposition was unacceptable; it must be the words of a traitor. There had never been any Holocaust! And Bach-Zelewsky was another of those liars he hated—though no less a liar than Goebbels, who had dared write in his diary on February 14, 1942:

The Fuhrer once more expressed his determination to clean up the Jews in Europe pitilessly. There must be no squeamish sentimentalism about it. The Jews deserved the catastrophe that has now overtaken them. Their destruction will go hand in hand with the destruction of our enemies. We must hasten this process with cold ruthlessness. We shall thereby render an inestimable service to a humanity tormented for thousands of years by the Jews. This uncompromising anti-Semitic attitude must prevail among our own people despite all objectors. The Fuhrer expressed this

idea vigorously and repeated it afterwards to a group
of officers who can put that in their pipes and smoke it.

Certainly Ernst Zundel, spared the glory of serving the
Fatherland, never brought himself to "put that in his pipe
and smoke it." But there was still more that Goebbels had
to tell which Ernst Zundel apparently cannot bear to hear.

On December 18, 1942, he wrote, "The Jewish question
is receiving big play in the enemy and in the neutral news
services.[8] . . . [The Jews] are now trying to stir up the entire
world merely to incite public opinion against the Nazi
Socialist Reich and its anti-Semitic convictions. There's
only one answer to this, viz., *to continue at present
rigorously and without compromise.* You are sunk if you
give the slightest indication of weakness."[9] (Emphasis
added.)

And on April 25, 1943, this later admission from
Goebbels: "The Jews tried to leave the [Warsaw] ghetto by
subterranean passages. Thereupon these underground passages were flooded. The Ghetto is now under artillery
fire . . . Conditions are chaotic not only in the Ghetto, but
also among sections of the Polish population."

How could Zundel account for such a tragedy when
Jurgen Stroop, the SS general in charge of the repression,
had shown how humane he had been when he put the ghetto
to the torch!

Thousands perished in the conflagration; the stench of
burning bodies was everywhere. Charred corpses lay on
balconies, in window recesses, on unburned steps.
Flames drove people from their shelters, forced them
from their hiding places in cellars and attics. Thousands staggered about the yards, easy prey for the
Germans. . . . Weary beyond endurance, they fell asleep
in driveways, beside doors, standing still, lying, and
were caught asleep by German bullets. No one as much
as noticed that an old man sleeping in a corner would
never awaken; that a mother nursing her baby had been

dead for three days; that a baby's cries and suckling were unavailing, for its mother's arms were cold, her breast dead. Hundreds committed suicide by leaping from the fourth and fifth story windows.[10]

All right, Ernst Zundel might admit, but this action was no gassing! And what do Zundel's readers think? Do they still question the veracity and accuracy of the historical record? They should know now that the Nazi beasts and their SS executioners caused not simply six million human beings to die, but ten million—Jews and non-Jews who were massacred only because the Master Race had dedicated itself to teaching and propagating hatred, to practising torture, to killing men, women and children, the old and the weak, the sick and the insane, the crippled, the intellectuals and the homosexuals, to sterilizing women and men of the "inferior races," and to carrying out hideous "medical" experiments—in a word, to behaving as unsocialized, subhuman animals unfit to share in the world of humanity. The Master Race!

Had the Nazis succeeded in their attempts, northern, central and eastern Europe would have been "purged." By the end of this century, perhaps a hundred million people, including the Slavs whom Hitler considered a hopeless second-class race, would have been annihilated or sterilized by the lunatics who presided over the "superior" destiny of the Third Reich.[11]

Finally, the reader can conjecture about the outcome of the war, and therefore the world, had the Nazis not been consumed by their pathological racism. Much of their military strength was sapped by the Holocaust agenda, effort wasted on people who posed no objective threat to the German program of conquest. For six years the German war machine held the world at bay while manpower and finances were drained away in the superfluous extermination of ten million unarmed souls. Instead, had Hitler enlisted the Holocaust victims in the service of his crusade of fascist expansion, the geopolitical realities of the contemporary world might look very different from their present arrangement.

An ironic epitaph for the ten million victims—Jews and non-Jews—might say that those who fell before a nation gone mad contributed to its demise. And to the extent that they did, their terrible martyrdom helped to pull the world back from the precipice of Naziism.

Appendix I

Security intelligence was obviously a euphemism for the foul tasks the *Einsatzgruppen* were assigned to accomplish. Heydrich's policy concerned the Jews who were to be concentrated in city ghettos "for a better possibility of control and later a possibility of deportation."

After Heydrich's conference with the *Einsatzgruppen* chiefs on September 21, 1939, a directive covering four points was issued: 1. moving the Jews, as fast as possible, into cities; 2. transferring German Jews into Poland; 3. moving the remaining 30,000 Gypsies, also to Poland; and 4. transporting in freight cars all systematically ejected Jews from Germany and German-occupied countries.

Heydrich's instructions were clear enough regarding the program and its future implementation. "The second ultimate stage of the Final Solution was to be synchronized with the attack on Russia, when *Jewish Bolshevism* would be destroyed."[1]

While the murders to be perpetrated by the *Einsatzgruppen* were limited to occupied Soviet Russia, they affected not only Russian Jews but also those Jews who were sent from Germany to be exterminated behind the army lines. The *Einsatzgruppen* were ordered to shoot as quickly as possible every Jewish man, woman and child that they encountered, and also to crush civilian resistance.

The *Einsatzgruppen* commanders were briefed at special sessions; Eichmann was present. Forgetting about civilian resistance, Eichmann commanded them to totally exterminate the Jewish population, including the murder of Jewish children.[2]

As the army co-operated fully with the *Einsatzgruppen* commanders, many local "volunteers" were enlisted into auxiliary units in some areas. They soon became the terror of the Jewish population; the Germans gave them the dirtiest jobs, such as shooting children, beating people to death with clubs, or dragging them from hideouts. Often their salaries were paid from money looted from Jews; thus, they became financially interested in the success of their actions.[3]

In time, the *Einsatzgruppen*, under the high command of Heydrich, chief of RSHA, performed special tasks with staggering competence. In the field, each unit was headed by an SS general: Franz Stahlecker, in Group A, was assigned to Army Group North; Artur Nebe, in Group B, attached to Army Group Central in White Russia and the territory farther east toward Moscow;[4] Otto Rasch, whose unit operated behind Army Group South in the Ukraine; and Otto Ohlendorf, in command of *Einsatzgruppe* D, which preyed over the southern portion of Ukraine and Crimea in the sector of the Eleventh Army. Ohlendorf had been the research director of the Institute for Applied Economic Science in Kiel, controlled by the SS Security Services, and in June 1941, he was the head of *Amt III* of the RSHA.[5]

Now, as chief of an *Einsatzgruppe*, Ohlendorf was an effective agent of death. In the first year of operation in his sector, until June 1942, he reported his unit had destroyed 90,000 people, including women and children.

The activities of his group soon became known when General Georg Thomas,[6] chief of the *Wehrmacht Oberkommando* (OKW) Economic Department, received a secret report (on December 2, 1942) from the Inspector of Armament in the Ukraine, regarding the progress of the campaign: "The shooting of Jews in Ukraine proceeded from east to west. It was done entirely in public with the use of the Ukrainian militia.... The way these actions, which included men, old men, women and children of all ages, was carried out, was horrible. The great masses executed make this action more gigantic than any similar measure taken so far in the Soviet Union. So far about 150,000 to 200,000 Jews may have been executed in part of Ukraine belonging to the *Reichskommissariat*."[7]

An often-quoted account of the atrocities committed by the men of the *Einsatzgruppen* in Ukraine is that of a German construction engineer, Hermann Graebe, who testified in Nuremberg to the killing sessions he had witnessed (U.S. Prosecution Exhibit 494).

At Dubno on October 5, 1942, his foreman told him that Jews from the town had been shot in three large pits, each about 30 metres long by three metres deep. About 1,500 persons had been killed daily. All the Jews who had been living in Dubno before the pogrom were still to be liquidated. The man had witnessed the shooting of some of the first victims, and he accompanied Graebe to the site where the slaughter had taken place. Several trucks were standing in front of the mounds which marked the location of the trenches.

To the Nuremberg court, Graebe said that "armed Ukrainian militiamen drove the people off the trucks under the supervision of an SS.... All these people had the regulation yellow patches on the front and back of their clothes, and thus could be recognized as Jews.... Now I heard rifle shots in quick succession from behind one of the earth mounds. The people who had got off the trucks—men, women and children of all ages—had to undress upon the orders of an SS man, who carried a riding or dog whip. They had to put down their clothes in fixed places, sorted according to shoes, top clothing and underclothing. I saw a heap of shoes about 800 to 1,000 pairs, great piles of under linen and clothing. Without screaming or weeping these people undressed, stood around in family groups, kissed each other, said farewells, and waited for a sign from another SS man who stood near the pit, also with a whip in hand...At that moment the SS man shouted something to his comrade. The latter counted off about 20 persons and instructed them to go behind the earth mound...I walked around the mound and found myself confronted by a tremendous grave. People were closely wedged together and lying on top of each other so that only their heads were visible. Nearly all had blood running over their shoulders from their heads. Some of the people shot were still moving. Some were lifting their arms and turning their heads to show that they were still alive. The pit was already two-thirds full...about 1,000 people. I looked at the man who did the shooting...who sat at the edge of the narrow end of the pit, with his feet dangling...He had a tommy-gun on his knees and was smoking a cigarette. The people, completely naked, went down some steps which were cut in the clay wall of the pit and clambered over the heads of the people lying there, to the place to which the SS man directed them. They lay down in front of the dead and injured people...Then I heard a series of shots. I looked into the pit and saw that the bodies were either twitching or the heads lying motionless on top of the bodies which lay before them. Blood was running away from their necks. I was surprised that I was not ordered away but I saw that there were two or three postmen in uniform nearby. The next batch was approaching already. They went down into the pit, lined themselves up against the previous victims and were shot...I noticed that another truckload of people had just arrived. This time it included sick and infirm persons...I left with my foreman and drove my car back to Dubno."

Graebe returned the next day and witnessed another spectacle. Thirty people were assembled there, lying near the pit, some of them still alive. "At that moment, we heard a first car approach and I noticed it was an SS detail. I moved away to my site. Ten minutes later we heard shots from the vicinity of the pit. The still alive Jews had been ordered to throw the corpses into the pit; they themselves had to lie down in it to be shot in the neck."[8]

If Ohlendorf did quite well from June 1941 until June 1942, killing 90,000 people during his first year of operation,[9] Artur Nebe in Group B liquidated only half that figure, though that was during only five months of his command. Group C reported 75,000 victims in a period of just over four months—June 22 to November 3, 1941—including a two-day massacre at Kiev on September 29 and 30 with a count of 33,771 alone (U.S. Prosecution Exhibit 410 at the Nuremberg Trial).

At the same time, SS General Stahlecker, with his Group A, had been breaking all records by wiping out 218,050 Jews during 1941, as is shown in his report and the map of Sector A attached to it.[10]

The *Einsatzgruppen*'s "methods combined guile, terror and systematic savagery."[11] One particular unit assigned to killing Jews would gather their victims somewhere under the pretext of resettlement. The Jews were forced to hand over their valuables and surrender their outer clothing; at that juncture, they had no illusions regarding what was to follow. Indeed they were led to the place of their execution where an anti-tank ditch had been excavated. Kneeling or standing, they were shot; they fell into the ditch or their bodies were thrown into it.[12]

The first shootings in Poland, which had lacked adequate organization, had shocked some witnesses. One of them even wrote to Hitler. He was Paul Kluge, a corporal in a German medical unit stationed at Schwetz. Out of curiosity, having heard that the execution of Poles would take place on Sunday, October 8, 1939, in a Jewish cemetery, he decided to attend and see if the rumors were true. He waited for some time with his friends before a large bus, full of women and children, drove in. "We saw a party consisting of a woman with three children, aged 3 to 8 years, led to an open grave about two meters wide and eight meters long into which the woman, her youngest child in her arms, was forced to descend. The other two children were then handed to her, and the four creatures had to lie face down, the children clinging to their mother's left side. Four men of the detachmen then climbed down into the grave and, with their revolvers aimed at about thirty centimeters away from the napes of the necks, they shot their four victims. I was called to help fill the grave, when I could see the next party of women and children shot in the same manner—nine or ten groups, all shot the same way, in the same grave."[13]

Eichmann observed one *Einsatzgruppe* at work near Minsk. Young troopers were shooting into a pit already full of writhing bodies. In Jerusalem, upon interrogation by prosecutor Gideon Hausner, Eichmann, quite composed, said: "I can still see a woman with a child. She was shot and then the baby in her arms. His brains splattered all around also over my leather overcoat."

A report sent to Warsaw in May 1942 by the Jewish Labour Bund and then via the underground to the Polish Government-in-exile in London, was the first documentation to reach the West regarding the action of the *Einsatzgruppen*.[14]

They applied the same techniques everywhere. Males from fourteen to 60 were rounded up, slaughtered, machine-gunned down or killed in the streets; children, in orphanages, and the old, in hospitals or in homes, were shot. In many towns, Jews were taken away to an unknown destination, and executed in nearby woods. The 1942 report to Warsaw lists a few towns where a total of 56,000 Jews were exterminated (30,000 in Lwow alone). There was a longer list of other cities where killings were carried out. "According to various estimates the number of Jews bestially murdered in the Vilna regions and Lithuanian Kaunas is put at 300,000." These were the actions of *Einsatzgruppen* A units, whose methods were applied similarly by the three other groups.

When, after year-long hearings, the International Military Tribunal at

Nuremberg delivered its verdict against the major German war criminals on September 30 and October 1, 1946, it said, in particular: "Adolf Eichmann, who had been put in charge of the program to exterminate the Jews, has estimated that the policy pursued resulted in the killing of 6,000,000 Jews, of whom 4,000,000 were killed in the concentration camps and 2,000,000 were killed by the *Einsatzgruppen*."

This is Zundel's Holocaust that never was!

In the summer of 1942, the *Einsatzgruppen* launched their second stage of operations which consisted of liquidating the remnants, the small ghettos and communities that had been by-passed earlier. Except for a few "absolutely essential Jews," all others were shot or poisoned in gas vans which were sent to relieve the shooting squads. Sometimes a whole ghetto, like that of Janow, was set on fire and burnt down with all its inhabitants. What is striking is the obsessive character of the whole anti-Jewish program: at the height of a most destructive and bloody war on two fronts, the destruction of the Jews took precedence over all war needs!

The ruthlessness and sadism of the killers reached a mad fury as 55,000 Jews were liquidated in Minsk; 16,000 in Lida; and 8,000 in Slonim—simply a few figures from the total list.

The story of the *Einsatzgruppen* is also found in their own achievement reports, articulated with "cold factuality," as they were described in the judgment of the Nuremberg Military Tribunal. In his office in Berlin, Eichmann had only to tick off one Jewish community after another. For instance, 23,000 Jews of Kamenets Podolsk were reported executed in the last three days of August 1941; and as stated earlier, 33,771 from Kiev were massacred on September 29 and 30 of the same year. Sometimes, the reports totaled the activity to date: thus, Group A reported killing 18,430 Jews and 3,387 Communist functionaries on October 15. Group B, on November 3, had "*so far* liquidated about 80,000 people," and Group D's execution rate rose to 54,696 on December 12, 1941.

A year later, on December 26, 1942, Himmler reported to the Fuhrer that during the period from September to December the overall total of Jews executed by the *Einsatzgruppen* had been 363,211.[15] Hitler was jubilant.

On the basis of a thorough study of all reports, it was estimated that the number of Jews liquidated by the *Einsatzgruppen* totaled about 1,400,000.[16] Yet this figure was soon to be surpassed. The greatest bloodbath in history was soon to flood an entire continent.

Appendix II

Kommandant Hoss has described the Birkenau crematoria, saying that No. III (his numbering) failed completely after a short time and later ceased altogether, while No. IV had to be repeatedly shut down. Then the gassed bodies were burned in pits behind the building. When such breakdown occurred, and No. I also failed, it was No. II which was relied upon as a "stand-by."

Hoss also mentioned Bunkers 1 and 2, which were gassing chambers, not crematoria. Later, No. 2 was wrongly named No. 5—wrongly because No. 5 now designated a site, not a barrack (near the actual Bunker 2) where the cremation was carried out in the open. Its huge pyre was used to supplement the burning of corpses in the crematoria, which were new buildings made ready for use in March and April 1943.[1]

Hoss' basic numbering (I to IV) was in fact the system used in Birkenau by the SS personnel, whereas Nos. II to V printed in the *Auschwitz Museum Guide-Book* and in *KL Auschwitz Seen by the SS* are those reproduced in Nazi documents.[2]

In the summer of 1944, said Hoss, "during the action in Hungary, using all installations except No. III [No. IV on the Nazi plan] the highest total of people gassed and cremated within 24 hours was rather more than 9000"—a total which survivors and post-war authors and investigators consider to be an underestimate (see Appendix IV).

This action in Hungary was ultimately called "Aktion Hoss." At the time, Hoss was no longer *kommandant* in Auschwitz; it had been six months since he had been transferred to the Inspectorate of Concentration Camps. But this recent change did not prevent Himmler from ordering Hoss to return to Auschwitz and to prepare and check over the planned liquidation of more than 400,000 Hungarian Jews. On May 8, 1944, therefore, Hoss was back in the camp. He hastily put the whole extermination factory into shape, adding several pits to the crematoria, a new hut where the doomed would get undressed, and completing the construction of the railway track extension and the ramp where the crowd of Hungarian Jews would be promptly handled and led directly to the gas chambers. Selections were no longer bothered with.

Once it had started (on May 16), the action was continued and intensified until it ended toward the middle of September.[3]

Appendix III

The horror of the pseudo-scientific experiments has been recounted by Olga Lengyel in Chapter XIII of her book, *Five Chimneys*.

"Once," wrote Lengyel *in fine*, "we asked an Aryan German inmate...for the basic reason for the sterilization and castration....He told us that the Germans had a geopolitical reason for these experiments. If they could sterilize all non-German people still alive after their victorious war, there would be no danger of a new generation of 'inferior' peoples. At the same time the living populations would be able to serve as labourers for about thirty years. After that time, the German surplus population would need all the space in these countries, and the 'inferiors' would perish without descendants."[1]

The doctors' trial in Nuremberg produced specific evidence of the hideous lengths to which Himmler's scientists went to gratify their chief's "humanitarian" ambitions. Twenty-three accused—sadists, perverts, though all trained physicians—went into the dock. An abridged version of the proceedings covers 1,000 printed pages. The criminals were charged by U.S. Chief Counsel, Brigadier-General Telford Taylor with "murders, tortures and other atrocities committed in the name of science. The defendants had treated their fellowmen as less than beasts who succumbed to their crimes in hundreds of thousands."[2]

Himmler, of course, had provided their inspiration. One of the *Reichsfuhrer*'s ideas had been to study a method of decimating the eastern population which would quickly and cheaply bear results. A Dr. Adolf Pokorny had suggested using a drug—caladium seguinum—which, if it could be extracted, would produce an imperceptible sterilization of human beings. "The thought, alone," wrote the man, "that three million Bolsheviks who are at present prisoners of the Germans could be sterilized so that they could be used as labourers, but be prevented from reproduction, opens the most far-reaching perspective."

The tests conducted in Auschwitz were disappointing, and Dr. Clauberg kept to the method of sterilization which he had first applied to several thousand Jewish women and Gypsies at Ravensbruck.

On March 28, 1941, another accused, Dr. Viktor Brack, also came up with a method of sterilization (mentioned earlier) which could be accomplished by means of powerful X rays, resulting in castration. "One way to carry out these experiments," Brack explained to Himmler, "would be to have these people lined up before a counter. They would be given a form to be filled out, the whole process taking two to three minutes. The official attendant behind the counter can then operate the apparatus and the switch which will start the rays coming from both sides. With such an installation 150 to 200 persons could be sterilized daily, while twenty installations would take care of 3,000 to 4,000 persons daily." Brack had also figured out that among the 10,000,000 Jews in Europe, two to three million were women fit for work. Therefore, they would be selected and preserved for the purpose but at the same time they would be rendered incapable of propagating.[3]

Appendix IV

As has been outlined earlier, No. I was the Auschwitz mother-camp crematorium and the smallest. It had two two-retort ovens. In 1941, a third oven was added and all three could burn 350 corpses in 24 hours.

The 65 square-metre morgue served to gas the doomed; its capacity was 600 to 800 people a day, and since it could not cope with the planned mass exterminations, the Nos. 1 and 2 Bunkers in Birkenau were turned into gas chambers; No. 2 was equipped with two of them, and had a capacity of 2,000 victims per day.

In 1942, cremation was carried on using 2,000-corpse pyres and, later, in pits. The operation went on day and night and at the end of 1942, the common pits, in which 107,000 corpses had been originally buried, were emptied. The corpses were then burned.[1]

It was not until the first semester of 1943 that Nos. II and III Crematoria, which had been installed in Birkenau, became operational. Nos. IV and V were added later.

In II and III, the 210 square-metre underground morgue was actually the gas chamber, which the victims entered down a flight of steps. In IV and V, three gas chambers and, later, a fourth one were on ground level, and could exterminate 3,000 people at a time. In May 1944, however, with the arrival of the Hungarian Jews, gassing in the crematoria proved inadequate and the two chambers in Bunker No. 2 were reopened. The capacity of all gas chambers then reached 60,000 persons in 24 hours—a number with which the crematoria could not cope.

With respect to the capacity of the crematoria, II and III each had five three-retort ovens.[2] The total, therefore, was 30 retorts, in which 350 people per hour could be cremated; in two twelve-hour shifts, including the time lost cleaning and removing the ashes, the two crematoria could swallow an average of 5,000 cadavers. Crematoria IV and V had a total of only sixteen retorts, and in the same working time they could dispose of 3,000 corpses daily.[3]

The overall capacity of 8,000 corpses a day was far below the production of the gas chambers. Consequently, in the spring of 1944, six enormous pits were dug beside Crematorium V. Olga Lengyel estimates their size was 60 yards long and about four yards wide. They were provided with a system of ditches to drain off the human fat.[4]

With burning going on night and day in these pits, and the non-stop cremation carried out in the crematoria, the incineration reached a daily total of 24,000 corpses in August 1944.

After the middle of 1943, the gas chambers were reserved for Jews and Gypsies, while Aryans died by hanging, shooting or phenol injections. Until June 1944, the arrival of new prisoners onto the ramp[5] was concealed from the rest of the camp, but then, when the railway extension from Auschwitz Station to Birkenau was completed, the branch line passed through the main entrance of the camp. It ran between Sectors B I and B II as far as Crematoria I and II (Hoss' numbering), and ended at a ramp with three platforms right beside the entrance of the extermination buildings. Transports carried up to 20,000 people daily. After gassing, which took about twenty to 25 minutes, the corpses were reduced to ashes in half an hour.

Jan Sehn's conclusion is that the overall figure of gassed and cremated victims in the five crematoria and the auxiliary bunkers, added to the outdoor burnings in Birkenau, certainly reached 4,000,000 total.[6]

According to the Nuremberg Trial records, however, the total monthly capacity of corpse burning in the five crematoria (Auschwitz No. I and Birkenau Nos. II to V) reached 276,000—an average of 9,000 corpses daily:

No. I burned 9,000 people monthly during 24 months.
Nos. II and III each burned 90,000 people monthly during nineteen and eighteen months respectively.
No. IV burned 45,000 people monthly during seventeen months.
No. V burned 42,000 people monthly during eighteen months.

The overall total of victims destroyed was thus 5,120,000. Further details are in Kraus and Kulka, *The Death Factory*, pp. 123-124.

Appendix V

Besides such items of useful recuperation as medicines and eyeglasses, Dr. Nyiszli has mentioned that there was also in the courtyard of Crematorium II (his number) "a refuse called *Canada* by the SS and the inmates. It was composed of objects that had belonged to the deportees, and considered not worth being salvaged: various foodstuffs, documents, diplomas, military decorations, passports, marriage certificates, prayer books, holy objects and Bibles that the deportees had brought with them into captivity. This little hill, called *Canada*, daily consumed hundreds of thousands of photographs...Sometimes there were flowers, culled from the graves of beloved parents in all the Jewish cemeteries of Europe, pressed between the pages and piously preserved. Prayer beads and odds and ends of all sorts rounded out the smoldering hill." A prisoner had been assigned to "watch the fires burn."[1]

This testimony, however, needs some clarification. With regard to the objects which had belonged to the prisoners, a large number, which had been piled on the ramp at the time the convoys arrived,[2] were immediately sorted and loaded upon trucks. This seized property or loot was at once sent to various distant Nazi posts. SS men on duty in the camp also benefited by receiving articles which had been snatched from their gassed victims. Applications, which were later retrieved, reveal that they used to ask even for baby carriages and layettes for infants.

What had not been seized for immediate disposal was then taken to special barracks known altogether as *Canada*, where clothes, shoes, crutches and artificial limbs, hair, spectacles, toys, valuables and hundreds of other items were sorted and stored, and some sent to be burned.[3]

In his report inserted in *Adam Bujak's Photo Album*, Adolf Gawalewicz wrote that prior to evacuation in 1945, the SS "burned 29 warehouses with their contents. After the liberation of the camp, in the remaining six warehouses were found, among other items, 348,820 complete sets of men's wear, 836,255 complete sets of women's wear, 13,964 carpets, etc...."

The SS, naturally, had arranged for the safe deposit of all pieces of jewelry, notes and gold in the *Reichsbank* vaults. Such looted precious material, when it was retrieved at the end of the war, was filmed and shown to the Nuremberg Court.[4]

Appendix VI

There was a fifth method of execution perpetrated against the deportees from the Milo ghetto. The deportees were loaded into box cars that were so dilapidated as to be of no use other than as scrap. Phosphorous bombs were then thrown inside before the doors were locked for the last time.[1]

There is also in the record the testimony of Paul Gottlieb Waldmann, who was serving as a driver in Ohlendorf's *Einsatzgruppe* D. Waldmann was captured in 1941 and testified that his work had taken him several times to Auschwitz, where he had witnessed a special method of killing Russian prisoners. "One room," Waldmann explained, "was reserved for undressing." Another was a waiting-room where a loud radio played for the prisoners. From this second room, one by one they were ordered into a passage leading to a small fenced-in room with an iron grid in the floor. Under that grid was a drain. As soon as a prisoner was shot, the corpse was carried away by two German prisoners while the blood was washed off the grid, pending the arrival of the following victim. What happened in that death chamber?

There was a slot in the wall 50 centimetres long; the prisoner was forced to stand with the back of his head against that opening, behind which a Nazi marksman was poised. From at most a foot away, he shot his victim. Strangely enough, the killer, despite being at so close range, missed at times. When the method changed, the prisoner was still made to stand against the wall but now an iron plate was slowly lowered onto his head as if the man's height was being measured. Not so. The plate, operated by a foot lever in the corner of the room, contained a ramrod which shot out suddenly and pole-axed the prisoner with a blow on the back of the head; he thus dropped dead.[2]

Frischauer states that apart from Auschwitz—in Dachau, Buchenwald, Treblinka and Bergen-Belsen—novel methods of mass killings had been developed: death by steam[3] and gas alternated with *Aktion Kugel*, an ingenious device by which inmates, who were forced to submit themselves to tests and measurements, were killed by automatic weapons installed in the measuring apparatus.[4]

210

Appendix VII

Hoss' affidavit of April 5, 1946, at Nuremberg went into the record as U.S. Prosecution Document PS 3868, and bore the heading:

OFFICE OF U.S. CHIEF OF COUNSEL
FOR THE PROSECUTION OF AXIS CRIMINALITY
APO 124A, U.S. ARMY
INTERROGATION DIVISION

After having identified himself, notably as "a member from 1 December 1934 of the SS Guard Unit, the so-called Deathhead Formation (Totenkopf Verband)," and eventually as commandant of Auschwitz, "Rudolf Franz Ferdinand Hoess, being first duly sworn, deposed and said as follows:"...

"2. ...I commanded Auschwitz until December 1943,[1] and estimate that at least 2,500,000 victims were executed and exterminated there by gassing and burning, and at least another half million succumbed to starvation and disease, making a total dead of about 3,000,000. This figure represents about 70% or 80% of all persons sent to Auschwitz as prisoners, the remainder having been selected and used for slave labor in the concentration camp industries. Included among the executed and burnt were approximately 20,000 Russian prisoners of war (previously screened out of Prisoner of War cages by the Gestapo) who were delivered to Auschwitz in Wehrmacht transports operated by regular Wehrmacht officers and men. The remainder of the total number of victims included about 100,000 German Jews, and great numbers of citizens, *mostly* Jewish from Holland, France, Belgium, Poland, Hungary, Czechoslovakia, Greece, or other countries. We executed about 400,000 Hungarian Jews alone at Auschwitz in the summer of 1944.[2]...

"4. Mass executions by gassing commenced during the summer 1941 and continued until Fall 1944. I personally supervised executions at Auschwitz until the first of December 1943 and know by reason of my continued duties in the Inspectorate of Concentration Camps WVHA that these mass executions continued as stated above. All mass executions by gassing took place under the direct order, supervision and responsibility of RSHA. I received all orders for carrying out these mass executions directly from RSHA....

"6. The 'final solution' of the Jewish question meant the complete extermination of all Jews in Europe. I was ordered to establish extermination facilities at Auschwitz in June 1941. At that time there were already in the general government three other extermination camps; BELZEK, TREBLINKA and WOLZEK. These camps were under the *Einsatzkommando* of the Security Police and SD. I visited Treblinka to find out how they carried out their exterminations. The Camp Commandant at Treblinka told me that he had liquidated 80,000 in the course of one-half year. He was pricipally [sic] concerned with liquidating all the Jews from the Warsaw Ghetto. He used monoxide gas and I did not think that his methods were very efficient. So when I set up the extermination building at Auschwitz, I used Cyclon B, which was a crystallized Prussic Acid which we dropped into the death chamber from a small opening. It took from 3 to 15 minutes to kill the people in the death chamber depending upon climatic conditions. We knew when the people were dead because their screaming stopped. We usually waited about one-half hour before we opened the doors and removed the bodies. After the bodies were removed our special commandos took off the rings and extracted the gold from the teeth of the corpses.

"7. Another improvement we made over Treblinka was that we built our gas chambers to accommodate 2,000 people at one time, whereas at Treblinka their 10 gas chambers only accommodated 200 people each. The way we selected our victims was as follows: we had two SS doctors on duty at Auschwitz to examine the incoming transports of prisoners. The prisoners would be marched by one of the doctors who would make spot decisions as they walked by. Those who were fit for work were sent into the Camp. Others were sent immedeately [sic] to the extermination plants. Children of tender years were invariably exterminated since by reason of their youth they were unable to work. Still another improvement we made over Treblinka was that at Treblinka the victims almost always knew that they were to be exterminated and at Auschwitz we endeavored to fool the victims into thinking that they were to go through a delousing process. Of course, frequently they realized our true intentions and we sometimes had riots and difficulties due to that fact. Very frequently women would hide their children under the clothes but of course when we found them we would send the children in to be exterminated. We were required to carry out these exterminations in secrecy but of course the foul and nauseating stench from the continuous burning of bodies permeated the entire area and all of the people living in the surrounding communities knew that exterminations were going on at Auschwitz.

"8. We received from time to time special prisoners from the local

Gestapo office. The SS doctors killed such prisoners by injections of benzine. Doctors had orders to write ordinary death certificates and could put down any reason at all for the cause of death.

"9. From time to time we conducted medical experiments on women inmates, including sterilization and experiments relating to cancer. Most of the people who died under these experiments hat [sic] been already condemned to death by the Gestapo.

"10. Rudolf Mildner was the chief of the Gestapo at Kattowicz *and as such was head of the political department at Auschwitz which conducted third degree methods of interregation* [sic] from approximately March 1941 until September 1943. As such, he frequently sent prisoners to Auschwitz for incarceration or execution. He visited Auschwitz on several occassions [sic]. The Gestapo Court, the SS Standgericht, which tried persons accused of various crimes, such as escaping Prisoners of War, etc., frequently met within Auschwitz, and Mildner often attended the trial of such persons, who usually were executed in Auschwitz following their sentence. I showed Mildner throughout the extermination plant at Auschwitz and he was directly interested in it since he had to send the Jews from his territory for execution at Auschwitz.[3]

"I understand English as it is written above. The above statements are true; this declaration is made by me voluntarily and without compulsion; after reading over the statement, I have signed and executed the same at Nurnberg, Germany on the fifth day of April 1946.[4]

(Signature) Rudolf Hoess
RUDOLF FRANZ FERDINAND HOESS

Subscribed and sworn to before me this
5th day of April, 1946, at Nurnberg,
Germany

(Signature) Smith W. Brookhardt, Jr.
SMITH W. BROOKHARDT., JR.,
Lt. Colonel,   IGD.

Notes

Introduction

1. Three weeks later, at the time of sentencing, Judge Locke called the convicted man a neo-Nazi, a fitting appellation which will be used here. And now, the trial over, Zundel has had the audacity to announce that he intends to launch a campaign to overturn the verdicts of the Nuremberg war-crime trials, which were conducted by American, British, French and Russian judges.

The huge, complicated and yet meticulous preparation of the Nuremberg trial, and subsequent hearings, in which the court, the prosecution and the defence each had their own part, constitute an unprecedented example in the annals of international justice. It was not merely four, but twenty-two, countries which were involved in setting up the tribunal, as noted by the American Chief Prosecutor, Justice Robert Jackson, in his opening remarks. Also in his final report to President Truman on October 15, 1946, Jackson emphasized that his delegation alone had numbered almost 700 people, which was still only one quarter of the total number constituting the prosecution teams. Not only had the staff members and their chiefs to scan more than 100,000 documents, sort through 25,000 still photos and analyse 100,000 feet of film, but during the trial miles of additional film had been shot; moreover, the daily transcripts of the hearings reached some 17,000 pages, just in English, which overlapped or confirmed the verbal exchanges which had been recorded on 4,000 discs. Finally, if one includes the material distributed to the defence, the court and the press, the tribunal actually produced 50 million typed pages and incorporated some 30,000 photostatic copies of scores of documents.

The whole organization was assiduous in assuring a fair defence. It is, alas, consistent with Zundel's hate mongering that his next project is to attack, forty years after the hearings, the judgment rendered by the Tribunal. (How the defendants were treated in Nuremberg by their jailer may be found in Burton C. Andrus's two books already quoted in the

215

Foreword. Ann & John Tusa in *The Nuremberg Trial* (1984), p. 125 et
seq., have also given a brief account of the defendants' lifestyle and the
welfare they enjoyed.)

2. "Freedom of expression, though fundamental, is not absolute. It
entitles to criticise and to question; it does not entitle to pervert the truth.
It does not entitle, by falsehood and deceit, to inflame racial animosity.
In a world sadly in need of reconciliation and friendship between all
peoples, they who seek to efface the remorseless inhumanity and
frightening terror of the Nazi regime serve but to incite further hatred
and ill-will. Above all, for the memory of those who perished, for the
anguish of those who survived and for the enlightenment of those to
come, the attempted falsification of the historic truths of that dark and
tragic era must not be allowed to remain unchallenged." Arthur Suzman
in *Six Million Did Die*, by Suzman and Diamond (1978), p. 73.

3. Indeed, the war Hitler waged cost humanity more than thirty million
dead including the victims of the Holocaust, 500,000 of whom still went
to the gas chambers between January and April, 1945, while four million
military and civilian casualties were recorded in central Europe during the
last three months of the war. A superb achievement!

In a translator's note signed V.H. (Victor Henry), the author's central
character of Herman Wouk's *The Winds of War* (Pocket Book Edition),
Hitler has been portrayed, on page 1017, as an "able and resolute
homicidal maniac using modern Germany as his murder instrument,
[who] directly caused between twenty-five and thirty-five million human
deaths; the exact figure will never be known. To stop him cost the world
billions, maybe trillions of dollars. Had the German people shut this
strange individual away in an insane asylum, instead of setting him up as
their adored leader and throwing their full strength behind him for twelve
years, these deaths and this waste would not have occurred. On the
historical record Adolf Hitler was certainly the worst liar, doublecrosser,
destroyer and mass murderer in the world's annals."

4. Zundel not only wore a helmet on which the *Totenkopf* of the SS
was missing, but in remembrance of the Fuhrer he worships, his study in
his Toronto house was transformed into a bunker from which he sallied
daily with his bodyguards.

5. Dr. Hottl's affidavit, dated November 26, 1945, was produced at
Nuremberg by US Prosecution as Exhibit 296. See the complete text in
Victor H. Bernstein, *Final Judgement*, London, 1947, p. 180. Also in
R.W. Cooper, *The Nuremberg Trial*, Penguin Books, 1947, p. 144 and
Gideon Hausner, *Justice in Jerusalem*, Schocken Books, 1968, pp.
378-379.

6. A brief description of the 485 tons of retrieved German archives will
be found in Ann and John Tusa's opus, pp. 97-101. Also, see William L.
Shirer's foreword to his opus, *The Rise and Fall of the Third Reich*, pp.
ix to xi.

7. *The Fall and Rise of Israel* (Reprint 1978), p. 224.

8. See Adolf Gawalewicz's history of Auschwitz-Birkenau in *Adam*

Bujak's Photo Album (n.d.)

9. The biased and deaf-to-truth lawyer was referring to Dr. Raul Hilberg's work, *The Destruction of the European Jews*, which is actually one of the most thorough accounts of the Holocaust.

10. Among other distinctive badges, the black cloth triangles worn by some prisoners indicated the category they belonged to—in this case asocial criminal individuals including prostitutes. (See folder p. 38 of Jan Sehn's *Le Camp de concentration d'Oswiecim-Brzezinka*, Warsaw, 1961.) Also Appendix 4, p. 283 of Kraus and Kulka's *The Death Factory*, and on p. 36 the Auschwitz Camp vocabulary.

11. The gruesome story will be found in Fenelon's narrative, pp. 212-222. Any reader motivated by curiosity and objectivity will also find in Jean-Francois Steiner's account, *Treblinka*, London, 1967, pp. 298-303, what significant purpose orchestras and their music really served in extermination camps.

12. As Suzman and Diamond write in the bibliography of their work: "All above writers [authoritative modern historians] recognise that Hitler's Final Solution envisaged the systematic annihilation of European Jewry, a policy which, but for the defeat of Germany, would almost certainly have been fully implemented." (Op. cit., p. 60)

Chapter I

1. How Hitler defined what a Jew was, will be found in John Toland, *Adolf Hitler*, New York, 1977, p. 694.

2. Toland, pp. 138-139.

3. Quoted by Toland, p. 157.

4. Toni Sender, a Socialist party member. See his *Autobiography of a German Rebel*, New York, 1939, p. 276.

5. They simply quit, and so did many Jews whose trades were boycotted. "In less than six months after Hitler's coming to power there was a decrease in the Jewish population of 11.5% in large towns and 17.1% in small towns. Some districts, where anti-Semitism was especially vile showed reductions up to 45%." (William L. Hull, op. cit., p. 195)

6. Ibid., p. 193.

7. *The Yellow Spot* (1936), a collection of facts and documents relating to three years' prosecution of German Jews, derived chiefly from National Socialist sources, was very carefully assembled by a group of investigators and published in London. For example, "Whoever buys from a Jew is a traitor to the people," proclaimed Julius Streicher in *Der Sturmer*—the filthy, repulsive rag of a sadist.

8. Ibid., p. 240.

9. Ibid., p. 241.

10. Toland, p. 440. What has Zundel to say about this mockery of freedom of expression?

11. Cf. Martin Gilbert's *Atlas of the Holocaust*, London, 1982.

12. There was further discussion when the delegates of 32 nations met at Evian, in France, at a conference to study the Jewish emigration to their countries. Canada did not even attend the meetings, and no large nation showed any willingness to open its frontiers to the refugees. "All that the Evian Conference accomplished," wrote William L. Hull, "was to establish the fact that the Jews were trapped in Europe." However, in October of the same year, 20,000 Polish Jews were rounded up in Germany for deportation to their country. To start with, only 8,000 were herded across the Polish border, and the balance, the larger figure in fact, were held in concentration camps or in trains pending departure. (See note 16.)

13. After Toland, op. cit., p. 563. The author added: "[Hitler's] last words, leaving no doubt that he meant to solve the problem by killing the Jews, were drowned out by a spontaneous mass scream of blood lust."

14. Bella Fromm, *Blood and Banquets*, New York, 1962, pp. 235-236.

15. The dramatic event is narrated in Hausner's *Justice in Jerusalem*, New York, 1968, p. 41.

16. After his arrest, the young killer protested that being a Jew was not a crime. "I am not a dog," he said. "I have a right to live and the Jewish people have a right to exist...Wherever I have been, I have been chased like an animal."

There was a later echo of the killer's trial in Goebbels' diaries when he wrote, on February 11, 1942, that Georges Bonnet (the former Minister of Foreign Affairs in the Daladier cabinet in 1939-1940) was ready to testify "that he opposed the declaration of war against Germany, but that the French government was put under such heavy pressure by the Jews that it could not avoid declaring war. This," Goebbels concluded, "shows in what an *irresponsible way this war was started and how heavily those must be punished who acted so rashly*" (emphasis added).

This is really the last straw! Wasn't Hitler *the* warmonger?

17. *New York Times*, November 11, 1938.

18. From 1933 up to October 1938, 150,000 Jews, that is 25 per cent of the original 600,000 Jewish population hastily left their country. Of the remaining 450,000, another 150,000 people emigrated after the Kristallnacht pogrom, while 30,000 were arrested and arbitrarily sent to Buchenwald, Dachau and Sachsenhausen.

19. Reverend William L. Hull has mentioned a letter received from Germany that same year at his mission in Jerusalem. The sender's father had been taken to a concentration camp. But if a certificate to Palestine could be obtained he would be released and could leave Germany. Again the futile effort at the Migration Office; again the blank refusal. Within less than six months, word was received that the father had died in the camp. No need to tell of the suffering and torture he endured to bring his untimely death. The story was multiplied millions of times in the succeeding years in Germany, Poland and other Nazi-controlled countries. (Op. cit., p. 200)

20. After Lucy S. Dawidowicz, *The War Against the Jews—1933/1945*, New York, 1975.

21. It was an old emigration plan that the Polish government had already contemplated. In 1937, Adolf Eichmann unearthed it, and the idea of the plan emerged again after the French armistice of June 18, 1940. Heydrich then charged Eichmann to prepare a covenant whereby the French would cede the island to Germany. Nothing resulted from his efforts. At his trial in Jerusalem, Eichmann claimed he had worked out the plan with the sole purpose of "putting solid ground under the feet of the Jews and allowing them freedom and statehood." Its true significance, remarked the prosecutor, Gideon Hausner, was in fact "the deportation of four million Jews into exile and their complete isolation from the outer world." (Hausner, op. cit., p. 415. Further details: p. 63)

22. Nora Levin, *The Holocaust*, New York, 1968, p. 89.

23. Hausner, p. 44. Four days after the Anschluss, Eichmann had already arrived in Vienna (March 17, 1938) to clear the place of Jews.

24. Helmut Krausnick, *Anatomy of the SS State,* New York, 1968, p. 44.

25. Willem Antonius Maria Sassen, a Dutch Nazi journalist who, in Argentina, was one of the two editors of *Der Weg*—The Way—a fascist, virulently anti-Semitic periodical. Sassen's conversations with Eichmann were recorded on tape, and Gideon Hausner retrieved them at the time he prosecuted Eichmann in 1961.

26. After Hausner, p. 40.

27. Ibid., p. 19.

28. Quoted by Toland, p. 700.

CHAPTER II

1. Up to the beginning of the war, the prison population rose to 5,300 in Buchenwald; 4,000 in Dachau; 1,600 in Flossenburg; 1,500 in Mauthausen; 2,500 in Ravenbruck; and 6,500 in Sachsenhausen—a total of 21,400, which more than doubled (to 44,600) the following year. The importance given to the development and maintenance of those, and other, camps is reflected in Frick's 1939 budget for his Ministry of the Interior. Close to 22 million marks were then allocated to the camps and the armed SS, that is, one fifth of the total budget.

What was going on in those camps was common practice: atrocities. One performance, among many others, has gone into the record. The stage was in Mauthausen where, early in 1941, some eight prisoners were to be led to the top of a quarry and were beaten, kicked and then thrown over the edge of the precipice—a drop of over 100 feet. It was a regular sport enjoyed by SS guards, who called their victims *paratroopers*.

2. The entire passage is after Lucy S. Dawidowicz, op. cit., pp. 86,

220   Hitler's Holocaust

104, 130 et seq.

3. Hausner, p. 56. Naturally, at his trial, Eichmann made all possible efforts in his defence to dissociate himself from that program.

4. Toland, pp. 798-799.

5. Hausner, p. 59. The 42-volume journal of Hans Frank's speeches and the minutes of his conferences and meetings during his governor generalship were produced at the Nuremberg trials. It is a unique relic of the Nazi era, revealing the barbarity and ruthlessness of a highly intelligent and well-read man who was ready to descend as low as necessary in the service of his Fuhrer.

6. Hausner, p. 60.

7. Toland, p. 958.

8. Ibid., p. 925. Heydrich had already conceived these groups as a paramilitary and police force in the 1938 Czechoslovakian campaign to repress any resistance of the population and, even more, "to carry out a political purge by terror methods." (Delarue)

Now the *Einsatzgruppen* were going to operate in the wake of the invading armies in Poland and Russia. Their basic task was supposedly "to insure security intelligence," but in fact the job to be done was the extermination of the Jewish population by the same terror methods which had already proved their worth in Czechoslovakia. See Appendix I.

9. Toland, p. 925.

10. These instructions encompassed the immediate opening of three annihilation camps at Belzec, Majdanek and Sobibor. The SS police leader thus became the head of a vast kingdom of death. He was also responsible for the creation of as many labour camps as the implementation of the SS program demanded. Thousands upon thousands of slave prisoners perished there and thus raised the overall figures of the systematic extermination carried out in the death camps. Eventually, a total of over two million people were killed under Globocnik's aegis, many of them having perished from starvation, as effective an instrument of mass murder as the executions. (Frischauer, p. 132) Globocnik's curriculum vitae will be found in *Encyclopaedia Judaica*, vol. 7, Col. 622. It mentions that the "Nazi executioner of Polish Jewry" is believed to have poisoned himself in May 1945.

11. Mercy killing or euthanasia had been authorized by Hitler to dispose of the mentally ill. Carbon monoxide had been used, and an officer of the Stuttgart police, Kriminal Kommissar Wirth, was put in charge of the program only to be later transferred to the Lublin camp and placed under the orders of Globocnik. It was in these circumstances that Eichmann could evaluate the new method of annihilation.

The mobile gas vans were known as "S" lorries, Becker having chosen the initial of the maker, whose name was Saurer. It also referred to the word *Sonder*, meaning "special" (treatment). On the use of these diabolical vans, see the astounding report of Becker in R.W. Cooper, *The Nuremberg Trial*, London, 1947, pp. 145-146. Dated May 16, 1942, Becker's report was produced at Nuremberg by the U.S. Prosecution as

Exhibit 288.

12. Willi Frischauer, *Himmler*, New York, 1962, p. 133. See also Ohlendorf's deposition in Nuremberg in Ann Tusa and John Tusa, *The Nuremberg Trial*, p. 171. Sentenced to death in 1948, Ohlendorf was hanged three years later with three of his colleagues, former *Einsatzgruppen* commanders.

13. The operation was also a matter of secrecy. Toland, pp. 926-927, has quoted Himmler's speech after Raul Hilberg's *The Destruction of the European Jews*, p. 218. But Erich Goldhagen in an article entitled "Albert Speer, Himmler and the Secrecy of the Final Solution," published in *Midstream*, October 1971, has questioned the accuracy of Hilberg's account. Goldhagen mentioned that *one* eyewitness, among eighteen, testified in 1959 in a German court that Himmler, unperturbed, drew his own pistol and finished off a Jew who had not been fatally shot—as if, added Goldhagen, to show that the *Reichsfuhrer* would not demand anything of his men that he would not do himself. In the same note 17, appended to his article, the author also quoted some members of former flying execution squads as saying that Himmler demanded of them deeds the very sight of which made him faint, break down and cry. But as a matter of "obedience to the highest law," as Himmler had put it, the mass killings were carried out as before, and a year after his visit to Minsk, the 16,000 Jews from the ghetto who remained were executed in a single day. (October, 1942)

14. All the records of the Gestapo were destroyed before Germany's collapse, except one. It concerned an order (to several Gestapo offices throughout the Reich, including one in Dusseldorf) to round up, detain and transport 50,000 Jews, and to confiscate and seal their apartments. The Dusseldorf police reported that the order had been carried out. The local "crop" had been 1,007 in Dusseldorf alone. (Hausner, p. 79)

15. See supra. Eichmann to Sassen: "I dictated it [Goring's directive]. These are my words. We had prepared the letter and submitted it to Goring for signature."

16. In Nuremberg, Goring and Kaltenbrunner (Heydrich's successor to RSHA) strongly denied any complicity in mass murder. It was too much to bear in broad daylight. Only those few Nazis who openly expressed contrition like Hans Frank and Albert Speer, the Minister of Munitions, or those who were actually caught red-handed, admitted the charges. Generally speaking, everyone put the blame on Hitler, Himmler, Heydrich and Eichmann. (Hausner, p. 86.)

17. Hoss was a member of the Nazi party since 1922. In 1928, Himmler met him by chance. In 1934, the SS chief suggested he join the *Totenkopf* guard corps of the concentration camps. On May 5, 1940, it was Inspector Richard Glucks who appointed him as *Kommandant* of the Auschwitz camp. Hoss was arrested by the British on March 11, 1946, and was interrogated forthwith. After he was taken to Nuremberg to testify as a material witness, he was transferred to Cracow. It was during the ten month period he spent in prison that Hoss wrote his autobio-

graphy. He was condemned to death in Warsaw and hanged on April 15, 1947, in Auschwitz, the site of his crimes. See: *Commandant of Auschwitz*, London, 1959. Translation by Constantine Fitzgibbon from the 1958 German edition of *Kommandant of Auschwitz*, published by the Deutsche Verlags-Anstalt. (The Polish original edition *Wspomnienia* was published in 1951.)

18. It is interesting to note that on February 28, 1944, Hans Frank wrote there were still perhaps 100,000 Jews in the General Government; 3.4 million had perished (Soviet Prosecution Exhibit 223 at the Nuremberg Trials).

19. Actually, it was Adolf Eichmann who had done the research and produced the plan to his chief, Heydrich. Later, Eichmann, remembering the Wannsee Conference, said everything went well; everyone was kind, polite and courteous. There was no useless talk. The orderlies were serving cognac and the affair was settled.

20. Hausner, pp. 94-95. Incidentally, Josef Buhler was tried before the Polish Supreme National Tribunal from June 17 to July 10, 1948, and sentenced to death.

21. In regard to his responsibility, at the time of his trial in Jerusalem, Eichmann declared that there was nothing personal in his job. He was one of many engaged in a political solution. But he had nothing to regret. He told Sassen while in Argentina: "To be frank with you, had we killed all of them, the 10.3 million, I would be happy and say: All right, we managed to destroy an enemy." He was alluding to a figure that Himmler's statistician Richard Korherr had fixed as the Jewish total to be comprised in the Holocaust. (Hausner, p. 11.)

22. The first time had been on January 30, 1942, on the Ninth Anniversary of the National Socialist regime. The second time was again on an anniversary—that of the promulgation of the Party—toward the end of February when Hitler said that, as was his prophecy (of January 30, 1939), "this war will not destroy Aryan humanity but it will exterminate the Jew. Whatever the battle may bring in its course or however long it may last, that will be its final course." His obsessional theme was not changing. These quotations are only a few specimens of Hitler's warnings and threats to the Jews, his repeated promises of extermination, his incessant flood of invectives. Earlier in *Mein Kampf*, his abuse and fierce hatred of the Jews is repeated hundreds of times. It is easy to see how all his murderous verbiage egged on the insults and sarcasms of Julius Streicher, the wild plans and actions of Himmler, Heydrich, Eichmann, Muller, Goebbels, Hans Frank and scores of murder-minded fanatics. The torrent of orders to kill and the subsequent reports of mass slaughters would amount to a multi-volume listing in testimony of the Nazi crimes against humanity.

23. Quoted from Prange by Toland, p. 964.

24. Toland, p. 968.

25. See testimony given in Jerusalem by Mrs. Hildegard Henschel from Berlin (Hausner, p. 104).

26. See note 11. In autumn 1943, Wirth was moved from Belzec to Trieste and was later assassinated by Tito's partisans. Further details are in *Encyclopaedia Judaica*, vol. 16, col. 553.

27. Toland, pp. 975-976, quoting Friedlander, p. 104 et seq. See also Gerstein's own testimony in Nora Levin, op. cit., pp. 311-312. (The episode has been reproduced by many authors.)

28. See Professor Wellers' testimony in Hausner, p. 107.

29. The story of the deportation of Jews from Germany and occupied Europe, under Eichmann's rule, is exposed in Hausner's *Justice in Jerusalem*, Chapter 8, pp. 98-131.

30. Jan Sehn's work, *Le camp de concentration d'Oswiecim-Brzezinka*, Warsaw, 1961—which is enriched with 43 illustrations—is one of the most complete and objective works on the history of the Auschwitz-Birkenau camps. It is based exclusively on documents and facts which served and were referred to during the trials which took place at the Supreme National Tribunal in Poland, the International Military Tribunal and the American Military Tribunal, both in Nuremberg. It includes accounts of how selections and "quarantine" of prisoners under SS yoke were carried out; how the inmates—Jews, non-Jews and prisoners of war—were housed and fed; how they lived, worked and were punished, tortured and otherwise treated before their extermination. One chapter deals with the ethics of the SS doctors who performed their inhuman pseudo-scientific experiments on the inmates—men, women and children alike. The detailed story of the gas chambers and the crematoria and the corresponding figures of "production" are treated in two separate chapters. The author has also listed the names of 23 SS personnel of Auschwitz-Birkenau who were condemned to death and sixteen to years of imprisonment, in Warsaw on December 27, 1947, by the Polish Supreme National Tribunal.

A map of the concentration, labour, extermination and special purpose camps operated by the Nazis in Germany and in German-occupied territories in the war years, and even prior to 1939, has been included on the inside back cover of the book. These camps (including sixteen located in the Berlin zone) were plotted according to the data provided by Rudolf Hoss during the inquiry carried out by the investigating judge, Jan Sehn. Sehn, a lawyer and a member of the Polish Chief Commission charged with the investigation of Nazi crimes, acted as examining judge while Hoss' trial was being prepared. He is quoted, or referred to, several times in *KL Auschwitz Seen by the SS* (Selection, Elaboration and Notes by Jadwiga Bezwinska, Ph.D., and Danuta Czech, M.A.), the reprint of which is by Howard Fertig, New York, 1984.

31. In 1934, Hoss' first post had been Dachau. SS *Obergruppenfuhrer* Theodor Eicke was then the *kommandant* of the camp and Hoss' superior. In July, that same year, Eicke was promoted to Inspector of Concentration Camps and, in 1941, General Inspector of the Death Division. In the spring of 1942 he was shot during a reconnaissance flight near Karkov. His body was never found.

32. Hoss, op. cit., p. 183. When Hoss was arrested after the war, he said: "I have been told, and it has been repeated to me since my arrest that I could have disobeyed that order and even assassinated Himmler. I don't think that such a thought could cross any SS officer's mind. It was absolutely unthinkable....Numerous officers have complained of the harshness of the orders given them, but nonetheless they have carried them to execution."

33. He was SS Lieutenant-Colonel, in charge of the Gestapo's Jewish evacuation office.

34. This 32-letter impressive appellation was the Superior Office of Reich Security. Himmler had created it on September 27, 1939, soon after the invasion of Poland, and entrusted Reinhardt Heydrich, *Obergruppenfuhrer*, Army General SS, with its direction.

35. *Goebbels' Diaries*, London, 1948, pp. 138, 147-148.

36. (a) The figures of quantities of Zyklon which were used in Auschwitz-Birkenau are incomplete. In Auschwitz alone, twenty tons were used in the years 1941-1944. At the same time, it is known that the manufacturer sold 300,000 marks' worth during the same time period; how much value and quantity went to Auschwitz-Birkenau is not specified.

(b) Poliakov correctly remarked that "we still know very little about the Auschwitz experiments," but since there was a stock of Zyklon on hand, "hitting on the idea of using this gas on condemned human beings probably required little imagination."

Philippe Aziz in *Les Medecins de la mort*, II, p. 41, gives no precise date for Fritzsch's experiment. Poliakov made no mention of it at all, and only one (p. 199), refers to the mass gassing that took place in the fall of 1941 (see infra). More about Zyklon B will be found in Poliakov, pp. 207-208.

37. *Auschwitz Museum Guide-Book*, p. 42.

38. Ibid.

39. "Quarantine" was where the prisoners suffered repeated sadistic torments imposed upon them, and were the victims of continual violence. During so-called sport drills, those who did not run fast enough or fell exhausted were led or dragged away by the *kapos* and finished off either by having a stick thrust in their mouths, or were shot. At roll call, some punished men had to stand at attention, their arms pulled up behind their necks from 9 p.m. until noon the next day.

40. Adolf Gawalewicz's brochure, pp. 3-5 in *Adam Bujak's Photo Album*.

41. Execution, by shooting, was also resorted to, as is evidenced by the killing of 40 Poles on November 22, that same year.

42. See Photos 34 and 43 in *Adam Bujak's Photo Album*.

43. Hoss' version is in *Commandant of Auschwitz*, op. cit., pp. 184-185 (and the event referred to again in Appendix I), whereas the second version is in *Les Crimes allemands en Pologne* (French edition), the result of the inquiry by the Commission of the Polish Government,

Warsaw, 1948, pp. 92-93. Perhaps the idea of using Zyklon B was Fritzsch's but Palitzsch actually served in the experiment as executioner.

44. The *kommandant* indicated that this crematorium (obviously the first in operation) "near the hospital building" was out of action for a considerable time in the winter of 1941-42. Unfortunately, he did not mention when exactly it was put to work nor how many bodies could be burned in its ovens. Nor did he give a number to this crematorium. See Appendix II. A photo of this crematorium is in Kraus and Kulka, *The Death Factory*, Pergamon Press edition, 1966, page 134.

45. From 1942 to 1944, some 40 of those sub-camps—*Nebenlager*—mushroomed in the region as far as Silesia. They were located near factories, mines and foundries, and housed the slave prisoners who were assigned to work there up to twelve hours a day.

46. Aziz in volume II, page 156, mentions that "the topic of the conversation with the *Reichsfuhrer* concerned the mass sterilization of Jewesses." There is no reference to animals in the author's quotation.

47. (a) See Appendix III. Transcending the limits of such criminal experiments, wrote Adolf Gawalewicz, remains the fact that in the nutritional kitchens of the Auschwitz Hygiene *Institut der Waffen SS und Polizei Sud-Ost*, soup was prepared from human flesh. (In the author's brochure inserted in *Adam Bujak's Photo Album*.)

(b) Details about Horst Schumann and his deadly experiments in sterilization and castration—which cost the lives of more than 14,000 mental patients in the "euthanasia" institution of Grafeneck and Sonnenstein, and to prisoners at Auschwitz and Buchenwald—will be found in *KL Auschwitz Seen by the SS*, pp. 314-316.

48. The assassination plan had been set up by the Czech government-in-exile in co-operation with the British Special Operations Executive, which was an underground warfare agency.

49. See Appendix II. Regarding offers for the delivery of cremation furnaces by the Erfurt firm and others, see Victor Bernstein, op. cit., pp. 139-140.

50. Hoss, op. cit., pp. 190-191.

51. Fenelon, op. cit., p. 194.

52. *Return to Auschwitz*, New York, 1983, p. 120.

53. See Appendix IV. The numbering of Birkenau Crematoria II, III, IV and V, now mentioned, will be found on the plan printed on the inner side of the *Auschwitz Museum Guide-Book* back cover.

54. Northwest of those, a sauna or bathhouse would also be built. In her narrative, Fania Fenelon, a member of the orchestra, said that their concerts were held in the sauna in the winter when it was raining. The interior of the immense building was odd and unpleasant. "Its precise function remained unclear: showers, disinfection centre, a sorting centre when numbers rose too high.... There were no windows, only long narrow skylights lost in the upper gloom." (Op. cit., p. 97) A more objective reference to the sauna is in Kraus and Kulka's opus, pp. 51-52.

55. The *Auschwitz Museum Guide-Book* mentions that the ashes, still

visible in 1950, furnished the most convincing evidence of the crimes committed in the camp. See Photo 107 in *Adam Bujak's Photo Album*.

56. After Anna Pawelezynska, *Values and Violence in Auschwitz*, Berkeley, 1979. See Photos 69 and 70 in *Adam Bujak's*. These Crematoria II and III (Hoss' numbers I and II) are those shown on the Birkenau plan referred to in Note 53. Crematorium I, not shown on the plan, was the one in operation in the Auschwitz mother-camp.

57. Hoss, op. cit., p. 126.

58. (a) From Seweryna Szmaglewska: *Dymy nad Birkenau* (Smoke over Birkenau), Warsaw, 1958. Publ. "Czytelnik", p. 121. A translation into English by Jadwiga Rynas was published in 1947 by Holt, New York. The Polish author, a former inmate in Auschwitz, testified as a prosecution witness in 1946 before the International Military Tribunal in Nuremberg. See her deposition in Kraus and Kulka's opus, pp. 112-116.

(b) In regard to the date when the slaughter of Gypsies started, the editors of *KL Auschwitz Seen by the SS* mention "the afternoon of August 2, 1944." Details of the liquidation will be found in the above-titled opus, p. 66, note 69.

59. *Auschwitz Museum Guide-Book*, p. 46.

60. The Revier, or men's hospital in B IIf, was part of the men's camp and was located between Crematoria II and IV, a choice location, since the weak and the sick, selected for elimination, had only a short way to reach the gas chamber.

61. Seweryna Szmaglewska, op. cit., pp. 298-299.

62. An ex-prisoner, Dr. Berthold E., at the time of Hoss' trial in Warsaw, has been quoted as saying that SS men used a 1.2 metre rod to select those children who passed under the rod; they were sent to the gas chamber. "Small children," said the witness, "knowing only too well what was awaiting them, tried hard to push out their necks when passing under the rod, in the hope to escape gassing." (In *Auschwitz Museum Guide-Book*, p. 64.)

63. Hoss, op. cit., p. 190.

64. Fenelon, pp. 169-170.

65. He was an SS colonel whom the author felt inspired to call Graf Bobby, "the name of a well-known character in Germany, the creation of a cartoonist of the Kaiser's time; corseted, monocled, he was elegance and snobism personified." (Fenelon, op. cit., p. 157)

66. Dr. Johann Paul Kremer, 58 years of age in 1942, was tried in Cracow by the Polish Supreme National Tribunal with 39 other defendants in the Auschwitz garrison case, and sentenced to death on December 22, 1947. He was granted clemency, owing to his age, and after ten years of imprisonment he was released and returned to his country. His diary has been reproduced on pp. 199-281 in *KL Auschwitz Seen by the SS*.

67. The whole passage that follows is after Adolf Gawalewicz, whose brochure has already been quoted.

68. At times, the SS used dogs for fun. "Being bored and wishing to

enjoy themselves,'' wrote Hoss, they "baited women prisoners with dogs.''(Op. cit., p. 141.)

69. See Photos in the *Auschwitz Museum Guide-Book*, pp. 74-75.
70. See Photo 33 in *Adam Bujak's Photo Album*.
71. Ibid., Photo 31.
72. Ibid., Photos 22, 23, 26 and 28.
73. Pages 79-80.
74. See Photo 10 in *Adam Bujak's Photo Album*. Also No. 29: Gallows inside Death Block 11.
75. Neither did the SS forget prisoners of war. As camp records show—other unrecorded figures being unknown—a total of 13,000 men were wiped out. Only 97 were found to have survived and were present at the last roll call, on January 17, 1945.
76. On August 29, 1942, 746 sick prisoners were disposed of in this way.
77. In *Auschwitz Museum Guide-Book*, p. 51.
78. Seweryna Szmaglewska, op. cit., p. 18.
79. The SS used to assign the job chiefly to priests and Jews since it was a particularly exhausting task.
80. See photo in *Auschwitz Museum Guide-Book*, p. 54.
81. A frequent sight on all sites and at every hour of the day.
82. (a) Plans to round up the Jews in Budapest in one day had been laid down by Eichmann much earlier. The deadline had been fixed for the middle of July. Apparently, Eichmann had had what he wanted. See details in Hausner, pp. 141-142.
(b) The "action in Hungary" which ended in the inferno of Auschwitz-Birkenau was renamed "Aktion Hoss" when the former *kommandant* was entrusted officially with the implementation of the program of extermination of the Hungarian Jews. See Appendix II.
83. Hausner, pp. 152-153.
84. It was exactly two years since Himmler had ordered that the increase of the transport of Jews to concentration camps be completed by January 1943, and, indeed, during those two years the pace had picked up momentum.
85. In his *Souvenirs d'une ambassade a Berlin*, French ambassador Francois-Poncet wrote that actually anti-Semitism in Germany was "a prejudice and a popular passion....In showing off [his] hatred, Hitler does not stand aside the people; he gets closer to them; he is their reflection; his frantic anti-Semitism does not harm his popularity; on the contrary, it is one of its elements.''
86. Toland, pp. 959-960.
87. Ibid., p. 1037.
88. Quoted by Poliakov, *Harvest of Hate*, Westport, Conn., 1971, p. 116, from Kersten's *Klerk en Beul: Himmler van nabij*, Amsterdam, Meulenhof, 1948, pp. 197-198.
89. Quoted by Poliakov, op. cit., p. 116.
90. This outburst of sincerity by Frank had come after the American

Prosecution had shown the court, during its afternoon session of November 29, 1945, a film of the concentration camps as they had been found by the advancing Allied troops. Victor H. Bernstein, who was in the courtroom, watched in shock the gory spectacle of "an endless river of white bodies flowing across the screen, bodies with ribs sticking out through their chests, with pipestem legs and battered skulls and eyeless faces and grotesque thin arms reaching for the sky...tumbling bodies and bodies in mounds, single bodies with holes between the eyes and bodies being shoved over cliffs into common graves, bodies pushed like dirt by giant bulldozers, and bodies that [were] not bodies at all but charred bits of bone and flesh lying upon a crematory grate made of bits of steel rails laid upon blackened wood ties." (See Bernstein's opus, *Final Judgement*, London, 1947, pp. 26-27.)

All other defendants in the dock had watched the film, and Dr. G.M. Gilbert, the psychologist in charge, wrote down at about one to two minute intervals the reactions of the men on trial.

In the evening in jail, Hans Fritzsche, breaking out sobbing, said to Dr. Gilbert: "No power in heaven or earth will erase this shame from my country!—not in generations—not in centuries!"

Most other defendants denied they had known that such things had been ordered and had been happening. It was then that Hans Frank, in his cell, spoke to Dr. Gilbert in the terms which have been reported. Keitel himself told Dr. Gilbert that the responsibility was "those dirty SS swine...I'll never be able to look people in the face again."

The next day, the defendants were outraged as they listened to General Lahousen's testimony. The witness, called to the stand by the American Prosecution, was Admiral Canaris' former assistant in the Abwehr. He now revealed what the resistance movement had been in his department. Goring, for one, called him a traitor. Other defendants thought he had betrayed the officers' honor. But Lahousen was unperturbed: "*Now* they talk of honor," he said later to Dr. Gilbert, "after millions have been murdered! No doubt it's unpleasant for them to have someone who can stand up and state these uncomfortable truths to their faces. I've got to speak for those whom they murdered. I am the only one left." (See Dr. Gilbert's *Nuremberg Diary*, New York, 1947, pp. 45-51.)

91. Toland, p. 1038.
92. Frischauer, p. 138.
93. See the complete 1,600-word quotation in Cooper, op. cit., pp. 113-115.
94. Quoted by Toland, pp. 1051-1052.
95. For further details on Speer's stand, see Erich Goldhagen's article "Albert Speer, Himmler, and the Secrecy of the Final Solution," in the October 1971 issue of *Midstream*.
96. Frischauer, pp. 126-127. See also Shirer's version of the destruction of the Warsaw ghetto (April 15 to May 16, 1943), op. cit., pp. 1269-1273.
97. See *Les Crimes allemands en Pologne*, vol. I, pp. 227-231, and the photos inserted between pages 234 and 235. The last two photographs

(#39 and 40) show a list of members of the police force who were decorated for the criminal action they had carried out in the ghetto. General Stroop's report of May 16, 1943, referred to in the above-mentioned work, was presented at the Nuremberg International Military Trial by U.S. Prosecution as Exhibit 275.

CHAPTER III

1. Odd Nansen, *From Day to Day*, New York, 1949. In the foreword, p. xiii, the author describes how he hid his diary in six hollowed breadboards, later transported to his home.
2. There were some 50 Jewish watchmakers in Sachsenhausen. "They were men of all ages, all...employed in the camp on the repair of stolen watches. Practically all these men had lost their families. Their wives and children had been sent into the gas chambers of Auschwitz and Lublin. It was their trade alone that had saved them from the same fate." (November 16, 1943)
3. See Dr. Nyiszli's description in *Auschwitz*, New York, 1960, pp. 27-28.
4. Its chief was *Oberscharfuhrer* Mussfeld.
5. Nyiszli, pp. 38-39. In her narrative, Olga Lengyel recalls how she had wanted to spare her older son, Arvad, who was not quite twelve, from the labours that might prove too arduous for him. The selector, who otherwise would have sent him to the right, was persuaded to send him to the left, where Thomas, Olga's younger son, had already been directed. Then she said that her own mother would like to remain with the children. The favour was granted but, unwittingly, "I had [just] condemned Arvad and my mother to death in the gas chambers." (In *Five Chimneys*, London, 1972, p. 27)
6. Nyiszli, pp. 41-42.
7. The *Sonderkommando* men would later take away the pile of clothes and shoes to disinfect them.
8. The Red Cross served as a cover. For every mass murder session, the Zyklon B in granule form would be transported into the camp. However, the compound was never stored in the administrative buildings or in the crematoria. Hoss confessed that Zyklon B had "a soothing effect" on him. "We had shortly to begin a mass killing of Jews and up to that time neither Eichmann nor I had any idea how to proceed with it....Now we discovered the gas and the means as well."
9. Nyiszli, pp. 42-47. In *Adam Bujak's Photo Album*, see Photos 40, 41 and 46 of Crematorium No. I in Auschwitz, where the slaughter took place. See note 11 below.
10. Nyiszli, p. 53.
11. All the events referred to by Dr. Nyiszli, as he recalled his time in Auschwitz in 1944, occurred in Birkenau and not in the Auschwitz

mothercamp. The "Number one krema," as the author called it, was in fact one of the four crematoria erected in Birkenau. They were designated by the Nazi administration (and are shown on the Birkenau plan printed in the *Auschwitz Museum Guide-Book*) as Nos. II, III, IV and V. Dr. Nyiszli's dissecting room was in No. II in Birkenau.

12. Nyiszli, pp. 59-60.
13. Ibid., pp. 61-62.
14. On June 2, one of those Frenchmen had arrived. He later left an account of camp life. See Vol. II of *Les Medecins de la mort*, op. cit., p. 46 et seq.
15. See Appendix V.
16. Nyiszli, pp. 68-71. See Appendix VI.
17. Nyiszli, pp. 72-74.
18. Ibid., p. 78.
19. Ibid., pp. 88-92.
20. Ibid., pp. 99-100.
21. Ibid., pp. 109-111.
22. Ibid., pp. 112-114.
23. By August 1944, Himmler had dictated to Hoss what he must do if the Russians advanced onto the camp. "Liquidate the site; destroy the documents; exterminate the prisoners and incinerate all the corpses without a trace. Keep on the job only the necessary squads, and exterminate them as soon as they have completed the liquidation of the camp." The Polish Resistance received a copy of these instructions in Cracow the very next day, and passed it on to the Polish Socialist Party. It had been two years since Joseph Cyrankiewicz, a Communist activist, was incarcerated in Auschwitz, and reorganized the already existing *reseau* of intelligence. Few succeeded in escaping but, through complex channels, the cell operating within the camp could keep the Cracow outsiders informed of what was going on in the death factory. Eventually, the Polish Socialist Party passed on all intelligence to the Polish Government in exile in London. In fact, the government had set up a committee to help the Auschwitz prisoners. Those who wanted to try their getaway clandestinely received various items which they could use on the chosen day. Meanwhile, agents working for the Resistance in the *Kommandatur* of the camp pilfered the files and copied the secret instructions Hoss received from Berlin. One of these agents was a German Sister, Marie, also a member of the Red Cross. It was through her that in February 1944 the original record of executions that had taken place in Auschwitz from the time it opened its doors until October 1943 was passed on. As these precious data and other secret messages reached London, the Polish Government turned them over to the BBC, which broadcast them immediately.

Either this way or through other channels, the Jewish agency in Palestine was also informed of the mass killings. Horrified, the executives urged that the British air force bombard the camp and destroy the crematoria and the track. No such action resulted.

24. Nyiszli, pp. 114-120.

25. The man's account of the events is in Dr. Nyiszli's narrative, p. 121 et seq.

26. According to the *Auschwitz Museum Guide-Book*, p. 91, it was Crematorium IV which was burned down and Crematorium II which was partially demolished. Dr. Nyiszli's crematoria numbering differs from that appearing on Nazi documents, but is actually the same as that used by Hoss. See Appendix II.

According to the same source—*Auschwitz Museum Guide-Book*, p. 93 —it was some women working in *Union-Werke*, the armaments factory, who stole the explosives that they smuggled into the Birkenau camp for the 12th *Sonderkommando*. Several of these women prisoners were arrested and consigned to the underground cells of Block II in Auschwitz. There they were tortured, and after long weeks of interrogation in which they betrayed no one, they were hanged.

27. See Dr. Nyiszli's narrative, pp. 128-132.

28. Nyiszli, pp. 133-134. Apparently the author did not know half of the story about the need for skeletons. There was at least one other institution, besides the Anthropological Museum, which was interested.

"A ghastly illustration of Eichmann's authority in the camp," writes Hausner, "was the story of the supply of skeletons and skulls to the Strasbourg University 'Institute of Ancestral Heredity.' The anatomy specialist there was Professor Hirth. With Himmler's approval, Sievers, the director of the Institute, applied to Glucks, the concentration camps inspector, to get the "goods" from the camps, but Glucks referred him to Eichmann. The latter then asked for a direct request from Himmler's headquarters. The still living people, who were to provide the skeletons, were picked out at Auschwitz by an anthropologist, and Eichmann's department sent 79 male Jews, 30 female Jews, 2 Poles and 4 of unidentified nationality to be turned into skeletons at the Natzweiler concentration camp for the use of Strasbourg University. The killing was done by none other than SS Captain Josef Kramer, the future commander of the notorious Bergen-Belsen camp.

"Professor Hirth supplied Kramer with poison gas and exact instructions on how to proceed. The bodies, which were then turned over to the scientists, were partly dismembered and partly preserved in alcohol. When the French took Strasbourg, they found these bodies and dismembered parts, which they photographed and marked as 'apparently Jewish.' We produced in court the twenty-one macabre photographs they took." (Hausner, op. cit., pp. 339-340)

Sievers was interrogated at Nuremberg (see Record Trial Transcript, p. 15, 325) and Professor Hirth's report to Himmler was produced as Document 085. Josef Kramer, who has been mentioned before, was an old rat of concentration camps, where he had been employed since 1932. In 1940 he was at Auschwitz as Hoss' adjutant. He left this post when he was transferred to Natzweiler, but returned to Auschwitz in May 1944, this time as successor to Hoss. It was six months later that he became *kommandant* of Bergen-Belsen; there he distinguished himself by his cruelties and earned the name Beast of Belsen. He was arrested by the British on April 17, 1945, tried in Lueneburg by a British court on November 17, sentenced to death and hanged on December 12, that same year, at Hameln prison. Further details on the beast will be found in Kraus and Kulka, *The Death Factory*, Chapter 7 ("Slave-Drivers, Jailers and Hangmen"), pp. 228-230.

29. Nyiszli, p. 136.

30. Ibid., pp. 137-139.

31. "The gas chambers were large and victims fooled into thinking they were going through a delousing process. Some groups were taken to the 'baths' to the accompaniment of light operatic music played by girls dressed in blue and white. The buildings at Auschwitz also conspired to delude the victims. The ground over the gassing cellars was converted into a well-kept lawn with flower borders; the signs at entrances merely said 'Baths.'" (Nora Levin, op. cit., p. 315)

William L. Shirer in *The Rise and Fall of the Third Reich* also recalls this episode of prisoners being led to their deaths to the accompaniment of sweet music.

32. Nyiszli, pp. 141-145. The date, November 17, 1944, indicated by Dr. Nyiszli may not be correct. In his deposition at Nuremberg, Dr. Rudolf Kastner said that Himmler's instructions to stop the gassing of Jews was released on November 25.

33. Kazimierz Smolen's account in the *Auschwitz Museum Guide-Book* does not mention the event but said that for the last time in the history of the camp, on December 30, 1944, three Austrians and two Poles belonging to the Camp Resistance Movement were executed by hanging.

Also, neither Smolen nor Dr. Nyiszli mentioned what happened to the children who were still in the camp. It was Olga Lengyel who recalled the episode. At the end of 1944, by order of the SS High Command, it was decided that the children should disappear. The author and other women received the order to bathe the youngsters. The camp road was coated with ice and it was snowing. The children, shivering, exhausted, and slashed with the SS whips when they fell, were beyond terror. When the showers were reached, they were bathed in icy water. Then, with their rags back on their dripping bodies, they had to stand for a five-hour roll call in the freezing cold and snow. The few of them who survived were like automatons, almost dead from exhaustion. According to regulations, the corpses had to be thrown behind the barracks, where rats fed on their emaciated bodies. (Op. cit., pp. 216-218)

34. Dr. Nyiszli completed his narrative by telling how the human column covered 300 kilometres in twenty days and reached Ratibor. The "herd" was by then reduced to 2,000, since 1,000 had been shot along the way. The last part of the journey to Mauthausen in box cars lasted five

days. There were still 1,500 of the original column; a few of the missing 500 had escaped and many had simply frozen to death. According to another source (Nora Levin), it was only on January 19, 1945, that the SS evacuated the camp and marched out the remaining 58,000 inmates, male and female, who had survived. Many died on the way to camps farther west where the prisoners were supposed to be resettled.

The number of evacuees is confirmed by Jan Sehn, who also mentioned that 5,000 to 6,000 sick inmates were left in the camp. However, according to the editors of *KL Auschwitz Seen by the SS*, p. 198, note 108, when the Army of the First Ukrainian Front encircled the camp on January 27, they liberated about 7,650 prisoners. The obliteration of the SS crimes had probably been ordered too late. On January 25, "only" 350 Jews were shot, while 200 prisoners were either shot or burnt in the sub-camp *Furstengrube*. In SS Pery Broad's reminiscences (quoted in the above book), the narrator mentions that all the prisoners who were left in the camp after the evacuation "would have been shot at the last moment but all SS leaders were scared and did not dare give the order." This probably explains why "so few" executions were carried out at the time.

Kraus and Kulka, *The Death Factory*, pp. 262-268, give a complete version of how the evacuation of the camp was carried out, starting on January 18. Their version includes the testimony of Karel Ornstein, prisoner No. 180,578 of Prague, who narrated the events of the evacuation and of what followed the departure of the prisoners on their trek.

35. The road that ran through the women's camp between two rows of barracks.

36. Three days later, the SS blasted Crematoria II and III; during the night of January 25-26, Crematorium V was also blown up. (According to Jan Sehn, II and III had already ceased operation and were dismantled in November 1944; Bunker 2 had also been destroyed.) As for Crematorium IV, it had been destroyed by the mutineers on October 7, 1944. See Photos 98, 100, 102, 103 and 105 in *Adam Bujak's Photo Album*. (The photo of Crematorium V is missing.)

37. Olga Lengyel, op. cit., pp. 202-207.

38. The appellation referred to the dehydrated, emaciated and bony creatures who haunted the camps area as the "living dead," "living skeletons" or "walking skeletons," terms which described most inmates in the Nazi concentration and extermination camps.

When these *muselmen* were rescued in 1945 in the various camps, they were too weak even to speak up and identify themselves. A university professor from Strasbourg remarked that kindness shown to them made no difference. They remained speechless and only stared blankly at their interlocutors. If they tried to answer questions, "their tongues could not reach their dried-up palates to make a sound." It was appalling. "One was aware," said the reporting witness, "only of a poisonous breath rising out of entrails in a state of decomposition." (*Temoignages stras-bourgeois*, Paris, 1949, p. 89)

39. Ann Tusa and John Tusa, *The Nuremberg Trial*, p. 13.

CHAPTER IV

1. *Train of Powder*, London, 1956. Ten years earlier, Rebecca West had attended parts of the hearings of the International Military Tribunal in Nuremberg.

2. Little has been said here of camps such as Dachau, Buchenwald, Nordhausen, Sachsenhausen, Mauthausen and others. Martin Gilbert, in his *Atlas of the Holocaust*, has pinpointed those German camps in several maps. Suzman and Diamond, in *Six Million Did Die*, include several reports on prevailing conditions in those camps at liberation (in Appendix IV).

On the eve of surrender, Himmler ordered the immediate evacuation of Dachau, and insisted that no living prisoner be allowed to fall into the hands of the enemy. Killings were thus speeded up, tripling in the first four months of 1945 to 13,000 as compared to a total of 4,884 victims for the whole of 1944. The investigators discovered "bodies piled up in the crematorium," which indicated that the death rate "far exceeded the daily capacity of the crematory."

Describing the general procedure of the Nazis, the Joint Committee representing the U.S. Senate and House of Representatives remarked in their report: "Vast numbers of nationals of overrun countries were abducted and brought into Germany, sometimes whole families, some-times just men. . . . Variously estimated at between 12 and 20 million those people were forced to slave labour and for slight infractions were placed in concentration camps."

In another report by the U.N. War Crimes Commission, it was mentioned that the Buchenwald camp record showed that 32,000 persons had perished in the camp. At Nordhausen, 50 miles northwest of Buchenwald, the same report stated that "although the methods of cruelty. . .differed in particulars, the general pattern of brutality at both concentration camps was similar, for example, beatings, tortures, starvation, etc. It was established that not less than 25,000 persons have perished at Nordhausen. The record of the SS in charge of the camp has been captured intact."

3. Hausner, pp. 156-159.

4. See the British report on Belsen by C.S. Coetzee and D.B. Sole in Suzman and Diamond, pp. 118-120. Illustrations on page 121 show "dead bodies strewing the ground like refuse" and "endless piles of corpses awaiting burial."

5. Two survivors from the labour camps told their stories at Eichmann's trial in Jerusalem: Dr. Leon Wells and Moshe Beisky. See

Hausner, 162-163.

6. The rest of the procedure was described by Dr. Kurt Gerstein, who saw it all at Belzec. See Hausner, pp. 91-92 and pp. 166-167.

7. Erich Goldhagen in the October 1971 issue of *Midstream*, p. 49.

8. The report by the Polish Government Commission has been quoted by Willi Frischauer, op. cit., pp. 129-130. This author has also referred to steam having been used not only in Treblinka but likewise in Maidanek. "The chambers were filled to capacity," the Polish Commission is quoted as having reported; "they were hermetically sealed and the steam was let in. In a few minutes all was over."

Frischauer, having failed to mention his source specifically—neither title, publisher, nor page number—I found no indication in the record that steam was used to burn victims to death. As confirmed by the Yad Vashem Institute in Jerusalem, it was gas, as in other camps, which was used in the chambers of Treblinka and Maidanek.

9. The prisoners had given this alias to SS *Untersturmfuhrer* Kurt Franz, who reigned in the camp. He was only a non-commissioned officer but because he was a member of the secret police, the camp *kommandant*, Franz Stangl, could not do anything without his subordinate's approval. (See J.F. Steiner, *Treblinka*, London, 1979, pp. 118-119 and 169) Nevertheless, Stangl was sentenced by a German court at Dusseldorf to life imprisonment for his co-responsibility in the murder of some 900,000 men, women and children, mostly Jews, inmates at Treblinka.

Kurt Franz, who presided over these operations of annihilation, was proud of his system, based on the precise timing of the various phases, from selection through to extermination of the newcomers. (Ibid., p. 169)

10. Sobibor also had an uprising—on October 14, 1943. About 100 men escaped, some 30 of whom lived to tell the story in court after the war. Majdanek was liquidated at about the same time as Treblinka. There, Odilo Globocnik, who was in charge of the obliteration of camps in Hans Frank's General Government, ordered the 18,000 surviving Jews shot. This slaughter marked the end of *Aktion Reinhardt*, that is, the seizure of the Jews' property and belongings, and their deportation to Globocnik's annihilation camps. (See Chapter II, note 10.)

11. J.F. Steiner, op. cit., pp. 313-335. See also Lucy Dawidowicz, *The Annihilation Camps: Kingdom of Death*, Chapter 7.

12. Kurt Gerstein. See Hausner, p. 167.

13. One Herbert Floss, "a specialist in the cremation of bodies," had been called upon to achieve what Kurt Franz's attempts had failed to accomplish. At the end of July 1943, the last ditch, containing 10,000 corpses, was opened. "The soil of Treblinka," wrote J.F. Steiner, "contained seven hundred thousand bodies, or an approximate weight of 35,000 tons and a volume of about 90,000 cubic yards." The bodies were burned by various methods and since the procedure was at first rather slow, "by rapid calculation, Lalka estimated the number of years to finish the job at 140. Even for the Thousand Year Reich, it was a long time."

However, under Floss' direction, in two weeks' time the last of all the graves would be emptied and the Germans would liquidate the camp. The mutineers, however, would strike before; the date of the revolt was set for Monday, August 2, 1943. (See J.F. Steiner, op. cit., pp. 278-288 and 314.)

14. Neither the specific location nor the name of the camp, nor the slave-labour group was mentioned in the testimony. See Hausner, p. 328.

15. Neither Kitty Hart nor Olga Lengyel, two survivors, has mentioned the number of ovens in operation in the Auschwitz-Birkenau crematoria, but referred to the number of *doors*. Assuming that they never entered the premises, the figures they produced in their testimonies—18,000 bodies burned per 24 hours—may not be accurate.

16. Yehiel Dinur, alias K. Zetnik, finished his testimony. "He rose, wavered back and forth on the witness stand and collapsed on the floor. He was carried to the hospital, where it took him several days to recover from the shock. I did not dare to put him on the stand again." (Prosecutor Gideon Hausner at Eichmann's trial in Jerusalem. See p. 171.)

Unless otherwise cited, the material in this chapter is based almost entirely on Hausner, pp. 156-171.

17. (a) After Lucy Dawidowicz, op. cit., p. 149.

(b) In the French edition of *Les Crimes allemands en Pologne*, op. cit., which deals in part with the story of the extermination camps of Chelmno, Belzec, Treblinka, Sobibor and Stutthof (about 23 miles east of Gdansk, a camp which Himmler visited on October 23, 1941), the estimated number of victims recorded by the Polish Commission investigating the German war crimes are, respectively, 340,000, 600,000, 700,000, 250,000 and 50,000. In Belzec and Sobibor, more than 90 per cent of the victims were Polish Jews. However, according to the Dutch Red Cross, 34,000 Dutch Jews were exterminated in Sobibor (not mentioned in *Les Crimes allemands en Pologne*). Although the report of the Commission has listed Majdanek as a concentration camp where extermination was carried out (as at Auschwitz) "not only on millions of people who were sent directly to the gas chambers upon their arrival, but also on hundreds of thousands of prisoners who worked as labourers and were condemned in advance to extermination," the report has left out the description and "production" of the camp in its Chapters IV and V (vol. I, pp. 101-156). Not only the Jews suffered extermination. It was estimated that between 1939 and 1945, close to 3,000,000 Polish non-Jews—intellectuals, professors, lawyers, doctors, businessmen, well-to-do citizens and their families—were also wiped out.

(c) Some of the gas chambers which were used for the "euthanasia" T4 program to do away with the insane were dismantled and reassembled in Majdanek, Treblinka and Belzec. (Dawidowicz, op. cit., p. 134)

18. See *Auschwitz Museum Guide-Book*, p. 19. Authors agree that the two million figure can never be fixed exactly. Hoss, in his affidavit of April 5, 1946, regards 2.5 million incinerated victims—as officially

recorded in a report to Himmler and signed by Eichmann—as the correct figure. This total, therefore, was accepted at the time of the Nuremberg trials, and can be found mentioned in the verdict. (See note 5 in *Conclusion*; also comments in note 52, pp. 126-127, in *KL Auschwitz Seen by the SS*, op. cit.)

CHAPTER V

1. Included are the victims of death march and death train evacuations. These tragic journeys of "resettlement" to camps farther west began during the second half of 1944, and were speeded up from January to April 1945. They continued until the very last days of the war when 300,000 surviving inmates, most of them living skeletons, were finally liberated.

These horrific episodes have been dramatically narrated and illustrated with maps and pictures by Martin Gilbert in his *Atlas of the Holocaust*, notably p. 211, et seq.

2. 5,978,000 in the author's balance sheet of February 1, 1946, and 6,093,000 in his *Crisis, Catastrophe and Survival*, New York, 1948, p. 60.

3. Gilbert, op. cit., p. 244.

CHAPTER VI

1. On liberating the camp, the Soviet Army found 7,000 kilos of women's hair that the SS had no time to send to Germany to be processed. (In *Adam Bujak's Photo Album*, see photos 50 and 51.)

2. I have reproduced, in Appendix VII, Hoss' affidavit (U.S. Prosecution Document 3868 PS). An abridged, annotated version of Hoss' deposition is also in Ann Tusa and John Tusa, *The Nuremberg Trial*, pp. 319-320.

3. See the story of Kurt Gerstein in Hausner, pp. 91-92. It has been referred to herein several times.

4. Veesenmayer has already been introduced; see supra, p. 68. Otto Winkelmann was SS Police Chief in Budapest.

5. This was a reference to the Kistaresa detention camp, seventeen kilometres from Budapest, where many Jews were detained as hostages or on alleged suspicion. Eichmann was known there as the *Sondereinsatzkommando* giving orders. See the whole episode in Hausner, pp. 143-145.

6. This is an absolute underestimate made by the court. Raul Hilberg, in *The Destruction of the European Jews*, p. 256, estimates the total number of Jews who perished during the Nazi invasion of the Soviet Union at 1,400,000, most of them by *Einsatzgruppen*. Hausner (op. cit., p. 83) mentions the same figure. But the International Military Tribunal

at Nuremberg claimed that two million Jews were killed by those units. See infra.

7. In regard to seeking a *cleaner* way to dispose of the Jews—by gassing—see Hausner, p. 90.

8. However, three weeks later, on May 14, *The Recorder* in Aden disagreed. There could not be any *second* liquidation because there had not been one in the first place. *The Recorder* simply claimed that all the figures of the Holocaust were forged and the extermination story a lie.

9. This chapter relates some of the highlights of Eichmann's trial, and has been drawn entirely from Gideon Hausner's book, *Justice in Jerusalem*, chiefly from pages 322 to 446. Students interested in the preparation of the case and some of the problems which confronted the prosecutor will find such data in Chapters 14, 15 and 16 of Hausner's work, pp. 277 to 321. To complement Hausner's narrative of his prosecution, the reader will find in Suzman and Diamond, pp. 101-107, the depositions of half a dozen of the eye-witnesses who testified in Jerusalem in 1961.

CONCLUSION

1. Hans Frank's reference to his diary was candid enough. He had noted down that during the three-year period from December 16, 1941, to January 21, 1945, between 2.4 and 3.4 million Jews had been eliminated. The feat was recalled by Major Walsh in his address at the Nuremberg Trial of major German War Criminals. See Suzman and Diamond, op. cit., p. 75 et seq.

In May 1945, at the liberation by the Seventh American Army, Frank's diary and 36 volumes of minutes and decrees of the General Government were retrieved. These later served to indict the governor. Many of the documents are speeches he delivered; excerpts of these, translated into French, were incorporated into volume I of *Les Crimes allemands en Pologne*, op. cit., pp. 11-44.

2. For instance, when the British troops entered Belsen in April 1945, they found 13,000 unburied corpses in Camp 1; a few days later, another 13,000 of the 40,000 who had survived the SS treatment died. The same situation, the same spectacle prevailed in all concentration and extermination camps.

3. (a) After the war, Dr. Jadwiga Bezwinska and Danuta Czech, as a contribution to the "mass of incontrovertible evidence including very extensive documentation obtained from Nazi sources," assembled in *KL Auschwitz Seen by the SS* three major testimonies by Rudolf Hoss, the first *kommandant* of Auschwitz at 40 years of age; by 21-year-old Pery Broad, who, in 1941 and until the liquidation of the camp, was a member of the Political Section (in other words, the Auschwitz Camp Gestapo); and by Dr. Johann Paul Kremer, 58, a physician who, on duty in

Auschwitz as of August 29, 1942, was assigned to the camp for three months. What these SS men had to say—Hoss in his memoirs, Broad in reminiscences and Kremer in a diary—was first published by Wydawnic-two Pranicze, Warsaw, in 1951, and its American edition was released in 1984 by Howard Fertig, New York. I have several times referred to this 300-page book, which includes two appendices, one being the deposition on August 6, 1946, of Stanislaw Dubiel to Dr. Jan Sehn, the investigating magistrate in the Auschwitz case. The witness had been in the camp from November 6, 1940, till January 18, 1945, and on April 6, 1942, he had been assigned to Hoss' house in the service of the *kommandant* and his family.

(b) When Justice Jackson spoke for the prosecution at Nuremberg, he said in reference to the indictment relating to the crimes committed against the Jews: "The conspiracy or common plan to exterminate the Jews was so methodically and thoroughly pursued that despite the German defeat and Nazi prostration this Nazi aim has largely succeeded. Only remnants of the European Jewish population remain in Germany, in the countries which Germany occupied and in those which were her satellites or collaborators. Of the 9.6 million Jews who lived in Nazi-dominated Europe, 60% are authoritatively estimated to have perished...History does not record a crime ever perpetrated against so many victims or one ever carried out with such calculated cruelty."

In his closing remarks, Sir Hartley Shawcross, the British chief prosecutor, spoke in much the same vein. "Twelve million murders!" he thundered. "Two-thirds of the Jews in Europe exterminated, more than six million of them on the killer's own figures. Murder conducted like some mass-production industry in the gas chambers and the ovens of Auschwitz, Dachau, Treblinka, Buchenwald, Mauthausen, Majdanek and Oranienburg."

4. H.R. Trevor-Roper, in his introduction to *The Testament of Adolf Hitler* (translated from the German by Colonel R.H. Stevens and published by Cassell and Company Ltd., London, 1961), has recounted (pp. 4-11) how this extra instalment of Hitler's 1941-42 *Table-Talk* was recorded and corrected; what role Hitler's secretary, Bormann, and Goebbels played; how the original document was secretly preserved and eventually burned after a copy had been made of it; and finally how that copy was retrieved.

Hitler's dictation to Bormann took almost the whole month of February 1945, from the 4th to the 26th. After a gap of a month, Hitler completed this statement on April 2. But he was not finished. The Fuhrer now added his official Political Testament, which he signed on April 29 in the presence of Bormann, Goebbels, Generals Krebs and Burgdorf, who also signed the document as witnesses. Hitler then proceeded with dictating his personal will. Excerpts of both the will and the Political Testament are in William L. Shirer, op. cit., pp. 1459-1464.

5. Before Hoss' trial by the Polish Supreme National Military Tribunal on March 11-29, 1947, when he was sentenced to death, Hoss had been

called as a witness in Nuremberg by Dr. Kauffmann, counsel for Kaltenbrunner. At one point, Hoss was questioned by Colonel Amen on behalf of the prosecution, and he then confirmed that his affidavit of April 5, 1946, was true in all respects, and Hoss reaffirmed the truth of each of the extracts of his testimony which were read to him. See Appendix VII.

Apart from Hoss' trial, there were many others. Among the cases listed in Suzman and Diamond (op. cit., pp. 41-45) will be found: 1. The Zyklon case, which was held before the Military Court in Nuremberg on March 1-8, 1946; 2. From December 23, 1963, to August 1965, a German court in Frankfurt heard the cases against Robert Mulka, once Hoss' aide, and 21 former SS personnel. The systematic mass killing in the Auschwitz gas chambers was not disputed by either the accused or their counsel. They merely denied complicity or relied on the defence of superior orders. Seventeen of the 22 defendants were found guilty of complicity in the mass extermination. (A photograph of Robert Mulka is reproduced in Kraus and Kulka, op. cit., p. 275.) A more complete list of trials other than the International Military Tribunal in Nuremberg is found in *Encyclopaedia Judaica*, vol. 16, col. 291 to 302.

It is important to note that when American, British, Russian, German and Polish courts tried Nazi criminals, the judges confronted not only the military but individuals of all ages and professions. In addition to ministers and low- or high-ranking departmental executives of the Nazi and SS apparatus, the defendants represented what Jerzy Rawicz called "the entire profile of German society," (in *KL Auschwitz Seen by the SS*). They included intellectuals, lawyers, professors, medical doctors, architects, bankers, artists, and all categories of tradesmen, social workers, labourers and skilled workers. They belonged to all generations of the Third Reich and represented nearly all social circles—all were candidates for the implementation of Hitler's genocide. Behind the Nazi and SS ideology, the whole nation was on trial; it was *their* Fuhrer who had put them there.

6. Scores of quotations from *German* sources dating from the pre-war years will be found in *The Yellow Spot*, op. cit. Here are two examples from this 287-page book:

(a) "Wouldn't one kill wild beasts, if they were man-eating, even if they happened to look like men? And are the Jews any different from man-eaters?" (*Dietwart*, the official organ of the German Reich Sports Leadership, July 1935), p. 201.

(b) "Only through radical extermination of the evil and alien part of our German blood can the future of our people be made eternally secure." (Hans Dietrich, National Socialist Deputy, in the *Coburger Zeitung*, upon his visit to Dachau Concentration Camp), p. 257. The date is missing; it is probably 1935.

7. Deposition in Nuremberg on October 24, 1947. Quoted by Poliakov, p. 212.

8. A reference to protests of Swedes and Jews in Jerusalem.

9. See also Goebbels' entries of March 20 and 27, 1942, quoted supra.

10. By Marek Edelman, a survivor, in *The Last Stand*. See *The Root and the Bough*, edited by Leo W. Schwarz, New York, 1949, pp. 60-61.

11. As Himmler said to his audience at the Wewelsburg Conference at the beginning of 1941: "The purpose of the Russian campaign is to reduce the Slav population by thirty millions...." Or perhaps more. They, too, were thus promised a holocaust!

APPENDIX I

1. Dawidowicz, p. 162. See also Heydrich's top-secret directive of July 17, 1941 (Document L.58 in *Nazi Conspiracy and Aggression*, published by the U.S. Government Printing Office, Washington.)

2. Hausner, pp. 69-70.

3. Ibid., p. 76.

4. Franz Walter Stahlecker, who was killed in March 1942 by the partisans, was never tried for his crimes as an *Einsatzgruppe* commander. Neither did Artur Nebe stand trial, as he became involved in the attempt to assassinate the Fuhrer on July 20, 1944, and was ordered to be hanged at that time.

5. He was a witness for the prosecution at the International Military Tribunal in Nuremberg. Part of his deposition is in Suzman and Diamond, op. cit., p. 81 et seq. In 1948, as an accused at one of the twelve trials of War Criminals by American courts, he was interrogated by Lt.-Commander Whitney R. Harris, a member of the American prosecution staff. "By far the most interesting of the three SS cases was United States v. Otto Ohlendorf et al.," wrote Brigadier General Telford Taylor, the Chief of Counsel for War Crimes. "The twenty-four defendants were commanders and subordinate officers of [the *Einsatzgruppen*], and their trial was, not unnaturally, publicized as the 'biggest murder trial in history.'" One defendant, Haussman, committed suicide after the indictment; another (Rasch) was severed from the case during the trial because of the physical and mental disability of the man. Twenty-two, therefore, out of 24 were actually tried.

It was indeed the biggest murder trial in history. It had been established that approximately one million Jews and non-Jews were liquidated in Russia by the *Einsatzgruppen*. The trial which commenced on September 29, 1947, before Military Tribunal II, ended on February 13, 1948, after 136 trial days. The charge of purposeful homicide in the case involved such incredible numbers "that believability must be bolstered with assurance a hundred times repeated...."

Of the accused, "eight were lawyers, one a university professor, another a dental physician, still another an expert on art. One, as an opera singer, gave concerts throughout Germany before he began his tour of Russia with the *Einsatzkommandos*. This group of educated and well-bred men did not even lack a former minister, self-unfrocked though he was." They had all been charged in the indictment as assassins. Indeed, their massacres had occurred beyond a shadow of a doubt, and their responsibility was stressed accordingly.

A few defendants endeavoured to deny personal participation in the murders; however, most leaned heavily on the pretext of "superior orders," whereas Lieutenant-General SS Otto Ohlendorf defended the killings on the grounds of "military necessity," up to and including the slaughter of Jewish children. As the main defendant, he was named several times in Taylor's report; two others, Haussman and Rasch, were named marginally (in a footnote); the names of the other men in the dock were not listed.

Judgment was rendered on April 8 and 9, 1948. Ohlendorf and thirteen other defendants were sentenced to death by hanging; two received life sentences, while six others were sentenced to prison terms of ten and twenty years.

See: (a) "The Nuremberg War Crime Trials," by Telford Taylor, in *International Conciliation*, April 1949, pp. 298-302.

(b) USA Department of the Army, Trials of war criminals before the Nuernberg Military Tribunals under Control Council Law no. 10, Nuernberg, October 1946-April 1949. Washington, D.C., U.S. Government Printing Office, 1953 (Green Series)—The *Einsatzgruppen* Case (no. 9), USA versus Otto Ohlendorf *et al.*, volume IV.

(c) Krausnicht, Helmut and Wilhelm, Hans Heinrich: *Die Truppe des Weltanschauungskrieges; die Einsatzgruppen der Sicherheitspolizei und des SD*, 1938-1942. Stuttgart, Deutsche Verlags-Anstalt, 1981. (This work includes the names and biographies of all the *Einsatzgruppen* commanders and eleven pages of bibliography.)

6. Poliakov, op. cit., p. 120, and other authors have also mentioned SS General Thomas as being in charge of *Einsatzgruppe* C. This commander was Dr. Max Thomas, who had been SS police leader in France from 1940 to 1942 and, ultimately, SS police leader in Ukraine. He was killed in action in 1944 and, therefore, was never tried for his crimes as commander of an *Einsatzgruppe*. He was no relation to the above-mentioned Georg Thomas, the chief of the armaments section at OKW.

It was Georg Thomas who challenged the Fuhrer's certainty of a Blitzkrieg leading to a quick peace at Hitler's military conference at Obersalzberg in August 1939. General Georg Thomas held at the time that instead Hitler's attack on Poland would turn into a catastrophical world war. (See Shirer, op. cit., pp. 690-691.)

7. The report was one of the U.S. Prosecution Exhibits at Nuremberg (#290). Ohlendorf had been in charge for six months, and the figures of the report are almost double the count he confessed to. (Nora Levin, p. 257) As to how the Jews and their children were tracked down, see Frischauer, op. cit., pp. 124-125.

8. R.W. Cooper, op. cit., pp. 118-120. The sworn statement of Herman Graebe was produced not only at the International Military

Tribunal (IMT) in Nuremberg, but also in an affidavit of the witness at Eichmann's trial in Jerusalem in 1961. Many authors have quoted from it.

9. See Ohlendorf's testimony at the IMT in Nuremberg (U.S. Prosecution Exhibit 2620 PS).

10. The original German map was reproduced on the first page of Leon Poliakov's *Harvest of Hate*. It indicates that at the end of 1941, the estimated number of Jews alive in the Baltic countries was 128,000. See further comments by R.W. Cooper, op. cit., p. 139.

11. Dawidowicz, p. 127.

12. At Eichmann's trial in Jerusalem, the testimony of Araham Aviel describing the action of an *Einsatzgruppe* at Dogliszow, near Grodno, in Soviet-occupied Poland, and that of Rivka Yoselewska at Azgorodski, near Pinsk, in eastern Poland, will be found in Hausner, p. 71.

13. Frischauer, p. 120.

14. Dawidowicz, p. 128. In her *Holocaust Reader*, New York, 1976, will be found the full report of the Jewish Labour Bund.

15. Interested readers should not fail to study Poliakov's Chaper Six, "Massacres of the Eastern Front, 1941-1942," in his *Harvest of Hate*; and Chapter 14 of Nora Levin's *Holocaust*. Each text is a comprehensive account of *Einsatzgruppen* organization, performance and achievement.

16. Hausner, pp. 80-83. Hausner's total does not tally with the 2,000,000 figure reached by the IMT, as mentioned above—which was also Eichmann's estimate. Jacob Lestchinsky, in his study, *Crisis, Catastrophe and Survival*, p. 60, claimed that there had been 1,500,000 victims in the occupied parts of USSR alone.

APPENDIX II

1. On the other hand, Hoss has reported no operation of the Auschwitz mother-camp crematorium (which he should have considered as No. I of the complex) when the four Birkenau crematoria started production in the spring of 1943 and later. In May 1944, it is true, the Auschwitz crematorium was transformed into an air-raid shelter. Actually it had already been closed down in June 1943, though the corpses of people still gassed in Auschwitz were, henceforth, burned in Birkenau (Kraus and Kulka).

However, the Polish Commission which investigated the German crimes in Poland has given this version of the "little crematorium" operations. On the basis of a 14-hour work day, sometimes even longer, 300 corpses were burned daily. Indeed, the equipment could cremate three to five corpses at the same time in each of the two (later three) "chimneys" of the oven. In their report, the Polish Commission also stated that, as of 1941, this crematorium could no longer consume all the corpses, and the incineration was then carried out in eight pits which had been dug for the purpose near the bunker-gas chambers Nos. 1 and 2.

2. See Kraus and Kulka's explanation regarding the double system of numbering, on page 14 of *The Death Factory*. On their own plan of the Birkenau camps (BI, BII and BIII), following page 16 (Fig. 5), the four crematoria are numbered (like Hoss') I to IV. A better and larger plan of the Birkenau camp showing Crematoria II to V is found in Anna Pawalczynska's *Wartosci A Przemoc. Zarys socjologicznej problematyki Oswiecimia*, published in Warsaw in 1973 by Panstwowe Wydawnictwo Naukowe; the plan also appears on page 27 of the English edition, published in 1979 by the University of California Press, Berkeley, California.

3. Further details are in *KL Auschwitz Seen by the SS*, op. cit., note 46, p. 124.

APPENDIX III

1. Op. cit., p. 187.

2. Telford Taylor was appointed by Justice Jackson on March 29, 1946, as Deputy Chief of Counsel to prepare the prosecution of war criminals other than those then being prosecuted before the International Military Tribunal (IMT).

At Justice Jackson's resignation in October, he was succeeded by Taylor as Chief of Counsel for War Crimes. Taylor, by then, had had the opportunity to prosecute the German General Staff and High Command at the IMT. In his summation in August 1946, he said, in reference to the Army and the *Einsatzgruppen*: "The idea that the extermination squads flitted through Russia, murdering Jews and Communists on a large scale but secretly and unbeknown to the Army is utterly preposterous."

3. Further details on the program of pseudo-scientific experiments can be found in Chapter 14 of Willi Frischauer's *Himmler...*; in Leon Poliakov's *Harvest of Hate*, pp. 250-254; in Philippe Aziz's four-volume *Les Medecins de la mort*; and in Shirer's *The Rise and Fall of the Third Reich*, pp. 1274-1288.

APPENDIX IV

1. After Himmler's visit in the summer, *Standartenfuhrer* Paul Blobel from RSHA, who was the chief of Department 1005, was rushed to Auschwitz to supervise the reopening of the original graves and the cremation of the corpses which had earlier been simply buried.

2. Kraus and Kulka, on page 137, have reproduced the photograph of one of the crematorium furnace-rooms. Four three-retort ovens can be seen; the fifth oven, unseen, is at the end of the line. Fig. 39 on page 136

shows the five ovens of the Crematorium II model.

3. Kraus and Kulka's total figures per day are respectively 6,500 bodies (2,000,000 a year) in Crematoria II and III, and 3,500 in Nos. IV and V (1,000,000 a year). See further details on pp. 14-15 in these authors' work.

Hoss, however—who, according to Gerald Reitinger, was "not very statistically-minded at Nuremberg"—has suggested more modest figures which do not tally with his previous estimates: "Depending on the size of the bodies," the former *kommandant* wrote in his autobiography, "*up to three corpses* could be put into *one oven retort at the same time.* The time required for cremation also depended on this, but in an average it took *20 minutes.* As previously stated, Crematoria I and II [Hoss' numbering] could cremate about 2000 bodies in 24 hours, but a higher number was not possible without causing damage to the installations. Numbers III and IV [again, Hoss' numbers] should have been able to cremate 1500 bodies in 24 hours, but as far as I know, these figures were never attained" (emphasis added).

Another estimate of Birkenau's cremation rate, by the Polish Commission of Investigation, is in volume I of *Les Crimes allemands en Pologne,* op. cit., p. 97. It states that "the four crematoria had 46 *chimneys* [overts] each of which could contain *3 to 5* corpses. . . . The four crematoria therefore, could incinerate together close to 12,000 corpses in 24 hours, i.e., 4,380,000 corpses per year" (emphasis added). This allowed for about half an hour for each loading and an hour every day to remove the ashes.

Nora Levin (op. cit., p. 316) and Leon Poliakov (op. cit., pp. 201-202) have adopted the 12,000 figure arrived at by the Polish Commission (for the four Birkenau crematoria), whereas Kitty Hart (op. cit., p. 89) has suggested an 18,000 daily total. Jan Sehn dropped his estimate to 8,000. Hoss eventually settled on a reduced total of 3,500 (see above).

In any case (even on the basis of Hoss' reduced figures), the 90,000 monthly total—which Richard Harwood denied—could be easily reached. (Concerning what Harwood called "fabulous claims" regarding the capacity of the crematoria, see Reitlinger, *The SS: Alibi of a Nation,* London, 1953, p. 287.)

4. In fact, the judgment of the Nuremberg International Military Tribunal did mention the Nazi attempts to use the fat of victims in the manufacture of soap. The Russian prosecution even presented to the court a document from a firm in Danzig which had constructed an electrically heated tank for making soap out of human fat. The firm also provided the recipe! (See pp. 4668 and 4672 of the Nuremberg Trial Record Transcript. Also Shirer's mention, op. cit., p. 1264)

Zundel does not like to be reminded of his Nazi friends' having turned human fat into soap. Yet, in 1943-1944, when he was four or five, his mother may well have cleaned his pants or washed his face with one of the new products generated by the Nazi war economy.

5. In Kraus and Kulka's *The Death Factory,* the folder facing page 17

is a photograph of the Birkenau area showing, in the centre between BI and BII, the three-line railway track and the original ramp.

6. See Jan Sehn, op. cit., p. 151.

APPENDIX V

1. Nyiszli, p. 143.
2. See photos in *Auschwitz Museum Guide-Book*, pp. 36-37.
3. Ibid., pp. 40-41. See also *Adam Bujak's Photo Album*: photos 47, 49-56, and 108-109. The whole operation of collecting, sorting, storing, marketing, reusing the belongings of the slaughtered Jews was known under a code name: *Aktion Reinhardt*.
4. See Bernstein, op. cit., pp. 143-146.

APPENDIX VI

1. Nyiszli, p. 142.
2. Frischauer, p. 132.
3. Frischauer does not mention his source. I have already indicated that I found in the record no mention of steam being used as a means of execution. But there is a method of killing which was just as horrible and was described by a witness, Mieczyslaw Sekiewicz of Konin, to the Polish Commission of investigators. The deposition of the witness has been recorded, among others, under the heading "The Methods of Execution" in *Les Crimes allemands en Pologne*, vol. I, p. 167 et seq.

Sekiewicz testified that he, a prisoner in Konin, had been taken one early morning to a place of execution near Kazimierz Biskupski where, in a forest clearing, there were collective graves. The witness and two other prisoners with him were then ordered to pick up the clothing, footwear and valuables of Jews—men, women and children—which the victims had left on the ground before being forced to jump into two pits, one of which contained a layer of quicklime. When toward noon the pit had been filled, all that could be seen, from above, were the heads of the doomed. It was then that a truck, with a pump and four containers supposedly filled with water, arrived on the site. Once the motor was started, the water was sprayed over the Jews; as it touched the lime, the wretched were exposed alive to the resulting ebullition. "Their screams became so horrible that as we stood close by a heap of clothes, we tore pieces out to stop our ears. To the sinister cries of the dying, Jews waiting for their turn added frightening lamentations. This lasted two hours, perhaps more." When Sekiewicz and his companions were brought back to the scene the next day to fill up and close the large pit, "it seemed full of dust. The mass of human bodies had settled down but the corpses were so tightly pressed together that they were still standing. Only their heads leaned to one side.'' (Op. cit., pp. 172-174)

4. Frischauer, p. 137.

APPENDIX VII

1. From then on, Hoss became Chief of *Amt* I in *Amt* Group D of the *Wirtschafts-und Verwaltungshauptamt* (WVHA), and in that office, he said he was responsible for co-ordinating all matters arising between Reichssicherheitshauptamt (RSHA) and concentration camps under the administration of WVHA.

2. Details concerning the organization of WVHA (Main Economic and Administrative Head Office) headed by *Obergruppenfuhrer* Oswald Pohl, and RSHA (Reich Central Security Office) headed by Heydrich follow in paragraphs 3 and 5 of the affidavit:

"While Kaltenbrunner was Chief of RSHA,'' declared Hoss, "orders for protective custody, commitments, punishment and individual execution were signed by Kaltenbrunner or by Mueller, Chief of the Gestapo, as Kaltenbrunner's deputy.'' At the time of sentencing Kaltenbrunner to death by hanging, the Nuremberg Tribunal stressed in particular that "the RSHA played a leading part in the Final Solution of the Jewish question by extermination of the Jews. A special section under the Amt IV of the RSHA was established to supervise this program. Under its direction approximately 6 million Jews were murdered, of which 2 million were killed by the Einsatzgruppen and other units of the Security Police. Kaltenbrunner had been informed of the activities of these Einsatzgruppen when he was a Higher SS and Police leader, and they continued to function after he had become Chief of the RSHA. The murder of approximately 4 million Jews in concentration camps...was also under the supervision of the RSHA when Kaltenbrunner was head of that organization....''

3. The following informative note has been added in the original document: "Handwritten insertion in opening sentence in paragraph replaces the last two sentences which were stricken out in ink: 'Mildner introduced one unique punishment at Auschwitz, nameley: binding an inmate's hands to his knees around a rod. The prisoner would then be revolved round the rod while he was beaten.'''

4. Four days later, Dr. Gilbert examined Hoss in his cell. The former *Kommandant* of Auschwitz spoke in much the same terms. "I pressed him further for some reaction to the enormity of what he was to undertake,'' said Dr. Gilbert, but "he continued in the same apathetic manner.''

Hoss admitted that "from our entire training the thought of refusing an order just didn't enter one's head regardless of what kind of order it was." It was "at the time of the collapse, when the Fuhrer died," that he realized for the first time that he would be brought to trial and hanged. (See *Nuremberg Diary*, op. cit., pp. 249-251.)

Bibliography

*Andrus, Burton C. *I Was the Nuremberg Jailer*. Coward McCann and Goeghegan: London, 1969.

———. *The Infamous of Nuremberg*. Leslie: London, 1969.

Aziz, Philippe. *Les Medecins de la mort* (4 vol.). Editions Famot: Geneve, 1976.

*Bernstein, Victor H. *Final Judgment: The Story of Nuremberg*. Latimer House: London, 1947.

*Bezwinska, Jadwiga, and Czech, Danuta, editors. *KL Auschwitz Seen by the SS*. Panstwowe Muzeum w. Oswiecimiu, 1965, 1972; Reprint by Howard Fertig, New York: 1984.

*Bujak, Adam. *Photo-Album of Auschwitz-Birkenau* (Text by Gawalewicz, Adolf). Wydawnictwo Sport and Turystyka: Warsaw, n.d.

Cooper, F.W. *The Nuremberg Trial*. Penguin Books: New York, 1947.

Dawidowicz, Lucy S. *A Holocaust Reader*. Behrman House: New York, 1976.

———. *The War Against the Jews 1933-1945*. Holt, Rinehart and Winston: New York, 1975.

Delarue, Jacques. *The Gestapo* (Transl. Mervyn Savill). Dell Publishing: New York, 1965.

Dickson, John K. *German and Jew*. Quadrangle Books: Chicago, 1967.

Encyclopaedia Judaica, 16 vol. (Cecil Roth, 1966-1970; and Geoffrey Wigoder, 1971, editors-in-chief). Kenter Publishing House: Jerusalem, 1971.

Fenelon, Fania. *The Musicians of Auschwitz* (Transl. Judith Landry). Michael Joseph: London, 1977.

Frank, Hans. *Im Angesicht des Galgen*. Beck: Munich, 1953.

* The author considers these works indispensable to an understanding of the Holocaust. Ernst Zundel, in particular, should acquaint himself with them if his goal is to arrive at the truth about Hitler's Holocaust rather than to exploit lies for nefarious purposes.

Freddborg, Arvid. *Behind the Steel Wall*. Viking: New York, 1944.

Friedlander, Saul. *Kurt Gerstein: The Ambiguity of the Good*. Alfred A. Knopf: New York, 1969.

*Friedman, Philip. *This Was Oswiecim—The Story of a Murder Camp* (Transl. from the Yiddish by Joseph Leftwich). United Jewish Relief Appeal: London, 1946.

*Frischauer, Willi. *Himmler: The Evil Genius of the Third Reich*. Belmont Books: New York, 1962.

Fromm, Bella. *Blood and Banquets*. Bles: London, 1943.

Gilbert, G.M. *Psychology of Dictatorship*. Ronald Press: New York, 1950.

*Gilbert, Martin. *Atlas of the Holocaust*.** Michael Joseph: London, 1982.

——. *Auschwitz and the Allies*. Holt, Rinehart and Winston: New York, 1981.

——. *Final Journey: The Fate of the Jews of Nazi Europe*. Mayflower Books: New York, 1979.

——. *The Holocaust* (Maps and Photographs). Hill and Wang: New York, 1978.

*Goebbels, Josef. *Goebbels' Diaries* (Transl. and edited by Louis Lochner). Hamish Hamilton: London, 1948.

Goldhagen, Erich. "Albert Speer, Himmler and the Secrecy of the Final Solution." *Midstream*, October 1971.

Gorzkowska, Jadwiga. *Nazi Criminals Before West German Courts*. Zachodnia Agencja Prasowa: Warsaw, 1965.

Gumkowski, J., and Rutkowski, A. *Treblinka* (An illustrated and documented publication). Council for Protection of Flight and Martyrdom Monuments: Warsaw, n.d.

Hart, Kitty. *Return to Auschwitz*. Sidwick and Jackson: London, 1981.

*Hausner, Gideon. *Justice in Jerusalem*. Schocken Books: New York, 1968.

*Hilberg, Raul. *The Destruction of the European Jews*. Quadrangle Books: Chicago, 1967.

——. *Documents of Destruction*. Quadrangle Books: Chicago, 1971.

Hitler, Adolf. *Hitler's Secret Conversations*. Signet: New York, 1961.

Holborn, Hajo. *Republic to Reich*. Pantheon Books: New York, 1972.

*Hoess, Rudolf. *Commandant of Auschwitz*. Weidenfeld and Nicolson:

** Martin Gilbert's *Atlas of the Holocaust* contains on pages 246-254 a bibliography of special interest which concerns the location of concentration and extermination camps, the deportations and evacuations of the Jews to those death factories, and the statistics of the killings which were carried out therein and in the field.

A more complete bibliography has been published jointly, as a bibliographical series, by Yad Vashem in Jerusalem and the Yivo Institute for Jewish Research in New York. The Jewish Book Council of America in New York can also provide pertinent lists of works dealing with the subject of the Holocaust.

London, 1959.

Hull, William L. *The Fall and Rise of Israel.* Zondervan Publishing House: Grand Rapids, 1954; (Reprint, 1978).

Jabotinski, Vladimir. *The Yellow Spot.* V. Gollancz: London, 1936.

Kerstein, Felix. *The Kerstein Memoirs 1940-1945.* The Macmillan Co.: New York, 1957.

*Kraus, Ota, and Kulka, Erich. *The Death Factory* (Transl. Stephen Jolly). Pergamon Press: Oxford and New York, 1966.

Krausnick, Helmut. *Anatomy of the SS State.* Walker: New York, 1968.

Lang, Jochen von, and Claus, Sibyll, editors. *Eichmann Interrogated* (Transl. Ralph Manheim). Farrar, Strauss and Giroux: New York, 1983.

Lengyel, Olga. *Five Chimneys.* Granada Publishing: London, 1972.

*Lestschinsky, Jacob. *Balance Sheet of Extermination.* Jewish Affairs, Feb. 1, 1946, New York; Office of Jewish Information, New York, 1946.

——. *Crisis, Catastrophe and Survival.* Institute of Jewish Affairs of the World Jewish Congress, 1948.

Levin, Nora. *The Holocaust.* Thomas Y. Crowell Cy.: New York, 1968.

Manvell, Roger, and Fraenkel, Heinrich. *Himmler.* Putnam: New York, 1965.

Nansen, Odd. *From Day to Day.* G.P. Putnam's Sons: New York, 1949.

Nyiszli, Miklos. *Auschwitz* (Transl. Tibere Kremer and Richard Seaver). Crest Books; Fawcett World Library: New York, 1960.

Pawelezynska, Anna. *Values and Violence in Auschwitz* (Transl. Catherine S. Leach). University of California Press: Berkeley, 1979.

*Piotrowski, Stanislas. *Hans Frank's Diary.* Panstwowe Wydawnictwo Namtowe: Warsaw, 1961.

*Poliakov, Leon. *Harvest of Hate* (From original French opus *Breviaire de la haine,* 1951). Greenwood Press: Westport, Conn., 1971.

*Reitlinger, Gerald. *The Final Solution: The Attempt to Exterminate the Jews of Europe, 1939-1945.* A.S. Barnes: New York, 1953.

——. *The SS: Alibi of a Nation.* Heinemann: London, 1956.

Reynolds, Quentin, et al. *Minister of Death: The Adolf Eichmann Story.* Viking Press: New York, 1960.

Robinson, Jacob (and Mrs. Philip Friedman). *The Holocaust and After: Sources and Literature in English.* Israel University Press: Jerusalem, 1973.

*Sehn, Jan. *Le camp de concentration d'Oswiecim-Brzezinka.* Wydawnictwo Prawnicze, 1961.

Sender, Toni. *Autobiography of a German Rebel.* Vanguard: New York, 1939.

Shirer, William L. *The Rise and Fall of the Third Reich.* Crest Books: New York, 1962.

Smith, Bradley, and Peterson, Agnes F. *Heinrich Himmler Geheimreden, 1933 bis 1945.* Propylaen: Frankfurt, 1973.

*Smolen, Kazimierz. *Auschwitz Museum Guide-Book 1940-1945.*

Panstwowe Muzeum, W. Oswiecimiu, 4th edition, 1972.

Steiner, Jean-Francois. *Treblinka* (Transl. Helen Weaver). Weidenfeld and Nicolson: London, 1967.

Suzman, A., and Diamond, D. *Six Million Did Die*. South Africa Jewish Board of Deputies: Johannesburg, 1978.

Taylor, Telford. *The Nuremberg Trials: War Crimes and International Law*. *International Conciliation*, April 1949, #450, pp. 241-371, Carnegie Endowment for International Peace: New York, 1949.

Toland, John. *Adolf Hitler*. Ballantine Books: New York, 1977; (c) Doubleday: New York, 1973.

Tusa, Ann and John. *The Nuremberg Trial*. Macmillan: London, 1984.

West, Rebecca. *Train of Powder*. Viking Press: New York, 1955.

Glossary†

Amt: Office
Anschluss: Political union (e.g., Anschluss of Austria and Germany)
Blitzkrieg: Lightning war
Bundestag: West German Parliament
Deutsche Arbeiter-Partei: German Workers Party
Durchfall: Diarrhoea
Einsatzgruppe: Task force of the SS (RSHA) for "special missions" in Poland and occupied Soviet territory where Communist commissars of the Soviet army and Jews were annihilated
Endgultige Losung (or **Endlosung**): Final solution; extermination of Jews
Entfernung: Removal, liquidation, expulsion
Frauenkonzentrationslager: Concentration camp for women
Fuhrer: Leader
Gauleiter: The highest ranking Nazi Party official in a Gau (province), responsible for all political and economic activity; also for mobilization of labour and for civil defence
General Government: Polish territory which was left after Hitler's annexation to the Reich of the four western provinces of Poland (October 8, 1939)
Gestapo (Geheime Staatspolizei): Secret State (political) police
Gruppenfuhrer (SA and SS): Major-General*
Hofbrauhaus: A beer hall in Munich where National Socialists often held meetings
Judenrein: Clean (free) of Jews
Kommandant: Commander, commanding officer
Kommandantur: Commander's office
Kristallnacht: Crystal night—the "Night of Broken Glass." Pogrom in Germany on November 10-11, 1938, after an official of the German Embassy in Paris had been shot and killed by a young Jew

†See page 19, footnote, regarding spelling and pronunciation of German words.
*Corresponding rank in the British Army.

Kurfurstendamm: A thoroughfare in Berlin

KZ (Kazet): Concentration camp

Muselman:** Derogatory slang term used by SS men for the dehydrated, emaciated, bony creatures who were inmates in Nazi concentration and extermination camps

Nazi: Abbreviation of Nationalsozialist (National Socialist)

Nebenlager: Sub-camp

Obergruppenfuhrer (SA and SS): Lieutenant-General*

Oberscharfuhrer (SS): Quartermaster Sergeant*

Obersturmbannfuhrer (SA and SS):Lieutenant-Colonel*

Ostjuden: Jews who had come to Germany from Eastern Europe or who lived in Poland or Russia

Panzer: Military tank

Rapportfuhrer: Sergeant-Major in the administration of a concentration camp

Reich (Deutsches Reich): Official name of Germany until 1945

Reichsbank: National Bank of the German Reich

Reichsleiter: Title of the highest ranking Nazi Party officials, comparable to the ministers of the government of the German Reich

Reichstag: German Parliament from 1871 to 1945

Reichsvereinigung: National union

Reichsvertretung der Juden in Deutschland: National representation of the Jews in Germany

RSHA (Reichssicherheitshauptamt): Reich Central Security Office. Administered by the SS, this office directed among other branches the activities of the Security Service (SD), the Criminal Investigation Branch of the Police and the Intelligence Service within and without Germany.

SA (Sturmabteilung): The "Stormtroopers" or "Brownshirts." The original para-military force of the Nazi Party

Sauberkeit: Cleanliness

Scharfuhrer (SA and SS): Staff Sergeant*

Schonungsblocks: Huts in which inmates received convalescent treatment

Schutzhaeftlinge: Prisoners detained without having been convicted by a court of law (for their own "protection")

(zur) Sektion: (for) autopsy

Sicherheitsdienst (SD): Security Service. The intelligence organization of the SS. Originally intended for the surveillance of the party, it was expanded after 1933 to keep under surveillance the entire population of the Reich.

Sonderaktion: Special action

Sonderbehandlung: Special treatment

Sonderkommando: Special duty unit

Sportpalast: Large hall in Berlin where the Nazis held meetings

SS (Schutzstaffel): Literally, protection or guard detachment. The

**German spelling

"elite" of the Nazi Party para-military force and its most powerful branch

Standartenfuhrer (SA and SS): Colonel*

Stammlager: Main camp, base camp

Stehzelle: A cell so small that the prisoner has to remain standing

Strafkompanie: Delinquent company

Sturmbannfuhrer (SA and SS): Major*

Todestransport: Death transport

Totenbuch: Registry of the dead

Totenkopf: Death's head, skull. Badge of special units of the SS responsible for the guard and surveillance of concentration camps

Transportjuden: Concentration camp inmates who were spared immediate death and instead were ordered by the SS to help with the transportation of new arrivals destined for immediate extermination

Untersturmfuhrer (SA and SS): Second Lieutenant*

Waffen-SS: The fully militarized formations of the SS which put nearly 40 divisions into the field during the war, 1939-1945

Wehrmacht: Name of the German Armed Forces from 1935 to 1945. They consisted of the Army, Navy and Air Force (Luftwaffe).

WVHA (Wirtschafts- und Verwaltungshauptamt): The SS's Economic and Administrative Central Office, responsible for the administration of the concentration camps

Zentralstelle: Centre

Zugangere (sic), Zugange: New prisoner admissions, registrations